BYZANTINE GOSPEL

BYZANTINE GOSPEL

Maximus the Confessor in
Modern Scholarship

Aidan Nichols O.P.

T&T CLARK
EDINBURGH

T&T CLARK LTD
59 GEORGE STREET
EDINBURGH EH2 2LQ
SCOTLAND

First Published 1993

ISBN 0 567 09651 3

British Library Cataloguing-in-Publication Data
A Catalogue record for this book is available from
the British Library

Typeset by Trinity Typesetting, Edinburgh
Printed and bound in Great Britain by Bookcraft, Avon

For Angela, Helen
and
Margaret who is working on the Fathers

Contents

Preface

The following study makes no claim to originality. It is essentially a synthesis of the European scholarship which has accumulated around the figure of Maximus the Confessor in the course of the last twenty-five years. Both Orthodox and Catholic theology, in Continental Europe, make ever greater use of the insights of this early Byzantine theologian. He is increasingly regarded as the giant of the Greek tradition, to be compared, as the author of its classical statement, only with Thomas Aquinas in the Latin West. Although one outstanding student of Maximus, Lars Thunberg, is Swedish, his work was published in English, thanks to the good offices of Canon A. M. Allchin, now Warden of St Theosevia House, Oxford. Otherwise, all the major monographs are in languages other than English — though the first large-scale American study appeared from the Notre Dame University Press in 1991. My aim has been to provide the English-speaking reader with a reliable guide to a selection of these 'major monographs', chosen — and commented on — in such a way that they provide a comprehensive overview of Maximus' theology: a 'Byzantine Gospel'. At the same time, sufficient primary texts have been included to give the reader a sense of Maximus' powers both as a summariser of the previous tradition, and as an original theologian in his own right. In both capacities he deserves to be remembered, and better known.

Blackfriars
Cambridge
Feast of St Gregory the Great, 1992

1

Background, Life, Work

Background

When did Byzantium begin? J. M. Hussey, in her *The Orthodox Church in the Byzantine Empire* has little hesitation in placing the true beginning of the Byzantine polity not with the foundation, on the site of the ancient Byzantion, of the city of Constantinople as capital of the eastern, and senior, half of the Christian Roman empire, but with the aftermath of what she terms the 'seventh century watershed'.[1] If true, then Maximus the Confessor, who was nineteen years of age when that century opened, lived at a time of momentous importance in the development of European Christian civilisation.

Why does Hussey attach so much weight to the seventh century? In the first place, the rise of Mohammed and the victories of Islam in the south and east contracted the boundaries of Christendom in a dramatic way while also bringing a fresh religious challenge. Secondly, the arrival of the Slavs on the border of Byzantium, and their acceptance of Christianity, brought a compensating 'enlargement and enrichment' to the Christian family.[2] Thirdly, the falling of those great cultural and theological centres of early Christianity Antioch and Alexandria under the Muslim yoke gave a new prominence to the see of Rome, which, with its venerated tombs of the martyr-apostles Peter and Paul was the apostolic see *par excellence* — as well as to the claims of Constantinople to share in the

---

[1] J. M. Hussey, *The Orthodox Church in the Byzantine Empire* (Oxford 1986), p. 9.
[2] Ibid., p. 10.

1

prerogatives of the 'elder Rome' as *Nea Rôma,* 'New Rome, Rome *redivivus.* Fortunately, as Hussey points out, the emperors of Byzantium in this period were of sufficient calibre to rise to the principal demands which a new situation thus placed upon them, above all in the administrative reform of their polity, its institutional reinvigoration.

Drawing on traditions both Christian and Roman-imperial, the early Byzantine state had a capacity to induce respect and even awe which matched the formidable problems — military, administrative and economic — that faced it in this period. As J. F. Haldon has written:

> The political system, with its formal ideology and its assumption of God-given jurisdiction, provided a focus for unity in a culturally, linguistically and economically diverse world, in a way that few autocracies have succeeded in doing.[3]

But there was, as the same author points out, a 'price to be paid': open criticism of the manner in which the emperor's guidance of the *oikoumenê* functioned, notably in its most delicate aspect — the religious, was a dangerous proceeding.

Not the least of the problems which faced the Byzantine ruling élites at the start of the seventh century was the continuing crisis over theological doctrine, endemic since the earliest years of the Christian empire but present in an especially acute form since the Council of Chalcedon, 451, 'unreceived' as this was by the numerous die-hard Cyrillians, or yet more extreme christological 'high Churchmen': the devotees of the Monophysite movement in Syria, Egypt and Constantinople itself. The effort to find some doctrinal instrument which would reconcile the Monophysites to Chalcedon, or at any rate would bring them back into the fold of the imperial Church without alienating Chalcedon's own fervent supporters, not least in the West, dominated the ecclesiastical policy of the Eastern emperors from the time of Zeno's *Henotikon* or 'Proposal

---

[3] J. F. Haldon, *Byzantium in the Seventh Century. The Transformation of a Culture* (Cambridge 1990), p. 23.

for Unity' of 482. None of the imperial interventions proved lastingly successful — not even the most ambitious of them, the General Council held under the auspices of Justinian at Constantinople in 553 and subsequently reckoned the Fifth Ecumenical Council of the Church. Though it condemned certain expressions of the (Antiochene) two nature Christology, and emphasised the hypostatic or personal identity which bound together the humanity of Christ with the eternal being of God the Word, the Monophysites remained dissatisfied and the separate organisation of their churches gathered momentum. Meanwhile, a related issue, new to the explicit agenda of doctrinal discussion, at once added fuel to the flames and also held out some hope, though this would prove deceptive, of ecclesiastical reconciliation.

This was Monothelitism and its twin brother Monoenergism. So far no Council had explored the question as to whether, in the Word Incarnate, there were two wills, a divine and a human, or simply one personal will that was somehow simultaneously both. Similarly, no Council had essayed an answer to the question whether the Saviour was characterised by a single activity, *energeia*, corresponding to the unicity of his hypostasis, or by a twofold acting, conformable to the duality of natures. The question was of no mere academic interest, for, as Hussey points out:

> to have agreed on one *energeia* or one will would have answered one of the principal Monophysite objections to the Chalcedonian definition, and therefore should have gained Monophysite support.[4]

The chronic problem of the Monophysites was compounded at this juncture by military threat from the Sassanid kingdom of Persia whose forces at one point reached the Asiatic shore of the Bosphorus. Aware of the close link between Chalcedonian faithfulness and loyalty to the empire, the Persians cannily persecuted Chalcedonians, favoured their Monophysite (and Nestorian) opponents. It was this conjuncture which led the

---

[4]Ibid., p. 13.

emperor Heraclius, supported by the Constantinopolitan
patriarch Sergius, to adopt a policy of conciliating the
Monophysites through a doctrinal instrument of concord: the
affirmation, as a reconciling article, of a single activity, *energeia*,
in the person of the Word Incarnate. There thus opened a new
chapter in the story of the Monophysite crisis. The new situation
formed the essential public context of St Maximus' life and
work. It will be, then, the subject of the rest of this brief account
of the Confessor's Byzantine background.

The collaboration of emperor and patriarch is certainly a
good example of the Byzantine notion of *symphonia* between
empire and Church, translated into action. Their co-operation
seemed indeed providential. To contemporaries Heraclius was
the saviour of the empire. The death of Justinian in 565 had been
followed by a period of increasing internal tension coupled with
external threat. The steps taken by Justinian's successor, Maurice,
to protect the outlying territories — for example by organising
the remaining Western provinces into exarchates, one based at
Ravenna, the other at Carthage, proved ineffective. In 602, in
the course of the failing military effort against the Slavs and
Avars, who had crossed the Danube and were both occupying
and devastating the Balkan peninsula, the semi-barbarian Phocas
came to power and inaugurated a reign of terror which only
embittered groups within — for instance the Monophysites
whom he repressed severely, and emboldened groups without
— above all the Persian king Chosroes II who undertook the
invasion of the East Roman polity in 605. The rallying of the
exarch of Carthage, Heraclius the Elder, against the régime in
608 was the signal for a revolt which in 610 led the citizens of
Constantinople to open their gates to his son, Heraclius the
Younger, whose fleet, with the icon of the Mother of God fixed
to the mast of its flagship, had appeared in the Golden Horn.
Phocas abandoned to the mercies of the mob, Heraclius the
Younger was crowned emperor on 5th October in the church of
St Stephen by a Constantinopolitan patriarch, Sergius, himself
but recently elected.[5]

---

[5]F. X. Murphy, C. Ss. R., — P. Sherwood, O.S.B., *Constantinople II et III* (Paris
1973), pp. 136-137.

Sergius acted as Heraclius' counsellor in both the governmental and the psychological senses of that word. To a man given to periods of self-doubt, he offered hope. More materially, he also put the financial resources of the Church at the emperor's disposal for the purposes of the empire's defence. During Heraclius' absence on campaign, Sergius was a principal figure in the administration of the great capital. When the emperor had to deal with Monophysite leaders, in the course of the military operations, Sergius provided him with suitable doctrinal texts. By 614, after some successes and many reverses, Heraclius was ready to retire to the West. What stopped him was Sergius' moral support as also the Persian capture of Jerusalem and the relic of the Holy Cross on 5th May. The Cross's parading in pagan triumph through the streets of Ctesiphon turned the Persian war into a Crusade.[6] Heraclius made peace with the Slavs; he re-organised the empire's administration by concentrating civil and military authority in the hands of those who headed the huge new territorial units of the empire, the 'themes'; in an effort of unification he made Greek its only administrative language. But the same necessary concern for unity also confronted him with the problem of the Monophysites, and here too the faithful Sergius could be of use. A particularly high degree of urgency was attached to this area of policy after 614 when a Monophysite synod, meeting at Ctesiphon under Persian auspices, took steps to strengthen the cohesion of the Monophysite community at large, over against the Chalcedonian 'Great Church'.

The Monophysite interpretation of the famous Cyrilline formula, 'One incarnate nature of the divine Word' was certainly regarded as heretical by both Heraclius and Sergius, though the formula itself was, as the work of the divine Cyril, thoroughly approved by them.[7] This circumstance suggested a way out of the dilemma — if only an understanding of Christology could be found which would satisfy at once the supporters of Chalcedon, the legal faith of the empire, and the theological

[6]Ibid., p. 138.
[7]Ibid., p. 139-140.

tendencies of those extreme Cyrillians so numerous among its
Armenian, Syrian, and Coptic peoples.[8]

During the opening years of his patriarchate Sergius was
engaged in assessing the strength of support for this policy,
and made approaches to bishops in Egypt and Armenia to
this end. The formula he hit on first was that of the single
energeia, 'operation' or 'activity', of Christ. From information
provided by Maximus the Confessor we learn of four letters
by Sergius in which he initiated the exposition of the single
energeia teaching. The first was addressed to the leader of a
small Monophysite body at Alexandria, George Aras, whom
Sergius commissioned to find patristic texts relevant to the
unique activity of Christ — the context being negotiations
taking place at Alexandria with the Monophysite patriarchs
of Egypt, Athanasius Gammala, and of Syria, Anastasius
Apozygares, under the aegis of the imperial prefect Nicetas.
Sergius' second letter was destined for Theodore, bishop of
Pharan, near Mount Sinai. By this point, Sergius had come
into possession of a most valuable document — the *libellus*,
'little book', sent, so it was claimed, to pope Vigilius by a
predecessor of Sergius, Menas of Constantinople, in which
the patriarch mentioned not only Christ's single activity but
also his single *will*. Theodore replied with enthusiastic
approbation. (Maximus would report that the defenders of
Monoenergism admitted that the articulation of their doctrine
came largely from Theodore of Pharan.) Sergius' third letter
was despatched to the leader of the Cypriot Monophysites,
Paul the One-Eyed. Later, Heraclius would send Paul, whom
he encountered during his Armenian campaigns, back to his
island, with a decree addressed to the archbishop of Cyprus,
Arcadius, forbidding all talk of two activities in Christ after
the Union. The fourth letter had as its recipient Cyrus, bishop
of Phasis, in Lazica. Cyrus did not understand how Heraclius'
instructions to archbishop Arcadius were compatible with
the Tome of Leo, which had clearly stated that 'each nature
does what is proper to it, in communion with the other';

[8]The whole story has never been better told than by W. H. C. Frend in his *The
Rise of the Monophysite Movement* (Cambridge 1972).

Sergius hoped to send him some more satisfactory explanations.[9]

Although Severus of Antioch had explicitly taught Monoenergism, in the course of his rejection of Chalcedon, the notion of reconciling Monoenergism with Chalcedon's Diphysitism was the brain-child of Sergius and Heraclius. It seems likely that the first real theologian of Monoenergism was not so much Sergius as Theodore of Pharan, that Chalcedonian whom Sergius had successfully won over to the new policy. Theodore's doctrine is known only from eleven extracts from writings ascribed to him, and discussed both at the Lateran Synod of 649 and the Third Council of Constantinople itself, in 681. In these extracts all of Christ's actions are seen as emanating exclusively from the Word. Though Christ knew the 'natural movements' of his humanity, their exercise, like their cessation, depended on the Word's activity alone. Will is also mentioned, as being single and divine.[10] Hence the names whereby in the history of doctrine these eirenic christological excursions became known: not only Monoenergism but also *Monothelitism*, the teaching on the single will. Theodore was not foolish: as W. Elert pointed out, *prima facie*, the literary image of Christ presented by the Gospels appeared to be taken with greater seriousness as a christological norm were the Church to affirm one single activity in Christ.[11] Nor, as the Redemptorist F. X. Murphy and the Benedictine Polycarp Sherwood, in their study of the antecedents of Constantinople III, candidly admit, were Heraclius' doctrinal interventions simply political in motivation. The enduring resistance of such Churchmen as Macarius and Stephen of Antioch, and Constantine of Apamea, to the final victory of Dyothelitism, as well as the survival of its Monothelite alternative in pockets of Syria and Palestine,

---

[9] F. X. Murphy, C. Ss. R., — P. Sherwood, O.S.B., *Constantinople II et III* (Paris 1973), pp. 140-142.

[10] Ibid., pp. 143-145. The texts are given in Mansi XI, 568B-569E and 572A. For an attempted reconstruction of Theodore's fuller identity, thought and significance, see W. Elert, *Der Ausgang der altkirchlichen Christologie* (Berlin 1957).

[11] Ibid., pp. 11, 224.

suggest that the doctrine eventually dubbed heretical represented an 'original religious position'.[12]

Between 622, when the new doctrine began to be employed for the first time, and its first notable success, the 'Pact of Union' with the moderate Monophysites of Alexandria in 633, its rôle in imperial policy was central yet patchily effective. The turn in Byzantine fortunes assisted matters. In 626, with Sergius leading the resistance, the armed might of Persians and Avars failed to take Constantinople. (The patriarch probably composed the *kontakion* to the Mother of Christ as protectress of the City, now incorporated in the Akathistos hymn, for this occasion.) In 628 the Persian king died, and in 629 Heraclius concluded an armistice which enabled the return of the Holy Cross to Jerusalem, where it was solemnly enthroned on 21st March. In 633 Heraclius called the Armenian catholicos Ezras to a council at Theodosiopolis (Erzerum) where all dissent from Chalcedon was foresworn — for the time being. In Syria, likewise, Heraclius used the instrument of a synod, with the Monophysite patriarch and twelve of his bishops participating, at Hierapolis (Mabboug). There, though with more discordant voices on the non-Chalcedonian side, a similar ecclesiastical peace was made on the basis of the one-activity and one-will teachings. In Egypt, things proceeded differently. In 630, or 631 Heraclius nominated Cyrus of Phasis as patriarch of Alexandria — ignoring the sitting Coptic patriarch, Benjamin, as the latter had indeed ignored Cyrus' titular Chalcedonian predecessors, living in Constantinople. The emperor gave Cyrus plenipotentiary powers, inclusive of civil and even military matters. But his primary task was the doctrinal peace.

When Cyrus arrived in his city, and, conveniently, his Coptic rival fled, he took the opportunity to publish a 'Pact of Union' to be accepted by all. The Pact condemned any denial that the incarnate Son 'worked both the divine and human by a single theandric activity' — a phrase drawn in part, it would seem, from the recently published writings of the anonymous master who wrote under the name of Denys the Areopagite.[13] Read out

---

[12] F. X. Murphy, C. Ss. R., P. Sherwood, O.S.B., *Constantinople II et Constantinople III* op. cit., p. 136.

[13] Mansi, XI. 565D. Denys, however, had spoken of a 'new' rather than 'single' such activity.

from the ambo of the patriarchal church in Alexandria, the Pact was accepted by both parties, and the union sealed with the Eucharist. So Cyrus reported joyfully to Sergius and Heraclius.

As luck would have it there arrived in Alexandria at this moment, *en route* from Carthage to Palestine, the monk Sophronius, whom Maximus had got to know and revere as a master in north Africa, and who would become, eventually, patriarch of Jerusalem. Though a Damascene, Sophronius had become a monk (along with the noted spiritual writer John Moschus) at the monastery of Theodosius, near Jerusalem. Driven out by the advance of the Persians they had fled first to Antioch, then to Egypt, and in 614 to Rome. On Moschus' death in 619, Sophronius returned to the East to bury his friend. He appears to have found things not to his liking, since Maximus' letters indicate that he was shortly back in the West, at Carthage. A second Eastern journey of return brought him to Alexandria, where he was known as the friend of the sainted patriarch John the Almsgiver.[14] Learning of the Pact of Union, Sophronius lost no time in denouncing its doctrinal contents to Sergius. Sergius hesitated. To avoid a controversy he temporised and, along with his permanent synod, issued a decree that henceforth neither one activity nor two should be taught, though all the actions of Christ, divine and human, should be ascribed, in conformity to the witness of the Fathers, to the single agent who was our Lord and true God.[15]

This text, the *Psêphos*, committed the church of Constantinople to a christological 'solution' which, as events would show, could gain the lasting support neither of the Latin West nor of many in the Byzantine East. Constantinople's 'Determination' put the emphasis, as one would expect of a Cyrilline Chalcedonianism, on the unitary agency of the God-man in the work of salvation. But it went further. While discountenancing the term 'one activity' as tending to eliminate

---

[14]On Sophronius and his teaching, see C. von Schönborn, *Sophrone de Jérusalem. Vie monastique et Confession dogmatique* (Paris 1972).

[15]F. X. Murphy, C. Ss. R., —P. Sherwood, O.S.B., *Constantinople II et Constantinople III*, op. cit., pp. 151-152.

the distinction of natures, it also frowned upon the phrase 'two activities' as seeming to introduce two opposed wills within the personhood of the Saviour. This option it rejected as impious, affirming instead its opposite: namely, that the Lord's flesh, as animated by his intelligence, did nothing of its own initiative but only when God the Word willed it, and as he willed it.[16]

The political situation which surrounded it was of the most delicate. While the provinces just re-conquered from Persia — Palestine, Syria, Mesopotamia — needed re-organisation, and the pacification of Egypt depended on the skills of a single ecclesiastic, Islam was emerging from the confusion which had followed Mohammed's death in 632. By 634 the Arabs would have invested Syro-Palestine. In 635 they captured Damascus; Jerusalem and Antioch would follow in 638. Before them much of the Greek-speaking population of the Near East fled. Chiefly Chalcedonian, and where theologically affected by the movements of the previous century, no doubt *Neo*-Chalcedonian, they were welcomed with open arms by a Latin Christendom faithful to the Tome of Leo and the Council of 451. In terms of *Realpolitik*, a balancing act — such as the *Psêphos* represents — was the best Constantinople could manage.[17]

For Sophronius, this would not suffice. Endowed with the blessed quality of turning up at the right place at the right time, he reached Jerusalem as the patriarch Modestus lay dying, and was elected to succeed him, either in late 633 or early 634. His synodal letter informing Sergius of his enthronement argued for both Cyril and Leo, and while defending the 'one incarnate nature' formula as capable of an orthodox meaning, insisted that, since Christ is in two natures he must enjoy all the properties of those natures, including activities.[18] At this stage, however, Sophronius did not directly affirm Dyothelitism, concentrating his fire instead on the Monoenergists. But his

[16]Mansi XI, 533c-536A.

[17]L. Bréhier — R. Aigrain, 'La nouvelle crise religieuse. Juifs, monoénergisme, Islam, 632-639', in idem., *Grégoire le Grand, les Etats barbares et la conquête arabe, 590-757* (= A. Fliche et V. Martin [eds.], *Histoire de l'Eglise depuis les origines jusqu'à nos jours*, 5, Paris 1938).

[18]Mansi XI, 481E.

démarche led Sergius to write an able self-defence to pope Honorius. Evoking in optimistic terms the union agreements reached via the instrumentality of the single activity idea, he was pleased to tell Honorius that Leo and his Tome were now liturgically commemorated even in Egypt, while, so far as substantial doctrine was concerned, he himself stood by the approved Fathers. But he also made it plain that, for him, affirmation of two activities leads to an assertion of two wills, and so to the allegation of inner contradiction in the Redeemer's person.

The Greek version of Honorius' reply survives. It praises Sergius for suppressing vain 'quarrels of words', and uses, commendingly, what would soon be marked out as an heretical expression: 'the single will of the Lord Jesus Christ'.[19] But in the context of the pope's references to the Letter to the Romans, with its 'law of the Spirit' and 'law of the members', it seems likely that Honorius was thinking of the moral or spiritual unity of Christ's willing.[20] Though the subsequent arrival of Sophronius' synodal letters reminded Honorius more forcibly of his Leonine inheritance, they do not seem to have modified his basic approval for Sergius' strategy.

Meanwhile in 638, shortly before Sophronius' death, a senior bishop of his patriarchate, Stephen of Dora, with his approval, took an oath at the shrine of Golgotha to journey to Rome, there to secure the canonical annullment of the new heresy. At the same time, the Arab advances had taken the heart from Heraclius. Sergius responded by writing, and gaining Heraclius' signature for, an *Ekthesis* or 'Exposition' of the faith, incorporating the *Psêphos* but including also an explicit confession of the Lord's single will.[21] Affixed to the doors of Hagia Sophia it was twice synodically approved, once before Sergius' own death in December, and once with the election of his successor Pyrrhus, who issued an encyclical letter requiring

[19]Ibid., 540B; see P. Galtier, 'La première lettre du pape Honorius', *Gregorianum* 29 (1948), pp. 42-61, and G. Kreuzer, *Die Honoriusfrage im Mittelalter und in der Neuzeit* (Stuttgart 1975), pp. 17-57, for studies.

[20]F. X. Murphy C. Ss. R. — P. Sherwood, O.S.B., *Constantinople II et Constantinople III*, op. cit., pp. 161-162.

[21]Manxi XI, 993E-996C.

adhesion to it, making play, not least, with the name of pope Honorius.

Honorius was already dead. His short-lived successor, Severinus, despatched his apocrisaries to Constantinople but they felt unable to give any assurance about the pope's possible support for the *Ekthesis*, news of which they brought back with them to the West. Pope John IV, a curial official consecrated in December 640, had, by the time of Heraclius' death in February 641, condemned the *Ekthesis* synodically and written to the new emperor, Constantine III, at once complaining of Pyrrhus' letter on the 'Exposition', giving an orthodox interpretation of Honorius' notorious slip, and asking the emperor to withdraw all copies of the offending edict. Constantine was probably orthodox, and docile, but his death in May and the ensuring dynastic struggle prevented any coherent imperial action until the accession of Heraclius' grandson, Constans II, in September. Meanwhile Pyrrhus defended Monoenergism zealously, but Constans replaced him with the patriarch Paul, while at Rome John IV himself died, and was succeeded by a Palestinian Greek, pope Theodore. In 645 or 646, as we shall see in the next section, Maximus arrived in Rome, bringing with him the deposed patriarch Pyrrhus, now temporarily returned to orthodoxy — until shortly the exarch of Ravenna, Plato, persuaded him otherwise. So the main figures of the Lateran synod of 649 were in place.[22]

From the Roman viewpoint, Paul of Constantinople proved no better than Pyrrhus. After much prevaricating, he made a clean breast of things in 643 with a long profession of Monothelite faith. Excommunicated by Theodore, he persuaded Constans II to issue, probably in 648, the *Typos*, 'An Edict Concerning the Faith'. Insisting on silence vis-à-vis the entire Monoenergist and Monothelite questions, for the sake of the peace of the churches and the good of the empire, it decreed severe sanctions for any malefactors.[23] What Theodore made of the *Typos* is unknown. Dying in the spring of 649 he was

[22]F. X. Murphy, C. Ss. R. — P. Sherwood, O.S.B., *Constantinople II et Constantinople III*, op. cit., p. 166.
[23]Mansi X, 1029C-1032D.

succeeded by an Umbrian deacon, Martin, who had been papal emissary at Constantinople. The new pope was consecrated without attempt to gain the usual imperial ratification. At the Lateran synod, opening on 5th October 649, he and Stephen of Dora would object to the *Typos* that it placed orthodox teaching and heretical on the same level, and, by its interdiction on discourse, deprived Christ of activity and will alike.

Though the Lateran synod was only a council of the Roman province, its essential inspiration, and theological structure, came from the Greek East.[24] Not only were its *Acta* in Greek as well as Latin; the Latin is hardly more than a translation of the Greek. With the exception of some materials from North Africa, its patristic documentation was entirely Greek. The explanation must be sought in the rôle at the synod of Greek (and other Oriental) monks, resident at Rome (as elsewhere in the West),[25] and, above all, of the personal contribution of Maximus — who, however, appears only once under his own name, among the last of the signatories of the formal complaint against the Byzantine authorities. Called by E. Caspar a 'battle-synod', *Kampfsynode*,[26] its effect was to *encourager les autres*— the orthodox groupings in the East Roman world. Pope Martin made great efforts to disseminate its decisions: by letter to Sigebert, king of the Franks, and to bishops in the new mission lands of the Low Countries; by envoy to Africa and Palestine; and, most perilous proceeding, to the imperial court — where the papal brief ascribed the *Typos* calamity exclusively to the patriarch Paul.[27] Murphy and Sherwood wrote finely of it:

> One may say that, in a sense, the distinctive mark of the council of the Lateran was to efface itself behind the Sixth

---

[24]F. X. Murphy, C. Ss. R. — P. Sherwood, O.S.B., *Constantinople II et Constantinople III*, op. cit., pp. 178-179.

[25]J. M. Sansterre, *Les moines grecs et orientaux à Rome aux époques byzantine et carolingienne; milieu du VIe. siècle — fin du IXe.siècle* (Brussels 1983).

[26]E. Casper, 'Die Lateransynode von 649', *Zeitschrift für Kirchengeschichte* 51 (1932), p. 123.

[27]F. X. Murphy, C. Ss. R. — P. Sherwood, O.S.B., *Constantinople II et Constantinople III*, op. cit., p. 182.

Ecumenical Council, just as Martin and Maximus the Confessor carried off their own victory in their effacement in an exile which made the Sixth Council inevitable.[28]

For Constans could admit no threat to his policy. On 17th June 653 he had Martin arrested, by the hand of the exarch of Ravenna, in the Lateran basilica itself. Tried in Constantinople in December on the charge of high treason (all discussion of religion being non-admissible), he was exiled to the Chersonese, in the Crimea, where he died on 16th September 655. He thus outlived Paul, who expired before Christmas 653, and Pyrrhus, who was restored to his patriarchal seat but died likewise in June 654. After the formal condemnation of Martin, however, the emperor sought no further formal act of adhesion by the Papacy to the *Typos*. Nonetheless in May 655, as we shall discover, the trial of the chief theological instigator of the Lateran synod, Maximus, and of his disciple, Anastasius, at last began.

The broader context to Maximus' life is, then, what Haldon has termed an argument of the State with 'the articulate and literate opposition', centred as that was on the Italian and African clergy, and notably those close to pope Martin, St Maximus, and the organisers of the Lateran synod.[29] As the trial accounts make clear, it amounted to a public debate about the sources of authority within the Empire — a foretaste of the more widespread and embittered, yet fundamentally similar debate of the Iconoclast crisis a few generations later. Yet, as this historian points out, the icons, and the saints themselves, had already begun to appear, in Maximus' own period, more desirable ways of access to the holy, more reliable mediations of God in Christ, than the 'Christ-loving' emperor.[30] In this

---

[28]Ibid., p. 181.

[29]J. F. Haldon, *Byzantium in the Seventh Century*, op. cit., pp. 365-366.

[30]For the title, see O. Kresten, 'Justinianos I, der "Christusliebende Kaiser", *Römische Historische Mitteilungen* 21 (1979), pp. 83-109; and for the image of the emperor, H. Hunger (ed.), *Das byzantinische Herrscherbild* (Darmstadt 1975). On the rôle of the emperor in East Roman Christendom, see A. Nichols, O.P., *Rome and the Eastern Churches. A Study in Schism* (Edinburgh 1992), pp. 133-151.

perspective it is, he thinks, significant that the most telling charge the Confessor's own enemies brought against him was not his opposition to the imperial court, but rather the slur — credited, apparently, among the soldiery — that he had spoken slightingly of Mary of Nazareth, the Queen of heaven. We shall return to that *motif* in the course of this study.

Life

For information about the life of Maximus we are mainly dependent on successive versions of the official *Vita*.[31] However, an important addition to our materials is furnished by the Syriac *Life*, published in 1973, which appears to be contemporary with the saint's own life and death.[32] Its anonymous Monothelite author, hostile to Maximus, presents a quite discrepant account of his early upbringing from that of the Greek hagiographical tradition. While admitting that the question is by no means a closed one, in what follows the early portions of the Syriac *Vita* will be ignored, and their picture of a Palestinian (indeed, half-Persian) Maximus, trained in the Origenistic-tending monasteries of Judaea, will be passed over in favour of its main rival, which locates his origins and education in the capital, and in humanist circles at that.

On this version: Maximus was born, in c. 580, to a Constantinopolitan family. From the extent of his familiarity not only with Scripture and such Christian theologians as Origen and the Cappadocians but also with philosophical writers, and notably Aristotle, Plato, Iamblichus and Proclus, he would appear to have enjoyed the kind of broad humanist education for which the great city was renowned. While still relatively young, he became 'protosecretary' at the court of the emperor Heraclius, who began to reign in 610 — though the date and significance of Maximus' appointment are still

---

[31]R. Devréesse, 'La vie de saint Maxime le Confesseur et ses récensions', *Analecta Bollandiana* 46 (1928), pp. 5-49.

[32]S. P. Brock, 'An Early Life of Maximus the Confessor', *ibid.* 91 (1972), pp. 299-346.

disputed.[33] From the continued part he played in official society after his entry into monastic life it has been suggested that his family belonged to an inner circle which provided the Byzantine capital with its intellectual and bureaucratic cadres.

Some three years after taking up his appointment, however, Maximus resigned it in order to enter monastic community at Chrysopolis (Scutari) on the Asiatic shore of the Bosphorus, opposite Constantinople. Whether he became *hêgumenos*, abbot, there, or whether this tradition is based on faulty inference from the memory that he was called *father (abbas)*, is disputed.[34] Some while later, for reasons obscure, he removed himself to the monastery of St George at Cyzicus (Erdek). Although political factors may have been involved in Maximus' withdrawal from court and city, he himself states, in a major autobiographical letter, that his chief reason for embracing the ascetic life was 'philosophy', that is, monastic spirituality.[35] His biographer stresses his advance in ascetical practice, and in the devotional life,[36] while his own writings show 'a considerable insight into the pastoral problems of a monastic community'.[37]

Probably in 626, when not only the Persians but also the Avars and Slavs were converging upon Constantinople and its environs, Maximus (together with many other Greeks) departed into exile. It is conjectured, on the basis of slightish evidence, that he spent periods in Crete and Cyprus.[38] He arrived in North Africa, home to numerous Byzantines since the reconquest under Justinian, in about 628. At Carthage, he probably occupied the monastery called 'Euchratas' which

[33]W. Lackner, 'Der Amtstitel Maximos des Bekenners', *Jahrbuch der Oesterreichischen Byzantinistik* 20 (1971), pp. 64-65.

[34]In his *Acta*, his signature to the Lateran council and his inscription to most of his works, he appears as simply 'monk': V. Grumel, 'Notes d'histoire et de chronologie sur la vie de Saint Maxime le Confesseur', *Echos d'Orient* 26 (1927), p. 32.

[35]*Epistle* 2 (PG 91, 392-408).

[36]PG 90, 72D-73A.

[37]L. Thunberg, *Microcosm and Mediator. The Theological Anthropology of Maximus the Confessor* (Lund 1965), p. 4.

[38]P. Sherwood, *An Annotated Date-List of the Works of Maximus the Confessor* (Rome 1952), p. 5.

had as its abbot the erstwhile companion of John Moschus, Sophronius, who in 633 would become the first Chalcedonian to combat the rise of the Monoenergist teaching. This encounter was crucial for Maximus' awareness of the fresh challenge to orthodoxy: new, yet in many respects comparable with the 'moderate' Monophysitism of Severus of Antioch. Though at first feeling the pain of exile very acutely, as letters to the bishop of Cyzicus testify,[39] Maximus came to regard his exile as a permanent state of affairs — though this is it was not to be, thanks to his developing rôle in the empire-wide dispute about both Monothelitism and Monoenergism which henceforth constituted the sole axis of his literary work.

There can be little doubt that Maximus made his mark in Africa, enjoying good relations with the imperial governors Peter the Illustrious and George.[40] Yet such friendships had their perils. The wealth of the province of Africa made it is a possible launching-pad for a *coup d'état* (as with the two Heraclii), while Maximus' very success in winning the support of the African church for his criticisms of the empire's religious policy (testified by the councils condemning Monothelitism which met locally after 646) testified to its ripeness for religious revolt. It cannot entirely be ruled out that Peter, strategos of Numidia, and George, prefect of Africa, had it in mind to make use of Maximus' name and prestige in their own politickings vis-à-vis the Byzantine state.[41]

His Western exile, which would last for a quarter century, contained two notable events of Church-historical concern. In 645, he engaged the deposed patriarch Pyrrhus of Constantinople in theological debate on the issue of the two wills and energies of Christ. Of that disputation, a scribal record has come down to us.[42] In the presence of the exarch, Gregory, and numerous bishops and other notables, they set

---

[39]*Epistles* 28-31 (PG 91, 620D-625D).

[40]P. Sherwood, *An Annotated Date-List of the Works of Maximus the Confessor,* op. cit., pp. 49-52.

[41]V. Croce, *Tradizione e ricerca. Il metodo teologico di san Massimo il Confessore* (Milan 1974), p. 11.

[42]*Disputatio cum Pyrrho* (PG 91, 287A-354B).

themselves to worry out the meaning of the key-terms involved and, through and beyond the question of language, to establish the basic theological principles on which christological doctrine should be set forth. At the close, Pyrrhus declared himself convinced, and ready to place a Dyothelite profession of faith into the hands of the pope, whilst at the same time expressing the hope that he would not be required to anathematise retrospectively his predecessors. It is presumed that Maximus accompanied him to Rome, to make in St Peter's his, as it proved, short-lived orthodox confession.[43]

The second signal event was, of course, the Lateran synod of 649 at which, as we have seen, Maximus was extraordinarily influential even though not necessarily physically present at its sessions.[44] While Maximus' rôle at the synod must be ascribed to the quality of his own teaching and personality, he may also have profited from the prestige enjoyed by Greek exiles in the West.

The emperor, Constans, reacted sharply to the Lateran synod's anathematisation of both Monothelitism and Monoenergism. But owing to the sympathy for pope and synod of the Byzantine exarch in Italy neither the pope nor Maximus were actually arrested until 653.[45] The trial of Maximus was delayed until the spring of 655, and ended inconclusively, as the imperial authorities were unable to prove either main charge against him. These were, that he had conspired treasonably against the emperor, and that his refusal to communicate with the church of Constantinople was both an ecclesiastical and a civil delict.[46] Sent into temporary exile at Bizia in Thrace, an attempt to convince him of the error of his ways, made by a court bishop, Theodosius, failed abjectly, but

---

[43]F. X. Murphy, C. Ss. R. — P. Sherwood, O.S.B., *Constantinople II et Constantinople III.* op. cit., pp. 166-167. At any rate, Maximus was in Rome by 646, according to the testimony of the *Relatio motionis inter Maximum et principes.*

[44]P. Sherwood, *An Annotated Date-List of the Works of Maximus the Confessor,* op. cit., p. 20.

[45]M. W. Peitz, 'Martin I und Maximus Confessor', *Historisches Jahrbuch der Görresgesellschaft* 38 (1917), pp. 225ff.

[46]The trial is described in the *Relatio motionis* (PG 90, 109C-129C).

has left an important record in the *Disputatio byzica*.[47] Summoned
to the capital, he was tempted to surrender to the will of the
emperor but finally refused, and was sent back to Thrace, this
time to another location, Perberis, for six years. In 662 an
overtly Monothelite council at Constantinople anathematised
him in his presence, and that of his disciples.

Condemned to mutilation, his tongue, by which he had
confessed the two wills and energies of the Redeemer, and his
right hand, with which he had refused to sign a compromise
statement of doctrine, were cut off. He was exiled to Lazica on
the south-eastern shore of the Black Sea, where he died on 13th
August 662 — a date which is kept liturgically in his honour in
both Eastern and Western traditions.[48] As the Swedish Maximian
scholar Lars Thunberg put it:

> His victory was soon to be won, but he himself could no
> longer take part in it.[49]

The American historian of doctrine, Jaroslav Pelikan,
commented:

> The title 'confessor', which he acquired soon thereafter
> and which is forever attached to his name, was a tribute to
> his steadfastness in confessing the faith of the undivided
> Church in the undivided hypostasis and the distinct
> natures of the person of the incarnate Son of God.[50]

The doctrine for which he died may seem narrow or technical;
the occasion of his martyrdom not especially momentous. Yet
the *doyen* of historians of Byzantine theology, John Meyendorff,
could write:

---

[47]PG 90, 136D-172B.

[48]J.-M. Garrigues, 'Le martyre de saint Maxime le Confesseur', *Revue Thomiste*
76 (1976), pp. 410-452.

[49]L. Thunberg, *Microcosm and Mediator. The Theological Anthropology of Maximus
the Confessor*, op. cit., p. 7.

[50]J. Pelikan, 'Introduction', in G. C. Berthold (ed.), *Maximus the Confessor.
Selected Writings* (New York 1985), p. 5.

These Christological commitments and debates imply a concept of the relationship between God and man, a theology of 'participation' which would, through the creative synthesis of Maximus the Confessor, serve as a framework for the entire development of Byzantine Christian thought until the fall of Constantinople to the Turks.[51]

Work

Maximus' literary activity appears to have begun with his transfer to Cyzicus in 624-5. From this period there dates Epistle 1, addressed to the chamberlain John, a letter which has been described as a 'magnificent hymn to charity',[52] as well as the predominantly ascetic discussions in Epistles 2, 3 and 4. But, above all, Maximus is beginning work on his first major treatise, entitled 'On Various Difficult Passages in the Holy Fathers Denys and Gregory', which will pass into history under the name of the *Liber Ambiguum* — the 'Book of Ambiguities'.[53] As the *Ambigua* (to give it its shorter title) testifies, the problem pre-occupying Maximus in this period is not yet Monothelitism but rather Origenism, especially as found in a quasi-popularised form through the activities of Evagrius of Pontus, not least in monastic circles. Indeed, Maximus is capable of using at this date turns of phrase which, in the later polemic against Monothelitism, he would take care to render more precise.[54] Maximus' principal aim was to confute the Origenist notion of the *henas tôn logikôn,* or aboriginal unity of all minds, in which he divined the root fault of the Origenist system. Since, in the wake of the Fifth Ecumenical Council, Justinian's Council of Constantinople of 553, Origen's name was not officially to be

[51]J. Meyendorff, *Byzantine Theology. Historical Trends and Doctrinal Themes* (New York 1979²), p. 5.

[52]V. Croce, *Tradizione e ricerca. Il metodo teologico di san Massimo il Confessore,* op. cit., p. 8. The 'grand chamberlain' was the senior official in the direct service of the Byzantine emperor, the administrator of his household: J. M. Hussey (ed.), *The Cambridge Medieval History, IV. The Byzantine Empire* (Cambridge 1967), II. p. 21.

[53]In question here is *Ambigua* 6-71 (PG 91, 1061-1417); *Ambigua* 1-5 come from a somewhat later date, around 634.

[54]E.g. 'one sole energy of God and of the saints', in *Ambigua* 7 (PG 91, 1076CD) — as noted by V. Croce, *Tradizione e ricerca,* op. cit., p. 8.

mentioned, Maximus' discussion takes the form of exegesis of some controversial passages in Gregory of Nazianzus that were capable of being understood in an Origenist sense. Its translation into Latin by John Scotus Eriguena achieved a critical edition in 1988.[55]

From the same 'monastic' period come several works of an ascetic-spiritual kind, works with which, until this century, Maximus' reputation was mainly bound up. Notable here are the *Liber asceticus* or 'Ascetic Discourse', and the *Capitula caritatis* or *Centuriae de Caritate*, the 'Chapters' or 'Centuries' on charity — so called because what Maximus has to say is arranged in one hundred points at a time. The first of these, the *Ascetic Discourse*,[56] takes the classic literary form of the dialogue; the second is a collection of apophthegms, or pithy sayings, originally a Stoic genre but launched on its Christian history by Evagrius of Pontus — to whose ideas on holy living these 'Chapters' are also indebted for their content.[57] Even more striking in its debt to that earlier master with an over-clouded reputation is another work, somewhat later, in the same genre — the *Capitula gnostica* or 'Gnostic Centuries', whose alternative title gives a better idea of their content.[58] The *Capitula theologica et economica*, 'The Chapters on the Theology and Economy', are not, of course, an early expression of the 'social Gospel' but a series of reflections on God in himself ('Theology') and in his self-disclosure for man's salvation ('Economy'). Both works exhibit Maximus' habit of drawing into a greater synthesis the contributions of his predecessors — having eliminated from the work of the former any elements which were ambiguous or even erroneous.

Before becoming involved in the struggle against Monoenergism and Monothelitism, Maximus produced a number of biblical commentaries, such as those on Psalm 59[59]

---

[55] E. Jeauneau (ed.), *Maximi Confessoris Ambigua ad Johannem, iuxta Johannis Scotti Eriugenae latinam interpretationem* (= *Corpus Christianorum, Series Graeca*, 18; Turnhout 1988).
[56] PG 90, 912-956.
[57] Ibid., 960-1080.
[58] Ibid., 1084-1173.
[59] Ibid., 856-872.

and on the *Pater*.[60] To these will shortly be added the much more compendious series of *Quaestiones*. The *Quaestiones ad Thalassium*, a major source for his theological doctrine,[61] and the *Quaestiones ad Theopemptum*[62] were, as their titles indicate, addressed to individual churchmen perplexed about knotty passages in the interpretation of Scripture. The *Quaestiones et dubia*, 'Questions and doubtful points', leave the original interlocutors in anonymity.[63] These writings exemplify another literary type quite widespread in Christian antiquity. This was the genre of *quaestiones et responsiones*, questions and answers on the Bible.[64] The ones Maximus wrote make plain his fundamental allegiance to Alexandrian principles in exegesis— something to be explained in the second chapter of this study.

We have already seen how Maximus' respect for the writings of Denys the Areopagite led him to refer to that unknown figure as 'holy father Denys', placing him, in the title of the *Book of Ambiguities*, on the same level as St Gregory Nazianzen, in the Greek church 'Gregory the Theologian'. Maximus' enthusiasm for the *corpus Dionysiacum* led him, at roughly the same epoch as the production of his biblical commentaries, to write the *Mystagogia* — an exercise in liturgical exegesis, a commentary on the rites of the Eucharistic liturgy in its architectural setting. This would remain not only one of the most crafted of his works (which are, in general, lacking in literary workmanship), but one of the most popular in later Byzantine readership.[65]

[60]Ibid., 872-909.

[61]Ibid., 244-785; C. Laga — C. Steel (eds.), *Maximi Confessoris Quaestiones ad Thalassium I, Quaestiones* I-LV (= *Corpus Christianorum, Series Graeca*, 7, Turnhour 1980); idem., II, *Quaestiones* LXI-LXV (= ibid., 22, Turnhout 1990).

[62]PG 90, 1393-1400.

[63]Ibid., 785-856; J. H. Declerk (ed.), *Maximi Confessoris Quaestiones et dubia* (= *Corpus Christianorum, Series Graeca*, 10, Turnhout 1982).

[64]Cf. G. Bardy, 'La littérature patristique des 'Quaestiones et responsiones' sur l'Ecriture sainte', *Revue Biblique* 41 (1933), pp. 205-212; 332-339.

[65]PG 91, 657-717; C. G. Sotiropoulos, *Hê Mystagôgia tou hagiou Maximou tou Homologêtou: eisagôgê — keimenon — kritikon hypomnêma* (Athens 1978). For the difficult problem of the authorship of the fragmentary *Scholia* on the Dionysian corpus, ascribed to Maximus, see M. L. Gatti, *Massimo il Confessore. Saggio di bibliografia generale ragionata e contributi per una riconstruzione scientifica del suo pensiero metafisico e religioso* (Milan 1987), pp. 83-86.

The place of origin of this literature was the proconsular Africa to which, in around 628, Maximus, in the confused situation attendant on the Persian advance towards Constantinople, had fled from the East to the West, where eventually, with the removal from the scene by death of Sophronius of Jerusalem in 638, Rome was left alone to maintain the Dyothelite teaching over against the great Oriental sees. From 641 onwards, all of Maximus' efforts would be devoted to the continuation of the christological struggle. Everywhere that there was need to defend the orthodox teaching, Maximus directed the little treatises which now form the *Opuscula theologica et polemica*, 'theological and controversial minor works', along with the remaining letters: taken together, these make up the content of that last stage in his literary production.[66]

Maximus' Roman activities, initiated in 646, reached their culmination in the Lateran synod of 649. The formulations of that synod, which have passed into the magisterial doctrine of Catholicism, reflect his theological thinking.[67] The synod's anathematisations of Monothelitism and Monoenergism provoked Maximus' arrest by the imperial authorities, his two trials and penal exile, all of which succeeded in bringing to an end his theological writing, though the records of his trials, especially the first, described in the *Relatio motionis inter Maximum et principes*, as well as the debate held at Bizia with the court bishop Theodosius, preserved as the *Disputatio byzica* in his *Acta*, are also important sources for his doctrine. It is to the content of Maximus' theological vision, and first of all to his understanding of the foundations of Christian theology, that we must now turn.

---

[66]PG 91, 9-286; for the *Opuscula*; Migne reproduces Combefis' collection of forty-five letters at PG 91, 364-649; they are analysed in M. L. Gatti, *Massimo il Confessore*, op. cit., pp. 48-60. She also notes four other authentic letters, ibid., pp. 60-63.

[67]V. Croce, *Tradizione e ricerca*, op. cit., p. 12.

2

Vitorio Croce on Maximus' Theological Method

Its Basic Formulation

As background to Maximus' account of theology, we can note that patristic theological method followed, in general terms, two principal routes. Its first major form is that of the exploration of images. Both the biblical doctrine of creation, with its corollary that finite realities can serve as expression for the infinite Creator, and the philosophical (Platonic) postulate that the sensuous world reflects the intelligible universe, help to account for this version of what theology is. As Gregory of Nyssa put it, 'Through conjectures and images, we bring the truth to its appearing'.[1] The other main way in which the Fathers approached theology was by the exploration of concepts. That the same theologian could pursue both paths simultaneously is shown by countless examples of this second way, in the context of christological and trinitarian theology, found in the writings of Nyssa. The concept of 'person' is a good example.[2] To these we may add that more elaborated structure of theological thinking (and relationship with God) found in the 'three-fold way' of affirmation, negation and 'eminence' associated especially with the fifth century Syrian writer, the Pseudo-Denys. Here a symbolic theology, whose limitations are signalled by the need to negate whatever we

---

[1] PG 44, 185A.
[2] A. Grillmeier, *Christ in Christian Tradition* (London 1974[2]), pp. 258-271.

affirm of the God of revelation through the language of this world, provides the starting-point for a more mysterious entry — at once affirming and negating our knowledge of God — into God's own life.[3]

Such intellectual *démarches* were, however, undertaken within the firm constraints of a controlling context: the acceptance of the intrinsic authority of Scripture, the Church's book, and Tradition, the Church's mind, itself formed by that book, and coming to expression, as the patristic age unfolded, in the teaching of Fathers and Councils (and popes). At the same time, patristic theologians did not neglect, in apologetic settings, rational arguments that might persuade their pagan (or Jewish) hearers toward the acceptance of the Gospel.[4]

The chief student of *Maximus'* method in theology, Vittorio Croce, insists that, in the course of the Monothelite controversy, Maximus found himself able to refine his theological method, and yet that method was already well-tested in his 'monastic' period with its attempted refutation, at once philosophical and theological, of Origenism.[5] His method became, however, more 'positive' or 'scientific', in the sense that the exigencies of the hour obliged him to collect texts, whether of Scripture, the Fathers, or the Councils where his ideas might find corroboration. But even in this activity he did not forget that the goal of theology is entry into the life of God. The defence of orthodoxy is at the service of 'piety'.

In *Tradizione e ricerca. Il metodo teologico di San Massimo il Confessore,* Croce opens by referring to Letter 6, which is dated by Dom Polycarp Sherwood to the years 624-625, and so counts among the earliest of Maximus' affirmations of theological principle.[6] Responding to a request from Bishop John, Maximus proposes to:

---

[3] J. Vanneste, *Le mystère de Dieu. Essai sur la structure rationelle de la doctrine mystique du Ps. Denys l' Aréopagite* (Louvain 1959).

[4] See A. Nichols, O.P., *The Shape of Catholic Theology. An Introduction to its Sources, Principles and History* (Edinburgh 1991), pp. 274-277.

[5] V. Croce, *Tradizione e ricerca,* op. cit., p. 12.

[6] P. Sherwood, *An Annotated Date-List* ... op. cit., p. 25.

demonstrate with natural arguments, without biblical or patristic testimonies, that the soul is an incorporeal creature.[7]

There then follows what Croce describes as a set of five syllogisms of a rigorously rational Aristotelean-Stoic kind. Maximus is aware that in this he is pursuing a piece of research rather than proclaiming a dogmatic affirmation (hence the duality in the title of Croce's study). But he also pronounces himself ready and willing:

> by the grace of God to spread out the cloud of divine witnesses, and of their testimonies, which surrounds us, so that, unencumbered of the weight of all the laborious disquisition which this argument has produced, and of the incessant verbal battle of these lovers of contests, we can peacefully possess real knowledge about God and his creatures.[8]

As Croce points out, what is significant here is the division of the argument into, on the one hand, an appeal to natural reasoning, and, on the other, the adducing of revealed testimony — as also the fact that the latter is itself subdivided into the biblical witness and the 'testimonies'; which Croce at once identifies as the writings of *the Fathers*.

At the opposite end of Maximus' life, in his final disputation, at Bizia, in Thrace, during the second trial of autumn 656, we find exactly the same tripartite scheme. For on that occasion Maximus vigorously rejected the expression 'hypostatic energy' as lacking all force 'whether scriptural or patristic or natural'.[9] Croce finds two other important occasions, one in *Ambigua* 7, in the course of a lengthy criticism of Origenism, and the other in the dispute with the ex-patriarch Pyrrhus on the christological issue, where the same trio make their bow.[10]

---

[7] PG 91, 425A.

[8] Ibid. (PG 91, 432CD). There may be an indebtedness of Maximus here to Nemesius of Emesa's *De natura hominis* 2 (PG 40, 536B-589D, and especially 589B).

[9] *Disputatio Byziae* 14 (PG 90, 152C).

[10] *Ambigua* 7 (PG 91, 1089A); *Disputatio cum Pyrrho* (PG 91, 344A).

However, the list is not quite complete: for Maximus also cites the Ecumenical Councils as a legitimating form of doctrinal testimony. He objects to his Monothelite adversaries that they are unable to put forward any use, *chrêsis*, of *Council*, Father or Scripture in support of their assertions.[11]

Looking more widely at Maximus' work, Croce offers an analysis of these principles as set to use in what he takes as representative works. For the more controversial writings, these test cases are *Ambigua* 7 and Maximus' 'tome' against the *Ekthesis* of Heraclius: thus a piece of argumentation against the Origenists in the first case, against the Monothelites in the second. In the former, Maximus proceeds to criticise Origen's notion of the aboriginal unity of rational intelligences principally by showing the absurd consequences to which that idea would lead, but he also lists the biblical passages that speak of *movement* as essential to man, and of the *future* character of the peace or *stasis* which will give human nature its completion. Maximus' explanation here is rounded off, significantly, by two citations from Gregory Nazianzen.[12] In this manner of proceeding, Maximus builds, in Croce's metaphor, a speculative bridge whose pillars are recourse to Bible and Fathers.[13] In the *tomos*, on the other hand, recourse to divine revelation is the fundamental procedure, with rational speculation serving as the cohesive mortar for joining together blocks drawn from Scripture, Fathers and Councils.[14] Somewhat anachronistically, Croce speaks of these two approaches in Maximus' work as his use of both the 'progressive' method (nature-Scripture-Fathers-contemporary magisterial teaching) and the 'regressive' method, where that sequence is reversed — anachronistically because these terms belong to the Western Catholic theology of the Roman schools, in the period from the mid-nineteenth century pope Pius IX to his namesake and successor of a century later, Pius XII! The Italian patrologist, however, sees things differently, writing:

---

[11] *Opuscula theologica et polemica* 15 (PG 91, 180BC).
[12] *Ambigua* 7 (PG 91, 1069B-1072D; 1072D-1076B; 1076B-1077D).
[13] V. Croce, *Tradizione e ricerca*, op. cit., p. 21.
[14] *Opuscula theologica et polemica* 15 (PG 91, 153B-184C).

Certainly there is nothing new in the articulation of this method of theological work in comparison with earlier patristic writing, at least where the heart of the matter is concerned. But what is found in no preceding Greek Father is, however, the explicit, formal enunciation of the methodological schema which we have described. For this reason, Maximus has rightly been regarded as a precursor of mediaeval Scholasticism.[15]

What of Maximus' method in his *spiritual* writings where — given the subject matter — these approaches characteristic of dogmatic theology are scarcely serviceable? Though there can be no question of a contradiction between properly theological effort and works of an ascetical or mystical kind, the 'dynamic' of the ascetical and mystical treatises belongs with a 'scheme of spiritual progress' familiar from the literature of early monasticism.[16]

And here three stages can be identified. Man's first task must be the overcoming of his disordered passions, not abolishing them so much as disciplining them, subjecting the 'concupiscible' and 'irascible' aspects of the soul to reason. In the second place, such 'active philosophy' leads one, via the virtues, to contemplate creatures in such a way that they disclose their *logoi*, which are simultaneously the 'reasons' for which they exist and their relationship to God as their beginning and end. But whereas such virtue and knowledge appear to be human works, carried out by way of the free and conscious actualisation of the capacities God gave man with human nature (though, as we shall see later when dealing with Maximus' soteriology, the somewhat Pelagian impression Croce gives here is distinctly misleading), the third stage — that of 'theology'

---

[15]V. Croce, *Tradizione e ricerca*, op. cit., p. 23. For the precedent tradition, see J. F. Bonnefoy, 'Origène théoricien de la méthode théologique', in *Mélanges Cavalléra* (Toulouse 1948), pp. 87-145; J. Plagnieux, *Saint Grégoire de Nazianze théologien* (Paris 1952), pp. 37-70; J. Conan, 'La démonstration dans le traité *Sur le Saint-Esprit* de saint Basile le Grand', *Studia Patristica* 9 (*Texte und Untersuchungen* 94; Berlin 1966), pp. 177-209; J. Beumer-L. Visschers, *Die theologische Methode* (*Handbuch der Dogmengeschichte* I.6; Freiburg 1972), p. 45.

[16]V. Croce, *Tradizione e ricerca*, op. cit. p. 25.

or 'theological mystagogy' — is the work of grace alone. As Croce synthesises Maximus' teaching on this point, such 'theology' is: a knowledge of God beyond all concepts; a direct sharing in his life; an *ekstasis* or 'standing out from' the natural condition of humanity, and, in its fulness, an eschatological event which will bring the process of divinisation by grace to its completion.[17] Although Maximus' vocabulary for the three stages of the spiritual life is, to a considerable degree, shared with Evagrius, who also treats of *phusikê* (the metaphysical), *praktikê* (the moral) and *theologikê* (the divine) — as well as echoing Gregory of Nyssa's *katharsis* (purification), *thêôria* (contemplation), *henôsis* (unity), the intellectualistic bias of Evagrius, and his pessimistic attitude towards material reality are foreign to Maximus' approach. The ascent to God always, for the latter, involves *agapê*, charity, while the passions, praxis, and 'natural contemplation' are not so much overcome as taken up.[18]

What most interests Croce here, in his specific concern with theological method, is Maximus' inclusion of theological research and demonstration in the *second* stage, that of the 'natural contemplation of beings'. It seems at first sight a strange thing to locate, within the material object of such 'natural contemplation', not only God's creatures but also the Bible, the Liturgy, the writings of the Fathers, and the declarations of the Councils. But we can at least take note of the fact that all of these disparate realities have it in common that they can be objects of human understanding. They are *materials* about which to reason.[19] In an important passage of the *Quaestiones ad Thalassium*, Maximus highlights the significance of this point.

The Word is familiar thanks to a twofold knowledge of things divine. One is relative, resting only on reason and concepts, and, furthermore, does not possess in actuated

---

[17]Ibid., pp. 26-27.

[18]L. Thunberg, *Microcosm and Mediator. The Theological Anthropology of Maximus the Confessor* (Lund 1965), pp. 351-381; vide infra, pp. 180-195.

[19]V. Croce, *Tradizione e ricerca*, op. cit., p. 28.

form the perception, by experience, of what is known.
With this kind of knowledge we are furnished in the
present life. The other, assuredly veracious, consists purely
in experience in act, without reason or concepts, and it
gains in an integral fashion the perception of what is
known, through grace, by participation. By way of this
kind of knowledge we shall, in the future rest, receive that
supernatural divinisation whose operation never comes
to an end.[20]

Ratiocinative, intellectual knowledge is distinguishable, in
other words, by its relativity when compared with the perceptual,
experiential knowledge that is the eschatological gift of God.
Theology in the modern sense of that word — a reflection on
divine realities by human beings in their present condition in
the world — has to move in the ambit of concepts. Such
thinking is summoned to transcend itself in a union with God
of a more than conceptual kind. Distinctive of Maximus'
theological epistemology is the fact that he displaces conceptual
thinking from ultimate centrality not, by a generalised appeal
to mysticism — not even the mysticism of the Age to Come, but
by his insistence on the need to develop a christocentric mind-
set. For the mystery of Christ, as the indescribable union of God
and man, is the true goal of all creation, and so the goal of
human thinking as well. As the Maximian passage cited above
continues:

This is the great, the hidden mystery. This is the blessed
goal for which all things subsist. This divine purpose,
thought out before the beginning of all beings, we define
as the pre-understood goal, to which all is ordered, while
itself it is ordered by nothing. Looking to this end, God
produced the essences of beings. This is truly the term of
Providence, and of those things that are subject to
Providence, by which, in God, there takes place the
recapitulation of all that he has made. This is the mystery
which circumscribes all the ages, and manifests the great

---

[20] *Quaestiones ad Thalassium* 60 (PG 90, 620C).

will of God, who is beyond the infinite, who is infinitely pre-existent to the ages, whose proclaimer was the Logos, divine by essence, when he made himself man. Thus was made evident, if I may speak so, the same revealed depths of the Father's goodness, and the end, for which all things received the beginning of their being, was shown for what it is.[21]

The Word of God

The basic pattern of Christian exegesis is already established in the New Testament's reading of its predecessor, the Old. It is the actualisation of Scripture in terms of the mystery of Christ. The Pauline letters exemplify this christological character of the distinctively Christian interpretation of Holy Writ with especial clarity, but it is far from confined to them.[22] This is not to say, however, that the Church was ignorant of interest in the history of Israel for its own sake (including there its moral and religious value). From pope Clement's ('First') Letter to the Corinthians onwards, a more 'literal' kind of exegesis existed side by side with its 'spiritual' (meaning, by and large, christological) counterpart. These two tendencies issue, after the sub-apostolic period, in the relatively stable exegetical traditions of two patristic schools: Alexandria and Antioch. While the Alexandrian school, in its early stages influenced by a Hellenised Judaism with a high level of culture, preferred to combine the by now traditional typological interpretation of the Old Testament with an allegorical concern for cosmology, anthropology and even angelology reminiscent of the local-born Jewish philosopher Philo, its Antiochene rival evinced a desire to cut back the more luxuriant growths of allegorical exposition. The contrast must not be too sharply drawn: Origen, a typical Alexandrian, is perfectly well able to integrate the letter into his ambitious scheme of book-by-book commentary of Scripture as a whole; the Antiochenes (a group

---

[21] *Ibid.* (PG 90, 620D-621B).

[22] M. Simonetti, *Profilo storico dell'esegesi patristica* (Rome 1981), pp. 14-18.

of divines with a family resemblance rather than a school in the institutional sense of the Alexandrian *didaskaleion*) were by no means innocent of the symbolic method.[23]

If the contrast of Alexandria and Antioch, though not antinomic, has any validity at all, then Maximus belongs firmly in the camp of the Egyptians. (The geographical reference is, by his period, otiose. Indeed Alexandrian-style exegesis was in favour within a century of Origen's death in places as far scattered as Asia Minor, Syro-Palestine and Cappadocia.) So far as hermeneutical theory is concerned, Croce finds Maximus' fullest account at a point in the *Quaestiones ad Thalassium* where his friend abbot Thalassius had sought help with construing II Chronicles 32, 20-21, a text describing how the Lord's angel, in answer to the prayers of king and prophet, was sent against the armies of Assyria. The explanation contains, so Croce reports, all the main terms and themes of Alexandrian exegesis, which he lists as: the 'incircumscribability' (that is, the transcendence) of the Word of God; its spiritual actuality, or relevance; the universal significance of what the Holy Spirit has inspired; its adaptability to each person (we have here, evidently, two sets of contrasting, yet correlative qualities); the counter-posing of the 'literal' and 'spiritual' senses of Scripture as, respectively, characteristic of Jewish and Christian modes of understanding, and lastly, in connexion with this, the necessity for the Christian to leave off the letter in search of the spirit. The passage is relatively lengthy, but Croce believes it important enough to present in full, and we shall follow suit.

> The Word of Holy Scripture, even if it admits of circumscription where the letter is concerned, limited as this is to the age of the facts narrated, remains, in what touches the spirit — the contemplation of intelligible realities — entirely *un*circumscribed. And no one will hesitate, finding that unacceptable, for they know well that the God who has spoken is by nature beyond circumscription. We must, rather, believe that the Word spoken by him is like him, if we sincerely wish to hear the

[23]Ibid., pp. 65-66.

counsel of Scripture. If indeed it is God who has spoken, and he is by essence uncircumscribed, it is clear that the Word spoken by him is uncircumscribed likewise. Therefore, contemplating spiritually these facts which happened as types... and limited to the outcome which, historically, they enjoyed, let us admire the wisdom of the Holy Spirit who in his writing adapted and fitting to each one who shares in human kind the meaning of what is written, so that whoever wishes can become a disciple of the Word of God....

And Maximus goes on:

For this too God came as incarnate — to fulfil spiritually the law, emptying out the letter, to stabilise and manifest the life-giving power of the law, eliminating from it the power of death. Now that which, according to the apostle, has the power of death in the law is the letter, just as, on the other hand, what has intrinsic life-giving power in the law is the spirit. For he says: 'The written code kills, but the spirit gives life.' Clearly then they have chosen the part opposed to Christ and have neglected the whole mystery of his Incarnation, not only burying in the letter their capacity for understanding, and not wishing to be in God's image and likeness, but, more than that, wishing to be earth, according to the decree of condemnation, and to return to the earth through their relation with the letter as with the earth.... They do grievous harm, since they offer many occasions for confirming the incredulity of the Jews. But we let them be as they will and return to ourselves and to the Scripture, beginning our spiritual research with the interpretation of the names in the text proposed.[24]

Maximus' idea of the 'spiritual' contemplation of the Bible belongs, however, to the wider context of his doctrine. In

[24]*Ibid.* 50 (PG 90, 465B-468C); the internal citation of Paul is from II Corinthians 3, 6.

language uncannily prophetic of Kant (and commentators on Maximus' exegetical methods recur to Kantian language at various points) three realities are said to offer themselves for our immediate consideration: oneself; the created order at large; and the Scriptures. Of these three we at first glance take in only the appearance: *hê epiphaneia, ta phainomena.* The truth, however, lives beyond, in the intelligible: *ho logos, ta noumena.* And so our search must take us too beyond the differentiated multiplicity of the sensuous towards the spiritual *logoi* of material things and finally to the supreme unity of the divine Logos.

> Human knowledge is, then, a passage, a transit, a going beyond (*diabasis*) which tends not to cancel out the sensuous manifold as though it were an evil, but to make of it a ladder of ascent towards the supreme Monad, God.[25]

Croce's findings are borne out by the detailed study of Maximus' exegetical vocabulary essayed by Paul M. Blowers, in his analysis of the *Quaestiones ad Thalassium*:

> I would conjecture [Blowers writes] that he concentrates on *diabainein-diabasis* because they [these terms] convey for him both a sense of *transcendence* — in keeping with the need to 'pass over', or to 'ascend beyond', sensible objects and the passions which they can spark — and yet also a crucial sense of *continuity*, namely, the necessity of first 'passing through' or 'penetrating' sensible objects en route to the intelligible or spiritual truth that, inheres, by grace, in those sensible things.[26]

In Scripture, what Croce terms, Kant-like, that 'sensuous manifold' is represented by the letter (*to gramma*), by which is meant a narration (*hê historia*) insofar as that is something written (*ta graphenta*). That letter is suitably transcended when,

---

[25]V. Croce, *Tradizione e ricerca*, op. cit., p. 35.

[26]P. M. Blowers, *Exegesis and Spiritual Pedagogy in Maximus the Confessor. An Investigation of the 'Quaestiones ad Thalassium'* (Notre Dame, Indiana 1991), p. 97.

thanks to its assistance, one gathers the spirit, *(to pneuma)*, the meaning (*to sêmainomen, hê dianoia*), what is intended by God (*ta noêthenta, ho logos*).

Although the Bible, in one way, simply illustrates a wider scheme, in another perspective, it is unique. For, as Croce's sub-heading indicates, it is itself, for Christian faith, the Word of God. Writing in the context of ancient Christendom, Maximus had no need to justify the claim that the Scriptures were divinely originated. However, he finds occasion to discuss the nature of that origination. The rôle of the sacred writer — normally indicated by the instrumental use of *dia*, 'through' — comes into view in connexion with the passage in First Peter where the apostle maintains:

> The prophets who prophesied of the grace that was to be yours searched and inquired about this salvation; they inquired what person or time was indicated by the Spirit of Christ within them when predicting the sufferings of Christ and the subsequent glory.[27]

Thalassius wishes to know what sort of research and investigation this might be. Maximus replies:

> It is not proper to say that grace alone by itself brought about in the saints the knowledge of the mysteries without those faculties which are by nature receptive of knowledge. Were it so, we would have to say that the holy prophets did not understand the force of the illuminations granted them by the Holy Spirit, and, in that case, how could the saying be true which has it that, 'The mind of the wise makes his speech judicious' (Proverbs 16, 23)? Again, it could not be without the grace of the Holy Spirit, searching with the natural faculty alone, that they arrived at the true knowledge of beings. Were it so, the breaking in of the Spirit would be useless to the saints, if in nothing did that Spirit co-work with them for the manifestation of the truth. But in that case, how could the text be true which has it that 'Every good

---

[27] I Peter 1, 10-11.

endowment and every perfect gift is from above, coming down from the Father of lights' (James 1, 17)?[28]

But not only is the *Spirit* the inspirer of Scripture; the Bible may also be regarded as the incarnation (in a certain sense) of the *Logos* of God. Notably in the *Capitula gnostica*, Maximus borrows from Origen the theme of the Word found in the Book.[29]

> The Logos of God is not called flesh simply by virtue of the Incarnation. The divine Logos, in the beginning with God the Father, was ever the Intelligible One, who possessed, manifestly and nakedly, the truth about everything, to the exclusion of parables, enigmas and narratives that demand allegorical explanation. [And yet] if this Word is made flesh, coming to dwell with men, who are incapable of understanding with the naked intellect nakedly intelligible things, and speak in ways they are used to, then he will unite with himself the variety of narratives, enigmas, parables and dark sayings.[30]

Maximus' tracing of the ultimate origins of Scripture to both the Spirit and the Son provides him, so Croce thinks, with his fundamental principles of biblical interpretation.[31]

The *first* of these principles is stated in the prologue to the *Quaestiones ad Thalassium: pneumatikôs pneumatika synkrinontes,* 'Seek with the Spirit what is of the Spirit'.[32] The exegesis of Scripture can only be 'spiritual', and that in virtue of three considerations: the knowing subject, the divine Object to be sought out, and the medium in which the knowing in question takes place. The *second* principle concerns, rather, the *Logos* of God. At one point in the *Quaestiones ad Thalassium*, Maximus turns to Christ with the splendid prayer:

---

[28] *Quaestiones ad Thalassium* 59 (PG 90. 604D-605A).

[29] On this, see R. Gögler, *Zur Theologie des biblischen Wortes bei Origenes* (Düsseldorf 1963).

[30] *Capita gnostica* II. 60 (PG 90, 1149C-1152A). Cf. Origen, *Commentarium in Matthaeum, fragmenta* (GCS 41, 1, p. 19, 11).

[31] V. Croce, *Tradizione e ricerca*, op. cit., p. 38.

[32] PG 90, col. 245B; cf. I Corinthians 2, 13.

Come, highly praised Logos of God, give us the revelation
of your words adapted to us. And once the enveloping
swathes are removed, show us O Christ, the beauty of the
intelligible realities.[33]

As the Logos is at the origin of the biblical word, so is he the
light for understanding it and its ultimate object.

The *logoi* of the biblical narrative are, like all creaturely
logoi, essentially referred to the unique Logos, from whom
they take their origin and meaning.[34]

And Croce sums up the groundwork of Maximus' hermeneutical
scheme in a little formula of his own: 'Seek the logos of
narrative according to the spirit', justifying the distribution of
terms with the thought that, for Maximus, the Spirit is more
frequently the medium of research, the Logos its goal.[35]

The scheme draws its own consequences in its train. First, if
the Word of God, like God himself, is uncircumscribed then
the biblical word will prove, as Maximus himself remarks,
'endowed with infinity of its own nature'.[36] A single passage can
justify an inexhaustible treasury of interpretations — where,
that is, the 'spirit' is concerned, since, as letter, the biblical
word is limited, as are all creatures. Maximus insists that every
syllable of Scripture has meaning for whoever 'desires virtue
and knowledge',[37] including there names and numbers.
Although Maximus was interested in etymology and
'arithmology', he did not, however, take this principle to
capricious extremes, maintaining that where, for example,
names are concerned, these must be interpreted 'in relation to
the underlying use and to the force of prophecy'.[38] What is in
view is, of course, spiritual contemplation and not notions of

---

[33] *Questiones ad Thalassium* 48 (PG 90 433A).
[34] V. Croce, *Tradizione e ricerca*, op. cit., p. 39.
[35] Ibid., pp. 39-40.
[36] *Quaestiones ad Thalassium*, prologue (PG 90, 294A).
[37] *Quaestiones ad Thalassium* 47 (PG 90, 424NA).
[38] Ibid., 26 (PG 90, 345C).

historical criticism. The salvific value of the meaning of past history is paramount, not that history itself, for its own sake. Taking his cue from Paul's account of the wilderness wanderings in I Corinthians 10, 11, Maximus declares:

> If in fact those things happened to them in figure according to history, for us, by contrast, they were written down for a spiritual warning — we for whom that which was written takes place always, in the way of understanding.[39]

It is not a matter of cancelling out the past, but its re-evocation in a different way. Maximus explicitly remarks that:

> What is past as regards history is always mystically present to us as regards contemplation.[40]

What is involved is the overcoming of the factual materiality of the past in order to grasp its spiritual force.

> Let us leave, then, the fact already achieved materially in the time of Moses and consider instead with the eyes of the mind the force of the fact in the Spirit, a force which is always at work and which, in working, enters ever more into vigour.[41]

As Croce puts it most felicitously:

> (History) remains, as sign and mystery, in the hands of the Spirit for the salvation of men. Once again, sense, flesh, letter, are not to be eliminated as impure, but to be transcended as insufficient.[42]

Such 'transcending' is, as already indicated, never done save in the Holy Spirit. Here purification and illumination go hand

---

[39]Ibid., 52 (PG 90, 497A).
[40]*Quaestiones ad Thalassium* 49 (PG 90, 449B).
[41]Ibid., 17 (PG 90, 304B).
[42]V. Croce, *Tradizione e ricerca*, op. cit., p. 43.

in hand—not as though that sequence constitutes an automatic succession, for divine illumination remains always grace, freely given, and yet, to be received it does require the mind's purification from the passions.[43] This is Maximus' way of applying to what the *Ambigua* call 'biblical gnosis' his general account of the steps in spiritual knowledge.[44] Biblical understanding can only be sapiential. Simultaneously, such knowledge requires the activity of the divine Logos also: he it is who invites readers of Scripture to the 'indescribable place of his banquet', where he feeds each in a way proportioned to each's capacity.[45]

> The unique and self-identical Logos becomes all things to all men, according to the capacity of each diffusing himself in each one... in some he is conversion, as precursor of the future righteousness; in others virtue, as presupposition of the knowledge awaited; in yet others knowledge itself, as seal of the future contemplative habit.[46]

But if Maximus underlines, in these ways, the varied comprehension that Scripture makes possible, he does not hesitate to draw out from his basic interpretative principles the equally necessary truth of the unity of Scripture, and, especially, its lack of all internal discordance.

> The word of God is, as an entire whole, neither *polylogos* nor *polylogia* but one single reality, formed out of many considerations *(teôrêmata)*, each of which is a part of the word.[47]

This is not so on the level of the letter, but on that of the spirit. Where difficulties of internal coherence raised by the biblical

---

[43] *Quaestiones ad Thalassium* 65 (PG 90, 737A).
[44] *Ambigua* 10 (PG 91, 1128D, 1128D).
[45] *Quaestiones ad Thalasium* 48 (PG 90, 433B).
[46] Ibid., 47 (PG 90, 429B).
[47] *Capitula gnostica* II. 20 (PG 90, 1133C). Cf. Origen, *Commentarium in Joannem* V. 5 (GCS 10, p. 102).

text are concerned:

> Since the solution... is impossible for those who give
> priority to the letter, and prefer what is said to its meaning,
> let us come to the spiritual understanding of the Scriptures
> and we shall find without labour the truth hidden in the
> letter, which shines like the light to those who love truth.[48]

Maximus signals an important difference in this regard, however,
as between the Old Testament and the New. In the *Capitula
gnostica*, at any rate, the Gospel is identified with truth itself.

> The law had the shadow; the prophets the image of the
> divine and spiritual good things of the Gospel. The
> Gospel in its turn made manifest to us the truth itself
> through words, that truth adumbrated in the law, pre-
> figured in the prophets.[49]

But since the Gospel truth is invested in words, which belong
to the sensuous world, Maximus can also say that 'the law has
the shadow of the Gospel, and the Gospel is the image [only]
of the good things to come'.[50] Maximus' view of the provisional
quality of Scripture is displayed in a passage of the *Ambigua*,
where he takes issue with Gregory Nazianzen for seemingly
downplaying St John the Baptist as a mere precursor of the
Gospel.[51] Yet the Gospel too, Maximus points out, is in one
sense itself only preparatory.

> John the great evangelist in his Gospel is also a precursor
> of that Logos who was more mystical and greater than he,
> the Logos indicated through him, the Logos who cannot
> be figured forth with words or pronounced with the voice
> that proceeds from a carnal tongue... Since in fact the law
> was a preparing, according to the knowledge disclosed up

---

[48] *Quaestiones ad Thalassium* 52 (PG 90, 492B-C).
[49] *Capitula gnostica* I. 93 (PG 90, 1121A).
[50] *Capitula gnostica* I. 90 (PG 90, 1120C).
[51] *Orationes theologicae* 28, 20 (PG 36, 53A).

to that time, of those who, by means of the law, were guided to Christ, the Logos in flesh, and led to the Gospel by his first coming, so also the holy Gospel is a preparation of those who through its instrumentality are guided to Christ, the Logos in spirit, and are led to the future world for his second coming. The Gospel too, in fact, is flesh and spirit, becoming the one or the other according to the knowledge of each one, given that every word (*logos*) happens by sounds and letters.[52]

Here the triad 'shadow, image, truth' covers the entire span of the economy of salvation.[53] So much so is maintained by Maximus himself in virtually those very words:

In fact, in shadow, image and truth there is wisely dispensed everything in the mystery of salvation which regards ourselves. As the great apostle says, 'The law has but a shadow of the good things to come instead of the true form of these realities' (Hebrews 10, 1). By its means, the Logos prepared for the receiving of the Gospel, through a certain obscure signification of the truth, those who lived according to the law in the way appropriate to them. The Gospel possesses the image of the truth, and holds it out clearly, right up to the present, for those who have the similitude of the good things to come. The Logos makes them ready through the hope of receiving the archetypes of those goods, of being enlivened by them and becoming the living images of Christ, and, indeed, one sole reality with him through grace and not just a likeness alone: they become, one might even say, if this manner of speaking did not seem to some too audacious, that self-same Lord.[54]

---

[52]*Ambigua* 21 (PG 91, 1244D-1245A).

[53]For Origen's use, see M. Harl, *Origène et la fonction révélatrice du Verbe incarné* (Paris 1958), pp. 139-153.

[54]*Ambigua* 21 (PG 91, 1253CD). For the theme of identification with Christ, see *Epistolae* 25 (PG 91, 613D) where it is explained that what is involved is total likeness, *kata panta homoios*, excluding identity of nature, *chôris tês kata tên phusin tautotêtos* — a caution against the Palestinian monks who claimed to be *isochristoi*: see J. Meyendorff, *Le Christ dans la théologie byzantine* (Paris 1969), p. 72.

Scripture's unity is its essential relatedness to the final truth, the definitive manifestation of the Logos, the completed achievement of the future good things.

For Croce, Maximian exegesis amounts to nothing less than a reading of the whole Bible in the light of the mystery of Christ. That mystery, already perceived in faith, provides the hermeneutical key to the interpretation of the Scriptures. As Croce puts it:

> It is the prior manifestation of the Logos in its all-embracing and unified quality which gives the point of departure to, and the foundation for, the analytic comprehension of the Gospels, the Law and the prophets. It is not so much that the Scriptures show us Christ, as that Christ shows himself in the Scriptures. Spiritual interpretation is therefore justified on the basis of this sort of pre-understanding of the mystery of Christ, which comes to illuminate all that could be obscure in the Bible, and not in the Bible alone but in all creation.[55]

Croce is able to substantiate this claim by two telling citations from the *Capitula gnostica*. In the first 'century', Maximus writes:

> The mystery of the embodiment of the Logos includes the force of all the enigmas and types of Scripture, and the knowledge of creatures visible and intelligible. He who has known the mystery of the Cross and Burial has known the *logoi* of all these afore-mentioned things. He who has been initiated into the indescribable power of the Resurrection, has known the goal for which God in the beginning gave subsistence to all things.[56]

And again, in the second 'century':

> When the Logos of God becomes in us clear and luminous, and his face shines like the sun, then too his garments

---

[55] V. Croce, *Tradizione e ricerca*, op. cit., p. 52.
[56] *Capitula gnostica* I. 66 (PG 90, 1108AB).

appear white: that is, the words of sacred Scripture in the Gospels appear evident and manifest, having nothing about them that is hidden. Moses and Elijah, too, come with him: namely, the more spiritual *logoi* of the Law and the prophets.[57]

However, Croce suggests that, by a kind of hermeneutical *perichôrêsis*, the mystery of Christ can also be found at the end of a process (and not just at the beginning), as the term to which a critical reading of the text leads. From the literal sense, one can move forward to the mystical (or intelligible, or spiritual) meaning and hence to the Logos himself — even though one *also* needs the light of the Logos to resolve the enigmas, to gather the archetypes from their types, to dispel the shadow of the Old Testament and to see the truth indicated by the images. In any case, Christology, or the mystery of Christ, is the centre, since that mystery expresses itself in humankind at large, in the individual human being, in the Church and in the cosmos. Not surprisingly, then, in the *Mystagogia*,[58] the four *archai* or founding principles (the word is Origen's) shown reciprocally inter-acting in that text — Church, Scripture, cosmos, man — are expressions of the single Logos, who is 'the beginning, middle and end of all beings that can be conceived and spoken of'.[59]

Maximus' attitude to letter and spirit depends, in practice, on the overall aim of his exegesis. And that is: the mystery of the incarnate Word conceived as, simultaneously, the mystery of our own salvation.[60] He presents 'biblical contemplation', *graphikê thêôria*, in terms of a dialectic of unity and multiplicity. In a lengthy passage of the *Ambigua*, he speaks of a unity that

> expands into a tenfoldness: place, time, kind, person, dignity or task, practical philosophy, natural philosophy, theological philosophy, present and future — that is, figure and truth...

[57] *Capitula gnostica* II. 14 (PG 90, 1132A).
[58] *Mystagogia* 1, 7 (PG 90, 308C).
[59] *Questiones ad Thalassium* 19 (PG 90, 308C).
[60] Cf. ibid., 62 (PG 90, 468D; V. Croce, *Tradizione e ricerca*, op. cit., p. 59.

But these ten modes also contract, and concentrate themselves:
the first five leading to the next three, and these to the final
duo, namely, the present and the future, while the latter take
us, finally, to what is 'most perfect and simple', namely:

> the all-comprehensive, ineffable Logos, from whom by
> progression (*kata proödon*) there derive the generality of
> the ten modes comprised within the contemplation of
> Scripture, and to which, as to a principle, the same
> tenfoldness by circumscription re-ascends (*anatatikôs*),
> led back once again to unity.[61]

Everything that we hold to be truth, Maximus goes on, is in
reality a figure, shadow and image of the 'higher Logos'. In the
incarnate Word of God, everything is gathered up: each human
truth, each divine truth, must be interpreted in terms of his
unique reality.[62]

All in all, Croce makes it clear that Maximus' hermeneutics
are definitely a *theology* of biblical language. They are not
notably indebted to a *philosophy* of what language may be.
There is here a contrast between Maximus and his Cappadocian
predecessor Gregory of Nyssa. The deviant account of the
'divine Names' given by the Cappadocians' arch-opponent
Eunomius forced Nyssa to consider, in the wake of the great
Constantinopolitan synod of 381, the relation between the
natural sense of the words found in human language and their
deeper meaning when taken up in revelation. Such a controversy
lay in a past but dimly remembered at the time when Maximus
himself wrote.[63]

The Faith of the Church

In Maximus' theological criteriology, Fathers and Councils are
inextricably combined; but since, to be authoritative sources,

---

[61] *Ambigua* 37 (PG 91, 1293AB).

[62] Ibid., 1296D.

[63] M. Canevet, *Grégoire de Nysse et l'herméneutique biblique. Etude des rapports entre le langage et la connaissance de Dieu* (Paris 1983), pp. 28-29.

both must be 'approved', *enkritoi*, they refer us to the more fundamental reality of the Church herself, as that from which they draw their probative force. Though Maximus has no dogmatic treatise *de Ecclesia*, and the Church is of interest in his writings primarily as place of proclamation of the orthodox *faith*, nonetheless this primary aspect belongs with a wider Maximian theology of the Church as a community both saved and mediating salvation, both one and unifying, both believing and teaching.

Maximus' most common way of denominating the Church is as 'holy Church' or 'the holy Church of God', a phrase which, as Croce indicates, suggests at once the Church's origin in God, her belonging to God, and her nature as the place of the presence of God.[64] In the *Mystagogia* he speaks of the Church as bearing the divine image, because she 'has the same energy, by imitation and figure'.

> For God who made and brought into existence all things by his infinite power contains, gathers, and limits them and in his Providence binds both intelligible and sensuous being to himself and to one another... It is in this way that the holy Church of God will be shown to be working for us the same effects as God, in the same way as the image reflects its archetype. For numerous and of almost infinite number are the men, women and children who are distinct from one another and vastly different by birth and appearance, by nationality and language, by customs and age, by opinions and skills, by manners and habits, by pursuits and studies, and still again by reputation, fortune, characteristics and connections. All are born into the Church and through her are reborn and recreated in the Spirit. To all in equal measure she gives and bestows one divine form and designation, to be Christ's and to carry his name. In accordance with faith she gives to all a single, simple, whole and indivisible condition which does not allow us to bring to mind the existence of the myriads of differences among them (even if they do exist) through

---

[64]V. Croce, *Tradizione e ricerca*, op. cit., p. 66.

the universal relationship and union of all things with the Church. It is through her that absolutely no one at all is in himself separated from the community since everyone converges with all the rest and joins together with them by the one simple and indivisible grace and power of faith.[65]

Here Maximus locates the Church within his wider theological vision, stressing, via his preferred language of exemplarity, the nature of the Church as sacrament of God in Christ. For it is by making his own Paul's doctrine of the Church as that body whose head is Christ that Maximus can go on, in a continuation of this passage, to say:

As the centre of straight lines that radiate from him [Christ], he does not allow, by his unique, simple and single cause and power, that the principles of beings become disjoined at the periphery. Rather does he circumscribe their extension in a circle and bring back to himself the distinctive elements of beings which he brought into existence. The purpose of this is so that the creations and products of the one God be in no way strangers and enemies to one another, having no reason or centre for which they might show each other any friendly or peaceful sentiment or identity, and not run the risk of having their being separated from God to dissolve into nonbeing.[66]

The echoes of the Letter to the Ephesians are unmistakable, yet, as Croce points out, all is recast in the characteristic Maximian metaphysical mould. Elsewhere Maximus stresses by way of a variety of biblical images that the Church's unity comes from Christ and inheres in him. He is the 'bond of union' between pagans and Jews; the 'entry-point and door of the Church'; the 'corner-stone' of the unity of the peoples bound in concord by the single word of faith.[67] Because the

[65] *Mystagogia* 1 (PG 91, 664D-668A).
[66] Ibid., at PG 91, 668AC.
[67] *Quaestiones ad Thalassium* 48 (PG 90, 433C-D); Ibic. 53 (PG 90, 501B).

Lord himself freely saved her by his own life-giving blood, and brought her into existence by his Passion, she can be herself the mediatrix of salvation. As Maximus writes in the *Mystagogy*:

We do not therefore abandon the holy Church of God, who possesses such mysteries for our salvation in the sacred ordering of the celebration of the divine symbols. By means of them she, in an outstanding way, creates each of us according to Christ, forming us as is appropriate, manifesting the grace of sonship through holy Baptism in the Holy Spirit...[68]

The Christian is then always *teknon*: a child born of the Church,[69] though Maximus does not, as we might expect, go on to call the Church our 'Mother'.[70]

In Maximus' ecclesiology, such a visionary, metaphysical, sacramental and Christic understanding of the Church is in no way incompatible with emphasis on her mystery as expressed in a visible community of a well-defined kind. Whereas, as the *Mystagogy* reminds its readers, there may be much human diversity in the Church, she must always remain one in her profession of faith. Though Maximus is aware that belonging to the Catholic Church is mediated by participation in a particular church, its faith and Eucharistic celebration, his focus of attention lies elsewhere. Croce, who considers many of Maximus' references to particular churches to be formulaic and stereotyped, declares roundly:

What mattered to Maximus was not the vindication of a variety in the expression of the faith in individual churches, but unity in the profession of the faith through the whole world.[71]

Those who maintain that, historically, Oriental ecclesiology has always been resolutely particularist, privileging the local

---

[68]*Mystagogia* 24 (PG 91, 712AB).
[69]*Epistle* 12 (PG 91, 497A).
[70]V. Croce, *Tradizione e ricerca*, op. cit., p. 69, for these references.
[71]Ibid., p. 71.

church as the locus (precisely) of truth and life, and regard a universalist ecclesiology, giving priority to the one Church from which the many churches proceed, as an isolated Latin phenomenon, should take note of this statement and its grounds in so important a Byzantine Father![72] The Church is catholic, universal, in the measure that she is not *merikon*, partial or particular, and to the degree that there reigns within her life not what is singular, *idion*, but that is *koinon*, 'common'.[73] Heresy for Maximus is a negation of catholic communion by misplaced particularity. Indeed, opposition to heresy enters into the very definition of the Church in the *Opuscula theologica et polemica* where he calls her 'the new Zion, where believers can find refuge from the wind of heresy'.[74] But what is heresy, and what orthodoxy? Maximus replies, the catholic, concordant or common is *what originates in the apostolic preaching*, 'the pious, right, true and saving word of the apostolic faith'.[75]

Such apostolicity of faith has two aspects: not only must what is believed and taught today in the Church be founded on the apostolic preaching, but the continuity of the apostolic faith with its contemporary expression must be established by way of those who, historically, provide for the Church a continuance of the apostolic succession. In this sense, in Croce's words, 'Tradition and hierarchy are inseparable principles'.[76] The orthodox faith is that which the saints *received*, transmitted to them as it was *kata diadochên, by succession*.[77] Over against the claims of the Byzantine emperors to a rôle in the determination of public doctrine, Maximus gives to the bishops the task of distinguishing between mere *kainotomia*, 'innovation', and genuine exposition of the original faith.[78]

---

[72]Cf. the discussion of 'the One and the Many' in the ecclesiological tradition, East and West, in my *Theology in the Russian Diaspora. Church, Fathers, Eucharist in Nikolai Afanas'ev, 1893-1966* (Cambridge 1989), pp. 177-187.

[73]*Relatio motionis* 6 (PG 90, 120C).

[74]*Opuscula theologica et polemica* 2 (PG 91, 52A).

[75]Epistle 18 (PG 91, 584).

[76]V. Croce, *Tradizione e ricerca*, op. cit., p. 74.

[77]*Ambigua* 41 (PG 91, 1304D); for the varied background to this term, both biblical and extra-biblical, in the ancient world, see A. M. Javierre Ortas, *El tema literario de la Sucesión. Prolegómenos para el estudio de la Sucesión apostólica* (Zürich 1963).

[78]*Disputatio Byziae* 9 (PG 90, 144c).

Croce gives short shrift to the idea that Maximus might be a theoretician of the idea of the 'sensus fidei' of the people of God. In a dogmatic context, 'faith' to him means the receptive attitude of the individual believer to the common doctrine, expressed in the teaching of the Church's Fathers whether living or dead.[79] But what Maximus looks for in a Church Father is custody of the 'right word of pious faith, changing nothing of its meaning',[80] and in this sense the hierarchy's ecclesiastical teaching is not autonomous in preceding and founding ecclesial faith, since by what Croce calls a 'kind of *perichôrêsis*' — a 'virtuous circle', we might term it — the profession of right faith constitutes the Church even as it is she who determines the dogmata of right faith.[81] At any rate, orthodoxy of believing is, for Maximus, the central reality of the Church: her holiness is 'piety' in holding this faith; her catholicity is continuity in its profession; her unity is identity of its acceptance. But the orthodox faith is thus vital because without true Christian gnosis, man cannot rise from the practice of virtue to the indescribable meeting with God.

In Maximus' account of tradition, the Liturgy and the Fathers play an outstanding part. At first reading, his *Mystagogia* has little to say about the dogmatic value of the Liturgy, concerned as that text so largely is with ascetical and mystical considerations. Yet he does present the Liturgy nevertheless as an initiation in knowledge of the mystery of Christ. Croce sums up Maximus' approach very well: for him

> the Liturgy is the place of faith, not in that faith is defined there but because it is mystically exercised in ascent towards God.[82]

In this sense, the Liturgy's rôle in his theological vision is closer to that of revelation than to the task of ecclesiastical teaching. It might usefully be compared with — in the modern period —

---

[79]*Epistle* 13 (PG 91, 532C).
[80]Ibid., 15 (PG 91, 549A).
[81]V. Croce, *Tradizione e ricerca*, op. cit., pp. 79-80.
[82]Ibid., p. 82.

Dom Odo Casel's *Mysterientheologie,* for which the symbols of the Liturgy are the effective invocation of the original revelatory experience.[83]

This does not mean, however, that the *regula fidei* of sound doctrine ever ceases to guide the spiritual life, and if asked where it can be found Maximus would reply: in the writings and sayings of the Fathers. *Kata tous pateras* is, Croce reports, one of his commonest phrases. But who *are* the Fathers? Basically, those great teaching bishops of the past whom the Church has approved — *hoi enkritoi Pateres* — and who are here identified in terms of a conventional choice of names in the discussion of Maximus' time. Maximus reinforces his references to their *authentia,* 'authority', by calling them *hagioi,* 'saints', and *didaskaloi,* 'teachers' — with the genitive phrase 'of the Church' frequently added, though Croce would leave open the question whether this be an objective genitive, indicating that the Church comes from their witness, or a subjective one, warning that it falls to the Church to distinguish 'her' Fathers from those who do not belong to her.[84]

Maximus is not afraid to couple the Fathers with the Bible and to use for both the same vocabulary of divine origination. For, like the biblical writers, the Church's Fathers were God-inspired, *theopneustoi*; they are *theokritoi,* approved by God; *theolêptoi,* carried away by God; *theophoroi,* God-carriers; made wise by God, *theophronoi*; and given eloquence by him, *theôgoroi.*[85] And yet since Maximus evidently regards it as the job of a theologian to show the concordance of the Fathers' teaching with Scripture, despite the grammatical parataxis he uses, the Bible is meant to be the primary reality here, and patristic teaching subordinate to it. The Fathers are agents of the tradition expressed in Scripture but so transmitted by them that it becomes *patristic tradition, hê patrikê paradosis.* Since it is then primarily the Fathers who secure for the Church her apostolicity, nothing could be less surprising than the proportion of Maximus' efforts, in the controversies over

[83]O. Casel, *The Mystery of Christian Worship* (London 1962).
[84]v. Croce, *Tradizione e ricerca,* op. cit., pp. 86-87.
[85]For references, see ibid., p. 88.

Monothelite and Monoenergist Christology, that went to showing the rootedness of the doctrine of the two wills and two operations of the Redeemer in the teaching of the 'approved Fathers'. For while the terms used by certain such Fathers might sound monophysitical, their meaning, according to Maximus, was much different: 'not in syllables, but in concepts and realities, *noêmai kai pragmai*, consists the mystery of our salvation'.[86] What we must look for is the meaning, *dianoia*, of the expressions, *ta phôna*, of the Fathers.[87] On any particular doctrine, it is the consensus of the approved Fathers which manifests the true belonging of some putative credendum with the faith of the Church. Because Maximus understood this requirement in a highly rigorist sense, such that one exception would invalidate it, he strove at times with what we might consider more zeal than wisdom to find a 'dyadic' meaning in such 'monadic' expressions as Cyril's 'one nature of the Word Incarnate' or Denys' 'single theandric energy'.

The topic of the Fathers leads by natural progression to that of the *Councils* of the Church. Croce actually introduces this subject by a text from the *Opuscula theologica et polemica* where Maximus remarks rhetorically that even if no patristic text confirmed the Chalcedonian definition, nothing would prevent that 'most holy Council of orthodox Fathers' from promulgating that definition 'with authority', *exousiastikôs*, and giving it, over against Eutyches, the force of law.[88] And yet, as Croce immediately points out, in concrete actuality Maximus believes the teaching of such Councils to coincide with that of the Fathers who link them to Christ's apostles.[89] More synthetically, then: the Christian faith comes from the witness of Scripture as reporting the preaching of the apostles, the eye-witnesses of Christ, a witness faithfully transmitted by the Fathers, the right understanding of whose faith the Councils sanction by their declarations.[90]

---

[86]*Epistle* 19 (PG 91, 596BC).
[87]*Disputatio Byziae* 13 (PG 90, 149A).
[88]*Opuscula theologica et polemica* 22 (PG 91, 257C).
[89]V. Croce, *Tradizione e ricerca*, op. cit., pp. 102-103.
[90]Ibid., p. 103.

How many such Councils are there? In his pre-649 writings, Maximus speaks of the 'five' Ecumenical Councils, but in the letter he despatched from Rome in the year of the Lateran synod, 649, he augments the number to *six*.[91] Though Maximus does not call that synod ecumenical, there can be no doubt, thinks Croce, that he treated it as such. For him, the *Lateratense* met all the conditions for ecumenicity that he regarded as essential. The patriarchs of the Eastern churches were absent, but he believed them to be heretics, and so outside the ecclesial *koinônia*. Croce does not enlighten us, however, as to what ecclesial significance Maximus might have attached to the presence of Orientals as such at this synod: for its personnel included two Palestinian bishops, and a number of monastic clergy from three of the four Eastern patriarchates (not Alexandria). The seventh century notion of the *consortium fidei apostolicae*, seen as binding together pope and bishops, monks and people, would have directed attention to this modest but genuine representativeness.[92] It did not trouble Maximus that the pope of the synod, Martin I, was subsequently deposed. To his mind, if a Council has been celebrated with canonical integrity, no subsequent event can cassate the binding force of its determinations.[93]

Among those determinations there was one absolutely vital *genre*, that of the Creed, the essential form in which the Christian message is contained. And yet it was clear enough that the Creed of Nicaea (meaning that of Nicaea-Constantinople) did not include the crucial formula of Chalcedon 'in two natures', whose defence underlay the Dyothelite and Dyoenergist action and passion of Maximus. He was obliged to confront, then, in however limited a way, the issue of doctrinal development. Maximus, despite his view of heresy as innovation, took courage from the example of

[91] *Opuscula theologica et polemica* 11 (PG 91, 137D).

[92] P. Conte, 'Il *consortium fidei apostolicae* tra vescovo di Roma e vescovi nel secolo VII, con appendice filologica e canonica', in M. Maccarrone (ed.), *Il primato di Pietro nel primo millenio. Ricerche e testimonianze. Atti del symposium storico-teologico, Roma, 9-13 Ottobre 1989* (Vatican City 1991), pp. 363-431.

[93] V. Croce, *Tradizione e ricerca*, op. cit., p. 107.

Gregory Nazianzen, who had not hesitated to develop, *prodiarthrein*, what Nicaea had to say incompletely, *ellipôs*, on the topic of the Holy Spirit, giving as his justification the fact that the question of the Spirit's *homoousion* had not yet been raised.[94] The Fathers of Chalcedon, according to Maximus, had simply brought to light and 'as it were explained' the Creed of Nicaea, for the benefit of those who were expounding that Creed erratically, indeed erroneously. In other words, vis-à-vis errors or misunderstandings, what is implicit and virtual in the Christian message delivered by apostles, Fathers and Councils may be rendered explicit and actual. This is not innovation, but a growth in understanding, *katanoêsis*, of the Gospel, in fidelity to tradition as received.[95]

Croce's final duty in offering an account of the ecclesial dimension of Maximus' fundamental theology is to signal the special place he gave — not least in the case of the Lateran council, already mentioned, to the Roman church. As the question is a delicate one, he approaches it with great care, setting forth Maximus' views in their chronological development.

The first relevant text is Maximus' defence of pope Honorius, written around 640.[96] The maligned pope, in writing 'We profess one sole will of our Lord Jesus Christ' did not intend to deny the duality of natural wills in Christ, argues Maximus, but only to exclude any inner division in the Saviour produced by human sinfulness. Maximus remarks that this view of Honorius' teaching was confirmed by a Greek priest, one Athanasius, who returning from Rome reported that the pope's synodal counsellors, 'most holy men of the great church', were grieved at the misinterpretation of the statement which had gained ground. Such a generous view was not, alas, shared by the fathers of the Sixth Ecumenical Council. Curiously, Greek

[94]Gregory's *Letter* 102 (PG 37, 193C) is cited in *Opuscula theologica et polemica* 22 (PG 91, 257B-260D).

[95]Maximus echoes here the position of Gregory Nazianzen, who regarded the doctrine of the Spirit's divinity as earlier 'indicated', but later proclaimed, when the Nicene confession of the Godhead of the Son made this appropriate: *Theological Orations* V. 25 (PG 36, 161ff.).

[96]*Opuscula theologica et polemica* 20 (PG 91, 228B-245, 245D).

controversialists in the Middle Ages made little of the 'heretical pope', while the West barely remembered the incident (the Latin originals of Honorius' letters were burnt at Constantinople) until cardinal Nicholas of Cusa blew the dust off it in his *De concordantia catholica* of 1431-1433. His case, however, was widely disputed among Catholics and Lutherans, and between Gallican and Ultramontane Catholics in the post-Renaissance period — not least during the preparation of the decree on papal infallibility of the First Vatican Council of 1869-1870. Though few scholars today regard the seventh century condemnation as an interpolation, it remains, of course, possible to hold that Honorius' replies to Sergius hardly fall into the category of *ex cathedra* definitions — and even that his lapse, in the eyes of his Dyothelite contemporaries, lay in negligence rather than open error. It is a topic where history and apologetics (both defensive and accusatory) are peculiarly intertwined.[97]

By the date of Croce's second text, which dates from 643 or 644, Maximus' tone has changed and his doctrine of the Roman see sharpened. Between his comments on the career of Honorius and the letter to Peter the Illustrious, the *Ekthesis* had been promulgated, and the Constantinopolitan patriarch Pyrrhus anathematised by pope Theodore I. In an East increasingly favourable to the one-will and one-energy doctrines, Maximus now calls on the Roman church as 'the most holy see of the apostolic men who guide well all the fulness of the Catholic Church and conserve her in order according to the divine law'. This letter contains, according to Croce, Maximus' strongest statements on the primacy, in which he identifies, as we shall see, the Roman see with the Catholic Church herself.

If in fact the Roman see is aware that Pyrrhus is not only reprobate but also thinks and believes erroneously, it is quite plain that whoever anathematises those who reprove Pyrrhus anathematises the Roman see, that is, the Catholic Church. We could say, indeed, that such an individual

---

[97]G. Kreuzer, *Die Honoriusfrage im Mittelalter und in der Neuzeit* (Stuttgart 1975), p. 226.

anathematises himself, at any rate if he is in communion with the Roman see and the Catholic Church.

And Maximus adds that, if someone wishes not to be considered heretical then let him give satisfaction to the Roman church, since, once that see is satisfied, 'everyone everywhere will together declare him pious and orthodox'. Maximus refers here both to the *sedens*, the 'most blessed pope of the most holy church of the Romans', and the *sedes*:

> the apostolic see, which from the ... Word Incarnate and from all the holy Councils, according to the sacred canons and definitions, receives and holds, in all, for all and above all the holy churches of God throughout the world, the command, the authority and the power to bind and loose.[98]

Here Maximus goes far beyond the idea of an appellate jurisdiction lodged in the Roman see to the notion that the local church of Rome carries the *persona* of the whole Church — a theme which Croce compares, illuminatingly, to Maximus' willingness, already touched on, to regard the voice of a Council as the voice of the Church likewise.[99]

Two years later Maximus turned to the question of other doctrinal differences between West and East, and notably the *Filioque*.[100] Since the doctrinal content of his comments on that much-debated theme will be described in the next chapter — when we shall be examining Maximus' Triadology and Christology with the aid of the Belgian Jesuit, Pierre Piret, it will suffice to note here the implications of his remarks for his view of the Western church and especially of Rome. In line with his primary concern for the unitary quality of the faith, in East and West alike, he defends the acceptability of the Latin account of the Spirit's procession, while maintaining that the Greek is the more precise. Croce comments on how this letter reveals a

---

[98] *Opuscula theologica et polemica* 12 (PG 91, 144A-D).
[99] V. Croce, *Tradizione e ricerca*, op. cit., p. 119.
[100] *Opuscula theologica et polemica* 10 (PG 91, 133A-137A).

Maximus far from servile vis-à-vis Rome but preoccupied above all with orthodoxy and the unity of confession.[101]

In 645 Maximus returned to the defence of Honorius, throwing in for good measure this time pope Vigilius likewise, whom Pyrrhus believed also to have accepted the Monothelite opinion. The interest of this apologia for our subject lies in Maximus' insistence that it is to the Roman pope as to the supreme court that Pyrrhus must betake himself so as to abjure his errors.[102]

Next, in the year of the *Lateranense*, 649, Maximus produces another lapidary statement on the primacy.

> In truth all the confines of the *oikoumenê* and those who anywhere on earth confess the Lord with right and sincere faith look fixedly, as to the sun of eternal light, to the most holy church of the Romans and her confession of faith. From the beginning, in fact, of the presence of the incarnate Word of God among us, all the churches of the Christians have acquired and possess as their only basis and foundation the very great church which the gates of Hell will never overcome, following the Saviour's promise, but which instead will hold the keys of faith and orthodox profession in her own keeping, the church which opens to those who come to her with devotion the true and sole piety, whereas she closes and impedes every heretical mouth ...[103]

Croce hardly goes too far in asserting of Maximus' use here of the Matthaean metaphors for Peter's pre-eminence that the Byzantine divine presents the Roman church as

> foundation of the faith of all Christians, indefectible and indestructible, the infallible measuring-rod of orthodoxy and heresy.[104]

---

[101]V. Croce, *Tradizione e ricerca*, op. cit., p. 122.

[102]*Disputatio cum Pyrrho* (PG 91, 353A).

[103]*Opuscula theologica et polemica* 11 (PG 91, 137C-140A).

[104]V. Croce, *Tradizione e ricerca*, op. cit., p. 125.

The last materials relevant to the issue of Maximus and Rome come from the documents of his trial. In both of the judicial enquiries to which he was subject, Constantinople and Bizia, the question of his relation with Rome was fundamental. Accused of supporting movements of political revolt in the West Maximus made clear that his interests concerned exclusively Gospel truth. As to the Lateran synod of 649, Maximus does not commend it as resting on papal approval, though he defends its validity despite its lack of imperial sanction. However, when the bishop Theodosius, in the course of Maximus' second trial, declared himself ready to subscribe to the doctrine of the two natures, wills and activities, Maximus refuses to accept his recantation on the grounds that what he must do is write to the bishop of Rome, as the Church's law requires.[105] Maximus' belief that the Roman primacy is traditional also for the Byzantine East is borne out by numerous patristic texts, if more feebly echoed in Eastern Orthodoxy of later times.[106]

Reason and the Logos

Croce's last subject is the rôle of rationality in Maximus' deployment of his theological vision. His basic methodological scheme comprised not only Scripture and Fathers but also nature. The *phusiologein* or 'natural discourse' already admitted as a source of understanding in Gregory of Nyssa becomes in Maximus, whose language is here more indebted to Origen, 'natural contemplation', *phusikê theôria*. Maximus' characteristic approach is found in *Ambigua* 10 on the Transfiguration which we shall have occasion to refer to later, in the context of the soteriological theme of the transfigured cosmos. Relevant to Maximus' foundational theology is his interpretation of the

---

[105]*Disputatio Biziae* (PG 90, 148A).

[106]O. de Urbina, 'Patres graeci de sede romana', *Orientalia christiana periodica* 39 (1963), pp. 95-154. On the question of the scope of the primacy there is of course no clear consensus in the first millenium — hence the possibility of competing courses of 'development' and 'fixation', and thus the schism between the Catholic and Orthodox churches.

shining vestments of the Saviour on Thabor as symbolic of *both* the words of the Scriptures *and* the creation itself. In both God veils himself in a way happy for us, lest his revelation discourage our reverence: in the Bible as Logos, in the creation as its Artifex. Yet, if our lives are to be directed to him, we need both the Scriptural understanding which' is in the spirit', *hê graphikê en pneumati gnôsis*, and that natural contemplation of beings which is' according to the spirit', *hê tôn ontôn kata pneuma phusikê theôria*.[107] The difference between the two phrases 'in the spirit' and 'according to the spirit' may perhaps suggest a diversity of value, a ranking of Scriptural knowledge and the knowledge of God in nature into superior and inferior. This is not, however, Croce's interpretation: he speaks boldly in this connexion of an 'identity of attitude' by the Christian thinker to nature and Scripture, and sees this as reflecting, in the last analysis, an identity of relation with the Logos of these two realities. As von Balthasar stressed in his *Kosmiche Liturgie*, nature ('natural law', creation) and history ('written law', Scripture) are related to the Logos-Revealer by perfect analogy. They complement each other in an eschatological way: Christ fulfils both, that is, by at once uniting them and transcending them in his own fulness.[108]

Before leaving *Ambiguum* 10 we can note with Croce that the eschatological reference saves all this from being cataphaticism run wild. Indeed, Maximus speaks of Bible and nature as merely *concealment* of the divine Word to those, whether Hebrews or Greeks, who stop at the letter of Scripture and the appearances of nature respectively, and only truly serving as divine revelation when these are transcended — as the believer in Christ must do.[109]

As this introduction of the dialectic of the cataphatic and apophatic ways may indicate, Maximus' interest in natural understanding derives chiefly from his hope that it will help in the knowledge of God and man's approach to mystical union

[107]*Ambigua* 10 (PG 91, 1128CD).

[108]H. U. von Balthasar, *Kosmische Liturgie. Das Weltbild Maximus des Bekenners* (Einsiedeln 1961²), p. 289.

[109]V. Croce, *Tradizione e ricerca*, op. cit., p. 135.

with him. Croce ascribes to him not so much an 'autonomous use of the method of natural knowledge' as an appeal to natural reason intimately connected with the deployment of biblical and patristic testimonies and the teaching of the Church.[110] And in any case for Maximus the capacity to recognise God in his creation has been limited by fallen man's subjection to the passions, being restored only by Christ.[111] Yet in and of itself the power of divine creation renders created things an evocation (Croce calls them 'una raffigurazione') of the Uncreated, and this extends to the sensuous realm itself.[112] As Maximus writes in the *Quaestiones ad Thalassium:*

> It was indeed proper to the supreme Goodness, not only to constitute the divine and incorporeal substances of intelligible realities as simulacra (*apeikonismata*) of the indescribable divine Glory, adept at receiving, to the degree allowed them, all the inconceivable splendour of the infinite Beauty, but also to place within sensuous realities, so far removed as these are from the intelligible substances, echoes (*apêchêmata*) of its own Greatness, which might draw the human mind, borne up by them, undeviatingly towards God, going beyond all the visible and intermediate things by which such a way is opened, and leaving all of them behind.[113]

More specifically, through the creation the human mind can come to know God as universal Creator and Provider, and Maximus appears to believe that both of these divine attributes can be shown to have reality by a strict rational demonstration, *logikê apodeixis*.[114] Indeed, commenting in the 'Questions to Thalassius' on Paul's famous declaration in the opening chapter of Romans that

---

[110]Ibid., p. 136.
[111]*Capita theologica et economica* II. 41 (PG 90, 1144B).
[112]V. Croce, *Tradizione e ricerca*, op. cit., p. 137.
[113]*Quaestiones ad Thalassium* 51 (PG 90, 476CD).
[114]*Ambigua* 10 (PG 91, 1189C).

Ever since the creation of the world his invisible nature,
namely, his eternal power and deity, has been clearly
perceived in the things that have been made (Romans 1, 20)

Maximus is willing to allow that created things can provide an
image of the Trinity, whose self-subsistent wisdom and power
they reflect in their own existence as specific kinds of things *en
route* to their perfection — interpreting here Paul's 'eternal
power' as God the Word and his 'deity' as God the Holy
Spirit.[115] The same confidence in natural reason recurs in
Maximus' treatment of the soul and its incorporeality.[116] An
orthodox (Roman) Catholic author such as Croce finds it
unsurprising, evidently, that Maximus should have anticipated
the teaching of the First Vatican Council on the natural
knowability of the existence of God, and that of the Fifth
Lateran Council on the philosophical demonstrability of the
immortality of the human soul.

However, Maximus is by no means a captive to the classical
tradition in philosophy, since he also wants to bring out the
distinctive novelty of *Christian* thought. Above all this is a
matter of the difference made by the doctrine of creation, with
its first postulate for thought of a free divine act on which all
things depend.[117] Croce does not hesitate to identify Maximus'
work as a mile-stone on the way to a Christian philosophy —
and notably a Christian *ontology*, with a very different
metaphysical 'horizon' from that of pagan Hellenism. In the
Opuscula theologica et polemica he contrasts two understandings
of such foundational ontological terms as 'nature', 'substance',
'individual', 'hypostasis': that of the 'philosophers', and that of
the 'Fathers', preferring always the second which turns out to
be a *re-lecture* of ancient philosophical definitions in terms not
only of the creation doctrine but also of an acuter feeling,
deriving no doubt from Christology, for the difference between

[115]Romans 1, 20; *Quaestiones ad Thalassium* 13 (PG 90, 296B).

[116]*Epistle* 6 (PG 91, 424C-433A).

[117]*Centuriae de caritate* I. 40 (PG 90, 1049A); V. Croce, *Tradizione e ricerca*, op. cit.,
pp. 142-143.

personhood and nature.[118] Nor would Maximus see this as merely a development in the history of ideas: *phusikê theôria* comes about 'according to the spirit', and it is the grace of the Holy Spirit which liberates created minds from slavery to material things and purifies them, enabling them to 'search and speculate' fruitfully on the 'divine realities'. Though grace cannot operate without the receptive co-operation of the natural faculties, the latter cannot deliver authentic knowledge of beings without gracious enlightenment: here Maximus anticipates the Thomistic adage, *gratia supponit naturam*.[119] As presented by Croce, true wisdom, for Maximus, is not, then, a purely mental activity, which can prescind with impunity from the concrete dispositions of heart and soul. Rather is it the fruit of the efforts of the whole person, under the guidance of the Holy Spirit.[120] The natural contemplation or consideration of beings has its own object, which can be stated independently of Scripture, but it is not an autonomous, self-enclosed activity. On the contrary, its instrument is reason and intellect as enlivened by the Spirit, and, as with the interpretation of the Bible, its 'sole law and measure is the Logos of God'.[121] Reality itself is according to the Logos, 'logical'. Whatever is *alogon*, without the Logos, or *paralogikon*, unrelated to him, Maximus relegates, as illogical, to the realm of non-being. Accordingly, by an application of the principle of non-contradiction, he picks up various aberrant philosophical beliefs, such as that in the eternity of matter, or the pre-existence of the soul, or the conviction, stemming from the work of Eunomius and his later disciples, that God can be known by us as he knows himself, and consigns these to the dustbin of the absurd. He does the same with the chief contemporary heresies — the Monothelite and Monoenergist positions themselves.[122]

[118] *Opuscula theologica et polemica* 26 (PG 91, 276AB).

[119] B. Stoeckle, *Gratia supponit naturam. Geschichte und Analyse eines theologischen Axioms* (Rome 1962), pp. 91-98.

[120] V. Croce, *Tradizione e ricerca*, op. cit., p. 151; cf. W. Völker, *Maximus Confessor als Meister des geistlichen Lebens* (Wiesbaden 1965).

[121] V. Croce, *Tradizione e ricerca*, op. cit., p. 154.

[122] Ibid., pp. 155-160.

By a kind of negative correspondence to this instinct for what is in radical disharmony with the Logos, and so illogical, Maximus felt equally strongly the harmony of orthodox doctrine, what Croce calls the 'logical coherence of the Christian message'.[123] Whereas opposing heresies cancel each other out, on the *via regia* of the orthodox dogmas come logical coherence and the internal harmony of divine revelation in its mutually reflecting facets. The later principle of the *argumentum ex connexione dogmatum* is fully anticipated in Maximus' work, above all in his exhibition of the inseparable linkage between the doctrine of the two wills and two energies and the mystery of man's redemption. More generally, for Maximus, Incarnation and salvation are always interrelated, and both require and furnish an anthropology, while Theology and Economy, God in himself, and God in his outreach to the world, are also in necessary unison.[124] As Croce puts it:

> The connexion of the dogmas is the consequence of the principle of non-contradiction. Counterposed theological affirmations cannot be held valid without thereby reducing to nullity all possibility of discourse. There inheres in the real a true logical unity, in the pregnant sense of that term, inasmuch as the Logos of God underpins the varied *logoi* of creatures, granting to them individual subsistence and unitary connexion.[125]

Not that this evacuates mystery. Though the mystery of God in Christ is at one level knowable, and this is the point of salvation through an *incarnate* Saviour, the dogmas nonetheless share, at another level, in the unknowability of God himself who, as the One above being, *huperousios*, transcends all man's cognitive capacity. Signifying discourse about God is possible,

---

[123]Ibid., p. 163.

[124]Ibid., pp. 164-165: for example, the ascription of the trinitarian activity and will to the divine *nature* cannot be contradicted by a subsequent (Monoenergist and Monothelite) allotment of Christ's activity and will to his person.

[125]Ibid., p. 167.

but only by way of a *synthesis* of affirmation and negation: the twist Maximus gives to Denys' theological epistemology. Negations of what God is and affirmations that he is, so Maximus writes, are 'bound together in an amicable way, *philikôs*, and are receptive of each other'. And to this we can relate the being of the Word Incarnate as the living synthesis of all apophasis and cataphasis. So Maximus presents him:

> The supersubstantial Logos, truly taking substance from our substance, conjoined to the affirmation of nature and what is natural their negation by super-eminence, and became man, holding in conjunction the *tropos*, ['mode'], of being above nature with the *logos*, [the intelligible substance], of the being of nature.[126]

Though there will be more to say, in a variety of contexts, about these crucial Maximian terms *tropos* and *logos*, it is to the mystery of Christ and the Holy Trinity that we must give pride of place in any account of the content of Maximus' Gospel.

[126]*Ambigua* 5 (PG 91, 1053B); cf. M. Wallace, 'Affirmation and Negation in the Theology of St Maximus the Confessor' (Thesis, Pontifical Athenaeum of St. Anselm, Rome 1960).

3

Pierre Piret on the Trinity and Christology in Maximus' Thought

Monad and Triad

To make sense of the Belgian Jesuit Pierre Piret's profound exposition of Maximus' doctrine of the triune Lord of the Church, we must contextualise his account — however summarily — in the setting of the development of trinitarian doctrine by the Greek fathers.

Although the sometimes bewildering variety of terms and images used by the New Testament, and by sub-apostolic authors, for the inter-relations of God, Jesus, and the Spirit, in themselves necessitated a gradual clarification of the Christian doctrine of God via the common mind of the Church, the single most important point in this process was the crisis caused in late second century Alexandria by Arius' treatment of certain ideas in the Church's most sophisticated theologian to date, Origen. As T. F. Torrance has written:

> The disturbing ideas that irrupted in the teaching of Arius ran back to Origen's blurring of the differences between the internal and external relations of God, that is, between the eternal generation of the Son within the one being of God and the creation of the cosmos by the eternal Son or Word of God. Origen was unable to think of God as *Pantokratôr* or the Almighty except in a necessary eternal conjunction with all things, *ta panta*. Thus for Origen the creation had to be regarded as concomitant with the being of God and as eternally co-existing with him.

And Professor Torrance adds for good measure:

> This failure to give clear-cut ontological priority to the
> Father/Son relation in God over the Creator/cosmos
> relation was aggravated by the fact that Origen was critical
> of the idea that the Son was begotten 'of the being of the
> Father', and appeared to think of the generation of the
> Son and the creation of the cosmos as both due to the will
> of the Father.[1]

It was Arius' implacable critic, Athanasius the Great, who
found in the *homoousion* ('of-one-being') clause of the Nicene
synod the key to the consubstantial relations within the Trinity
of Father, Son and Spirit, and so to the consubstantiality of the
Holy Trinity as a whole. God is Trinity in Unity, Unity in Trinity.
Moreover, Athanasius pressed into prominence the idea of the
fully inter-penetrating, or co-indwelling, quality of Father, Son
and Spirit — eventually to achieve celebrity as the doctrine of
divine co-inherence (*perichôrêsis*). As a result, the concept of
ousia, being, was transformed: henceforth, *ousia* would refer
not simply to that which is, but to what it is is in terms of its own
internal reality. Similarly, *hypostasis* ('person') will now indicate
being not just in its independent subsistence, but also in its
objective otherness as well.

The Cappadocian Fathers, in the course of their defence of
the Nicene faith, placed more stress on the distinguishing
properties of the three divine hypostases — this was especially
true of Basil of Caesarea. The latter's attempt to preserve the
unity of the triune God by exploring the ways in which the
modes of being of Son and Spirit are derived from the Father
carried with it a danger of a new subordinationism, reviving the
claim to a less-than-divine status for the Son made by Arius
(and for the Holy Spirit by Macedonius, somewhat later). In
reaction, Gregory of Nazianzus, like Epiphanius of Salamis,
preferred to develop Athanasius' thought with a different
emphasis — in a doctrine of God as 'the consubstantial unity
of three perfect co-equal enhypostatic Persons in the one

---

[1] T. F. Torrance, *The Nicene Faith* (Edinburgh 1989), pp. 84-85.

indivisible being of the Godhead'.[2] It is as we shall see, above all Nazianzen's doctrine which is Maximus' starting-point. Piret's magisterial study of Maximian Triadology itself begins, however, with Maximus' 'real' rather than 'notional' *point de départ*, and the true provenance of trinitarian orthodoxy — salvation in Jesus Christ.

Piret's *Le Christ et la Trinité selon Maxime le Confesseur* opens with an explication of Maximus' commentary on the Our Father: an emblematic text because, for the Confessor, the Trinity is revealed above all in the mystery of the Saviour. 'The incarnate Word teaches the Theology', as Maximus himself has it.[3] Or, in the words of Felix Heinzer:

> This expression of Maximus' in the introduction to his commentary on the *Our Father* reveals his profound awareness of the intimate and inseparable bond between what the Greek Fathers call the 'Theology' and the 'Economy': between the trinitarian mystery of God and the mystery of Incarnation and Redemption — and therefore, on the level of our mediation and reflection on these mysteries — between trinitarian theology on the one hand, and Christology and soteriology on the other.[4]

In this text, Maximus names the Father as dispenser, *chorêgos*, of the gift of salvation, while the dispensing of his promises takes place, successively, 'through the Son' and 'in the Holy Spirit'. At the same time, Maximus can also call the incarnate Son the author, *autourgos*, and mediator, *mesitês*, of the gifts of

---

[2]Ibid., pp. 10-11. J.-M. Le Guillou, O.P., in his *Le Mystère du Père* (Paris 1973) argues indeed that the Cappadocians' concern with the *homoousios* of the Trinity endangered the personalism of earlier Trinitarian theology, replacing the 'order' of the persons by an essentialism in which a Trinity of equal persons acts through a single and common energy proceeding from their common transcendent essence. However, given that contemporaries accused them of the opposite intellectual vice of tritheism it might seem that they had the balance right! Maximus' thought does justice to both aspects: one *and* three.

[3]*De oratione dominica* (PG 90, 876C).

[4]F. Heinzer, 'L'Explication trinitaire de l'Economie chez Maxime le Confesseur', in idem., and C. Schönborn, (eds.), *Maximus Confessor. Actes du Symposium sur Maxime le Confesseur* (Fribourg 1982), p. 159.

God, and see his activity as taking place at once 'through the Spirit' and 'through the flesh', directed simultaneously as it is 'to the Father' and 'to human beings'.[5]

> The Lord Jesus, by his own flesh, 'manifests' to men the Father whom they do not know. The unique, self-identical Lord Jesus 'leads' to the Father, by the Spirit, the men he has 'reconciled' in himself. In his affirmation of the mediator between the Father and human beings, Maximus indicates the relation between the Incarnation and the paschal mystery.[6]

The Son, Jesus, can show, in himself, the Father and the Holy Spirit, for they are essentially and perfectly immanent in him according to their Godhead, simply common to them as this is. Because Father and Holy Spirit are wholly in the Son, they are equally present with him in the Incarnation which he, the Word, brings about. The Father projects his loving design onto the Son, and the Spirit cooperates with the Son in its realisation. Thus the one God presides, through his philanthropy, over the Incarnation as a whole. As the living Word of God, the Son is only known and attained, in what he immutably is, by the Father and the Spirit. Only Father and Spirit know his Incarnation in terms of the being of the hypostasis of the Son. And so, in his flesh, the Son makes manifest the 'Theology' which remains invisible to men: the Father with the Spirit in the Son, the one God. The hypostasis of the Son, in other words, is communion with the Father and the Spirit.[7]

---

[5]PG 90, 872D-909A; the importance of this text had already been pointed out by I.-H. Dalmais, 'Un Traité de théologie contemplative: le commentaire du *Pater noster* par saint Maxime le Confesseur', *Revue d'ascétique et de mystique* 29 (1953), pp. 123-159.

[6]P. Piret, *Le Christ et la trinité selon Maxime le Confesseur* (Paris 1983), p. 60.

[7]Ibid., p. 61. Cf. the reasons given by Karl Barth for accepting Aquinas' doctrine of appropriation: for Barth, 'While only the Son became a man, the fact that the Father and Spirit are also subjects of reconciliation and redemption means that we do not grasp the deity of the Logos in abstraction from the Father and Spirit; this excludes both abstract independent Logos-Incarnation speculation and Jesus worship and any *Logos asarkos* which would imply a God behind the God *actually* revealed in Christ'. Thus P. D. Molnar, 'The Function of the Immanent Trinity in

For Maximus, the opening of the *Pater* concerns this 'Theology': when we invoke the Father, his 'Name' and his 'Reign', it is Father, Son and Spirit, respectively whom we are invoking. They exist *from* the Father and *with* him, as well as *in* him, in a fashion which is 'above cause and reason'.[8] These prepositions express what Maximus, following Gregory Nazianzen, calls 'the relation', *schêsis*, of Son and Spirit to the Father.[9] This relationship enables the Persons to be, in Maximus term, 'co-indicated'. Indeed, in the Commentary on the *Pater*, he appears to present the recognition of the identity of the single divine *ousia* as following on that of the simultaneous inter-relationship of the trinitarian Persons. The threefold Name is not, therefore, in Piret's words:

> an intermediary between what we are and what God is: we are created, and the Creator is the divine Trinity.[10]

I take this to mean: here Maximus decisively overcomes the temptation, endemic in much patristic Triadology, to imagine the Trinity, or at any rate the Son and the Spirit, as media of the world's creation and salvation. The triune life is no mere economic accommodation of the Godhead to the world's condition. It *is* the only God himself. Nonetheless, the names of Son and Spirit, as indeed of Father, do indicate not only their inner-trinitarian origins but also, through the 'missions' which replicate those origins in the context of the world and its history, the relations which the divine Trinity would enjoy with ourselves. And so, in calling on God as Father, by following the instruction of Jesus Christ, we not only confess that we are created: we also affirm our divine sonship by grace, and commit ourselves to leading a life in conformity with our words: 'thy Kingdom come, thy will be done on earth'. The man who desires to possess the Kingdom, so Maximus warns,

---

the Theology of Karl Barth: Implications for Today', *Scottish Journal of Theology* 42 (1989), p. 382.

[8] PG 90, 884C.

[9] Gregory Nazianzen, *Third Theological Discourse* 16 PG 36, 96A.

[10] P. Piret, *Le Christ et la Trinité selon Maxime le Confesseur*, op. cit., p. 65.

must be willing to be confirmed in the Holy Spirit to Christ, and, among other things, this means ceasing to be either Greek — one who distends the divinity into polytheism, or Jew — one who compresses the divinity, excluding the Word and the Spirit and thus becoming, in Maximus' harsh term, 'atheistic'. In Christ, by contrast, we know of the selfsame God that he is Monad and Triad.

Continuing this commentary on the *Pater*, Maximus now fills out this bare assertion with fuller trinitarian content.[11] The God we contemplate is Thought, Word and Life. Everlastingly, God is presence to himself: Thought without cause, engendering the Word who abides without beginning and originating the Life which is for ever. How are *monas*, the unicity of God, and *trias*, his threefoldness, related? Not, Maximus insists, in such a way that the Triad is simply an accidental modification to the being of the Monad, or the Monad merely a quality of the Triad. Nor are Monad and Triad simply heterogeneous (in his phrase 'one and another'), for the Monad does not differ from the Triad by any otherness, *heterotês*, of nature. Nor is one 'according to the other', *par' allên*: Monad and Triad are not distinguished by a subordination of power. No more is the Monad distinguished from the Triad as common or generic being, grasped simply by a mental act, when all particularity about Father, Son and Spirit has been subsumed under some wider notion. Neither, again, is one through the other, *di' allês*, since what is altogether self-identical and non-relative can in no way be mediatised by a relation, in the way that a cause is vis-à-vis a source of causality. Further, Monad and Triad are not 'one from another', *ex allês*, for the Triad does not have its provenance in the Monad but exists 'without genesis'. And thus bringing his negative statements to an end, Maximus goes on to counsel that, positively, we must *speak and think the same reality as truly Monad and Triad*, with reference for the former term to God's *principle of being, ho kat' ousian logos*, and for the latter term to the *mode of his existence, ho kat' huparxin tropos*: the self-same Monad, whole and entire, not shared out among the hypostases, the self-same Triad whole and entire, not confused by the Monad.

---

[11]PG 90, 892C-893A.

Noting, however, that Maximus speaks successively of Monad and Triad, Piret feels able to ask after the rationale of this 'movement' from God as One to God as Three, and finds enlightenment on the subject from the second set of *Ambigua*, or 'Book of Ambiguities', written around 629, as also from the first set, edited rather later, after 634.[12] Basically, what is involved here is Maximus' interpretations of various ambiguous passages in Gregory Nazianzen's theology, which had left open too many doors whereby an Origenist account of the God-world relation might enter.

In his *Third Theological Oration*, Gregory had spoken of the Monad as, from the beginning, in movement towards the Dyad and halting at the Triad.[13] Maximus invokes the assistance of Denys in insisting that God can only be said to 'move' inasmuch as he is desire and love, moving towards him those who are apt to receive him. God is in movement in that he inaugurates a relationship of desire and love in those capable of welcoming him, while attracting by nature those in movement towards him. Where God as Trinity is concerned, Maximus can say only that the Godhead is 'in movement' as *cause of the search by spiritual creatures for God's mode of existing* — which we know by faith to be as Father, Son and Spirit. What Nazianzen had called the 'movement' of the divinity is for Maximus the fecundity of God for created rational spirits. God manifests himself — as the Good, as the Word or Wisdom, and as Sanctifying Power — to suitably disposed human beings, and he reveals himself via the witness of Scripture as Father, Son and Holy Spirit. The first of these disclosures is, evidently, the preamble to the second which Maximus calls, with good reason, 'more perfect'.[14]

With the revival of Monoenergism in the Alexandrian Pact of Union, Maximus returned to this subject in the text which now forms the opening chapter of the first set of *Ambigua*.[15] His

---

[12]P. Piret, *Le Christ et la Trinité selon Maxime le Confesseur*, op. cit., pp. 70-71.

[13]*Discourse* 29, 2 (PG 36, 76B).

[14]II *Ambigua* 23 (PG 91, 1257C-1261A).

[15]For dating, see P. Sherwood, *An Annotated Date-list of the Works of Maximus the Confessor* (Rome 1952), pp. 31-32, 39.

main purpose here is to show that, just as the Monad is not the beginning of a process of expansion, terminating in a contraction, so the Triad is not the accomplishment of a composition presupposing a division.

> The Monad is truly the Monad. It is not a beginning, afterwards taking the form of a contraction of its expansion, as if it tended naturally to move towards a plurality, but rather the enhypostatised being of the consubstantial Triad. The Triad is truly the Triad. It is not, as if by accomplishment of numerical diversity, a composition of monads presupposing division, but rather the monosubstantial (*enousios*) existence of the tri-hypostatised Monad.[16]

And Maximus tells the addressee of this explanation that if he has learnt from Nazianzen of a *movement*, he should not need to ask how the more-than-infinite *Divinity* can be in movement, for the passibility, *to pathos*, in question comes from *us, not* from God. The movement is *in ourselves*. And as Piret stresses, this discussion closes a gap in Maximus' earlier efforts on the theme: the manifestation of the Triad is not an intermediary between the divine Monad and created being — the economic Trinity is not a demiurge — for God discloses himself to us as he is in his own reality.[17] As we have already seen, in the context of the Commentary on the *Pater*, the Triad *is* the Monad: the three hypostases *are* the divine being. Père Juan-Miguel Garrigues would go further here. Interpreting Maximus' thought in the light of the Thomist affirmation of the trinitarian Persons as 'subsistent relationships', he argues that, since in God's case 'to exist' signifies the identity of the hypostases in *their* subsistence with the divine nature in *its* being, the subsistent relations of the hypostases among themselves *are* the very being of God.[18]

If such austerely metaphysical divinity seems *prima facie* lacking in spiritual or pastoral potentiality, the student of

[16]I *Ambigua* 1 (PG 91, 1036B).

[17]P. Piret, *Le Christ et la Trinité selon Maxime le Confesseur*, op. cit., p. 82.

[18]J.-M. Garrigues, 'La Personne composée du Christ d' après saint Maxime le Confesseur', *Revue Thomiste* 2 (1974), pp. 197-199.

Maximus can note that the axiom of patristic orthodoxy according to which 'the Unity expands into the Trinity without increase, and gathers the Trinity into the Unity without diminution' provides, according to the abbé Jules Monchanin, the answer of the Gospel to perhaps the greatest of pagan religious cultures — that of India. For Monchanin, only this doctrine responds to the insoluble problem self-set by Hinduism: that it 'cannot reconcile God and the world, the One and the many', and so 'oscillates between a personal and an impersonal God, between a hidden and a manifest God, between an impersonal metaphysics and a personalist religion'.[19] More widely, the 1989 'Letter to the Bishops of the Catholic Church on Some Aspects of Christian Meditation', promulgated by the (Roman) Congregation for the Doctrine of the Faith, finds in the dogma of the Holy Trinity, where 'the Son is "other" with respect to the Father and yet, in the Holy Spirit, he is "of the same substance"', the foundation for a positive notion of difference, that removes the sting from the tail of the doctrine of creation, with its positing 'otherness between God and creatures, who are by nature different'.[20]

What more does Maximus have to say on the topic of the *inner* relations of the Godhead — Father to Son, and Father and Son to Spirit? Among the second collection of *Ambigua*, chapters 24, 25 and 26 deal with the first of these issues. Maximus' point of departure is, once again, a text of Gregory Nazianzen: this time an anti-Arian passage in the *Third Theological Oration*. Faced with the Arian challenge that *either* the Father engendered the Son without willing him — in which case the

---

[19] *L'Abbé Jules Monchanin. Témoignages, notes biographiques, textes* (Bruges 1960), p. 192. An earlier passage in this collection is illustrative:

> The trinitarian rhythm, beginning in the unfathomable abyss of the Father, passes through the Word and has completion in the Spirit; then returns from the Spirit through the Son to the abyss of the Father. We are seized by the last Person who is, so to say, on the 'border' of the Trinity. He leads and configures us to Christ, who in his turn leads us into the abyss of the Father.

Ibid., p. 165. Cf. J. Monchanin, 'Théologie et mystique du Saint-Esprit', *Dieu Vivant* 6 (1953), pp. 72ff.

[20] Congregation for the Doctrine of the Faith, *Letter to the Bishops of the Catholic Church on Some Aspects of Christian Meditation*, 14.

Father was constrained, but, being constrained, cannot be God, *or else* the Son was engendered by will and is, then, not consubstantially God, Gregory affirms that the Son, willed by the Father, is Son of *the Father who wills him* and not of will, or volition, as such.[21] Analogously, Gregory ascribes the Son's being to the Father as *he who speaks*, and not to (merely) the Father's word. Maximus, however, noticed an important ambiguity in Nazianzen's presentation. In differentiating the willing subject from his own voluntary power, Gregory could be said to have fallen into the Arian trap: if the Father is not identified with his own will in engendering the Son, he has brought him forth by some kind of contrariety. In contrast, Maximus considers the willing and the willed to be identical with the will: such simultaneity could not be proposed for human volitional activity, but it may for the Godhead, which is, as divine, without movement. Engendered Son and engendering Father are in a simultaneous relation which is none other than their divine being.[22]

In the same discourse, Gregory Nazianzen had considered a second objection thrown up by the Arian crisis on the basis of antecedent hesitations in the christological reflection of the early Church. As cause of the Son, the Father must surely be greater than the Son by nature.[23] Gregory's reaction had been: greater *as Father*, yes; but *not* by his nature, as God, for the Son is equally God with him. Maximus takes Gregory's response further by adding that to introduce a factor of comparison into the divine nature as the Arians and Eunomians had done is to deny that the divine nature 'absolutely', *pantôs*, is. And this in turn is to deny Father, Son *and* Spirit![24]

Nazianzen's last problem in the important oration which had so captured Maximus' attention concerns the notion that the Son is who he is by the Father's 'operation' or 'activity', *energeia*, and is, therefore, a mere 'enactment', *energêma*, of the

---

[21]*Discourse* 29, 6 (PG 36, 80C-81C): the Son's existence is that of him who is willed, *thelêsis*.

[22]II *Ambigua* 24 (PG 91, 1261B-1264B).

[23]*Discourse* 29, 15 (PG 36, 93B).

[24]II *Ambigua* 25 (PG 91, 1264C-1265BO).

Father.[25] Gregory had replied that 'Father' names neither being nor operation but relation. Maximus goes on to enquire more deeply into the link between the *energeia* whereby nevertheless the Father *does* engender the Son, and the self-identical divine being which he possesses. And here Maximus insists that in the case of Father and Son the *energeia* concerned and the being which it engenders (the Son) remain wholly immanent within the substance, *ousia*, of the energising being (the Father). The Son is, Maximus concludes, 'an essentially subsistent activity', *energeia ousiôdôs hupestôsa*. And so 'Father' does not name an operation vis-à-vis the Son, but rather the operation concerned *identifies the divine being of the hypostases of Father and Son alike.* However, Maximus now adds a *rider*. That eternal generation cannot altogether succeed in signifying Father and Son: above it is, he remarks, 'the ineffable and incomprehensible existence of the Only-Begotten One from the Father — and simultaneously with him and in him'.[26] The statement seems to undermine the force of everything that Maximus has said so far — by calling into question the revelatory force of the naming of the Word as Son, in history. Piret, however, proposes that we should take it, simply, as a *caveat*. He suggests two reasons which may have prompted Maximus to enter such a warning. First, the notion of a common kind identifying Engenderer and Engendered fits the species-identity of human nature better than it does the unique identity of the divine nature. Secondly, given that Maximus regards the trinitarian hypostases as existing in the form of enhypostatised relations of the divine being, it would seem to follow that, for him, the divine existence, signifying as it does the relation of the hypostases, goes beyond the activity proper to the divine substance. To speak of the Father's generation of the Son before all worlds, correct as that is, has the disadvantage, in Piret's words, of letting one

> suppose that the relation of the Son to the Father is only that of an object to an acting subject, or of a passive

[25]*Discourse* 29, 16 (PG 36, 95D-96B).
[26]II *Ambigua* 26 (PG 91, 1268B).

operation to an active one. But the Son must be recognised, rather, as the active subject of his relation to the Father who is his origin, since he is 'simultaneously with the Father and in him'. It is his relationship, therefore, that determines his operations and his hypostasis.[27]

It is time to turn from the binitarian communion of Father and Son, to the full Holy Trinity: what of the rôle of the *Holy Spirit* in Maximus' Triadology? And here Piret moves from the *Ambigua* to the *Quaestiones ad Thalassium*, published in all probability between the two 'Books of Ambiguities'. In the course of this work, Maximus offers his exegesis of the prophet Zechariah's vision of the sevenfold golden lampstand in chapter 4 of the book that bears his name.[28] Presenting thereby his doctrine of the Spirit and his sevenfold gifts, Maximus has two basic affirmations to make. First, we possess the Holy Spirit thanks to the Word Incarnate. Secondly, the Spirit proceeds in a fashion beyond all telling from the Father, through the Son. The Word who became man 'through what is mine gives in return what is by nature properly his own'. By inscribing his own divine power, *dunamis*, in human lives which show forth that power in the virtues, the Incarnate Word *gives* in such a way that we can *possess*, which is, as Piret happily comments, to 'give the gift until its very term'.[29] And the divine gift, as term of the divinity which gives, *is* he whom we confess as the Holy Spirit. What in turn the Holy Spirit gives is *the capacity to exercise his own gift*. As Maximus puts it, in the imagery of Zechariah:

> He gives to the candelabrum, that is, the Church, as light, his own operations ...[30]

activities which elsewhere in these 'Questions' Maximus speaks of in terms of grace, the interpretation of Scripture, and the knowledge of God. So far as the Spirit's relation to Father and

---

[27]P. Piret, *Le Christ et la Trinité selon Maxime le Confesseur*, op. cit., p. 94.
[28]Zechariah 4, 2-3, in *Quaestiones ad Thalassium* 63 (PG 90, 665A-688B).
[29]P. Piret, *Le Christ et la Trinité selon Maxime le Confesseur*, op. cit., p. 97.
[30]*Quaestiones ad Thalassium* 63 (PG 90, 672C).

Son are concerned, a neuralgic issue in the history of doctrine, and not least in Catholic-Orthodox relations, Piret glosses Maximus' text in a delicate way. Originated by the Father, the Spirit 'comprises' or 'includes', *comprend*, in his relation with the Father, the very relation of the Father and the Son.

To gain a fuller account of Maximus' teaching on this point, Piret now turns his attention to a doctrinally meatier text, the tenth of the 'theological and polemical opuscula'.[31] Copy of a letter to the Cypriot priest Marinus, Dom Polycarp Sherwood dated this document to the years between the disputation with Pyrrhus and Maximus' departure for Rome, that is, 645 or 646. Maximus concentrates on the classic question: if the Latins say that the Spirit proceeds from Father and from Son, do they not deny the primordial causality of the Father? Maximus was aware that Latin theologians claimed the convergent testimony of their own Fathers together with Cyril of Alexandria' commentary on John for the view that the Spirit proceeds through (*dia*) the Son. But, he goes on, they think of the Father as sole cause, *mia aitia*, of the Spirit in terms of 'provenance', *ekporeusis*; what they are drawing attention to is the Spirit's 'progressing', *proienai*, through the Son. The single starting-point of the Spirit in his provenance is the Father; but in his progression he passes from the Father through the Son. It is this distinction between two Greek verbs — one denoting hypostatic origination, the other trinitarian ordering — where Latin possesses only the one, *procedere*, that has allowed another Maximian scholar, J.-M. Garrigues to offer his attempted resolution of the Filioque problem in ecumenical discussion, *L'Esprit qui dit 'Père'*.[32]

Much of Piret's discussion of Maximus' trinitarian theology has been couched in the classical terms of *ousia* and *hypostasis*, which were also highly pertinent to the christological debate centering, in Maximus' period, on the right interpretation of

---

[31] *Opuscula theologica et polemica* 10 (PG 91, 136AB); P. Piret, *Le Christ et la Trinité selon Maxime le Confesseur*, op. cit., pp. 99-102.

[32] J.-M. Garrigues, *L'Esprit qui dit 'Père'* (Paris 1981); see also for a summary of the argument A. Nichols, O.P., *Rome and the Eastern Churches. A Study in Schism* (Edinburgh 1991), pp. 224-227.

Cyril and Chalcedon. Before moving on to deal with Maximus' Christology Piret understandably, therefore, pauses so as to reflect at some length on the implication of these two favoured words.

The vocabulary of *ousia* and *hypostasis* was first systematically employed to express *identité et altérité*, 'difference and otherness', in the Holy Trinity by the Cappadocian Fathers. Subsequently, the same terms were chosen for the same purpose, but this time in Christology, by Chalcedon. Piret suggests that the equivalence of these terms invites us to 'recognise in a unified way the christological and trinitarian realities'. Furthermore, if at the same time this doctrinal vocabulary is to succeed in showing the coherence of each of these realities, it must hold onto the self-same meaning when applied to Christ as to the Holy Trinity.[33] Such continuity of signification was, Piret reports, denied by those Monophysites who argued that the term 'hypostasis' should be reserved for Trinitarian theology unless it is being applied to the single concrete nature of Christ, and maintained that 'ousia' and 'phusis', though identical in the theology of the Trinity must be distinguished when it comes to Christology. The Severan Monophysites contrasted *ousia* to *phusis* as abstract to concrete, ascribing the general properties of an *ousia* to the sole relevant concrete reality, the individual *phusis* of the Word Incarnate.[34]

The Severans were not without arguments. They maintained that if, in the theology of God, the divine *ousia* is the true concrete object of our study, then we must surely say that what became incarnate was the Holy Trinity as such, and, correlatively, the human *ousia* of Christ must be all that there is to his concrete human totality. Then again, on the issue of the *hypostasis*, they proposed that, Christ being God and man, the difference between the two *ousiai*, crucial for other men vis-à-vis God, is irrelevant to the Incarnate Word. The hypostasis of Christ as presented by Chalcedon cannot be the hypostasis of the Son, since the latter is identical with the divine *ousia*,

[33]P. Piret, *Le Christ et la Trinité selon Maxime le Confesseur*, op. cit., p. 105.
[34]J. Lebon, *Le monophysisme sévérien* (Louvain 1909), pp. 242-283.

whereas the former is different from it.[35] Maximus encountered
the Severan critique of Chalcedon among bishop-sympathisers
in Cyprus and attempts to answer it in the ten paragraphs of his
Opuscula theologica et polemica 13.[36] In a minor *tour de force*,
Maximus runs through the list of the major trinitarian and
christological deviations of the patristic centuries showing how
their various errors stem from mis-constructions of the rôle of
either *ousia* or *hypostasis* in Christ and the Trinity. The 'royal
and irreproachable faith', Maximus tells the bishops of Cyprus,
consists in maintaining for the Trinity 'homoousia' and 'heterohypostasia', but for Christ the 'hetero ousia' of the Logos and
the flesh, together with 'idiohypostasia' for his single person.
Here the 'divine Cyril' and the 'ecumenical council'
(Chalcedon) concur. To the terminology of Chalcedon he
adds his own, that of identity and otherness, asking how this
'extreme union' can possess both *tautotês*, sameness, and *heterotês*,
'alterity'. The natural assumption would be that Maximus is
speaking here of the Incarnation, but Piret gives reasons for
thinking that he is, rather, stating a general law: all beings are
identity and alterity, thanks to their two distinct principles of
being, *ousia* and hypostasis.[37] Not of course that Maximus is
abandoning the field of Christology altogether. What allows
him to disengage his general law is awareness of the
extraordinary union of the two different natures in Christ
which cannot naturally be united. And furthermore, the law,
once arrived at, enables him both to affirm and to make more
precise his christological and trinitarian doctrine. As Piret re-
states that doctrine on Maximus' behalf:

> The alterity of the divine *ousia* and the human is also their
> proper, irreducible identity, in their union through the
> single hypostasis of One of the Trinity. The alterity of this
> same trinitarian hypostasis by reference to the other

---

[35]C. Moeller, 'Le chalcédonisme et le néo-chalcédonisme en Orient de 451 à
la fin du VIe siècle', in A. Grillmeier-H. Bacht (eds.), *Das Konzil von Chalkedon* I
(Würzburg 1951), pp. 696-699.

[36]PG 91, 145A-149D.

[37]P. Piret, *Le Christ et la Trinité selon Maxime le Confesseur*, op. cit., p. 123.

hypostases is also their own identity, in the single divine *ousia*.[38]

As Piret interprets him in this *opusculum*, to consider a trinitarian hypostasis in itself is always to consider it 'towards' the other hypostases and 'with' them. The hypostases are 'towards their union', a union which is their *ousia* and which exists hypostatically, since 'union of *ousia* is difference of hypostasis'.[39] In the trinitarian order, the Father and Son are towards their union, their hypostatically existing *ousia*, namely the Spirit. God is Spirit; yet the Spirit is a divine hypostasis. We can, then, acknowledge the possibility of a unique 'ex-stasis' of One of the Holy Trinity, a 'standing forth' *both* towards the divine *ousia* which is the union of the trinitarian hypostases *and* towards the human *ousia* in its difference from the divine. Here Piret rejects the view of such twentieth century Eastern Orthodox exegetes of the later Greek patristic tradition as Vladimir Lossky and John Meyendorff that a 'real distinction' disjoins the trinitarian hypostasis from the divine *ousia*. For Piret, to say that the hypostasis of Christ is one of the Trinity is to accept that the divine *ousia* of Christ is the trinitarian *ousia*. The 'ex-stasis' of one of the Trinity towards the divine 'homoousia' is his own divine *ousia* itself. By the same token, his 'ex-stasis' towards human *ousia* is that of the divine *ousia* while the union of his assumed human *ousia* with himself is the 'ex-stasis' of human *ousia* towards the *ousia* of God. Moreover, since the individuality of human *ousia* is at one and the same time the union and the differentiation of species and hypostasis, Piret rejects likewise Lossky's proposal that there is a tension between the human *person* in his or her openness and a human nature composed of *individuals* closed in on themselves. Lossky, to Piret's eyes, risks confounding the individuality of Christ's human *ousia* in the hypostasis of One of the Trinity. It is better to say, then, that:

> United to the hypostasis of the divine nature the individual [human] nature symbolises the union and difference of

[38]Ibid., p. 124.
[39]Ibid., p. 133: emphasis added.

human hypostases, and becomes the human *ousia* of that divine hypostasis itself.[40]

Or, as in a further lapidary statement, Piret sums up his disagreement with these members of the modern Paris School in Orthodox theology, and, at the same time, Maximus' criticism of the aberrant doctrinal positions of Arius and Nestorius:

> One of the Trinity is his own union with the divine *ousia*, which is the union of the trinitarian hypostases in the difference of their hypostatic properties. He is his own union with human *ousia* which is itself the union and difference, according to their nature and individuality, of human hypostases The divine *ousia* and the human are not united naturally; their nature is their own self-identity. But their identity with the unique trinitarian hypostasis is their union, hypostatically.[41]

As Maximus himself expresses this — a good deal more pithily! — in Letter 15: 'Homo-ousia is hetero hypostasia'. The divine *homoousion*, as the being common to the hypostases in their communion, is the direct and immediate expression of those Persons in their otherness.[42]

Piret's reflections on this dialectic of identity and difference in the holy Trinity undoubtedly owe something to a fascination with this topic in nineteenth and twentieth century European philosophy, seen most clearly, perhaps, in Hegel's thoughts on the matter in the section of his *Wissenschaft der Logik* devoted to 'essence' as a 'reflection' of being.[43] Yet they also illuminate Maximus' own less systematic concern with the same interrelation as revelation discloses it in the triune God.

---

[40]Ibid., p. 136.

[41]Ibid., p. 138.

[42]*Epistle* 15 (PG 91, 549B).

[43]G. F. W. Hegel, *Wissenschaft der Logik* II. 1. ii, = *Sämtliche Werke* IX (Leipzig 1970), pp. 26-62; for an account of the varieties, and importance of this theme, from Hegel to J. Derrida and E. Lévinas, and an original resolution of the issues it raises, see W. Desmond, *Desire, Dialectic and Otherness: An Essay on Origins* (New Haven 1987).

The Incarnate Son

If the Holy Trinity is disclosed for us in the mystery of the Saviour, then Maximus will have much to say, inevitably — and even had the christological controversies of his day never been — about the being and work of the *Incarnate* Son. The great Jesuit patrologist Pater Alois Grillmeier considered that, within Greek theology, Maximus had so superbly interpreted the teaching of Chalcedon that, all mythological elements of expression left behind, his Christology is well-situated to enter into dialogue with 'modern knowledge' — the contemporary understanding of the world.[44] Piret's austere exposition, now addressing itself to the mystery of the Incarnate Son, certainly leaves few mythopoeic elements behind. Like Maximus' own work, it presupposes the truth, and consummate doctrinal importance, of the Chalcedonian definition: the single Lord Jesus Christ is in two natures, intimately, indeed inseparably, united, but never confused, much less merged.

Today the Chalcedonian formula has a poor press. Contemporary pietists contest any intellectual elaboration of the original Gospel, spurning the philosophical pretensions of its drafters while unconscious of philosophical assumptions of their own. Modern-day rationalists deny the possibility of any supernatural incursion upon history, excluding the very possibility that Jesus Christ might be truly God as he is truly man. Some call in question the particular 'static' ontology in which the Definition explores the mystery of Jesus, contrasting it with the 'dynamic' quality of Scripture's own salvation-historical approach. Others claim that the doctrine of the two natures amounts to no more than an oscillation between Nestorianism and Monophysitism, and lay at its door the tendency of many in the Great Church to superimpose a sentimental Nestorianism on an intellectual Monophysitism — a phenomenon, certainly, which can be observed. Those criticisms which do not simply derive from a position that is —

---

[44]A. Grillmeier, 'Moderne Hermeneutik und altkirchliche Christologie', in idem., *Mit ihm und in ihm. Christologische Forschungen und Perspektiven* (Freiburg-im-Breisgau 1975), p. 547.

logically or actually — outside the Christian community altogether, generally stem from a failure to appreciate the place of the Definition in the context of the developing christological doctrine of the Church. That context will be sketched out briefly here, by way of preamble to an account of Maximus' Christology through Piret's eyes.[45] But first, let us have the text of the Definition itself.

> In agreement, therefore, with the holy Fathers, we all unanimously teach that we should confess that our Lord Jesus Christ is one and the same Son, the same perfect in Godhead and the same perfect in manhood, truly God and truly man, the same of a rational soul and body, consubstantial with the Father in Godhead, and the same consubstantial with us in manhood, like us in all things except sin; begotten from the Father before the ages as regards His Godhead, and in the last days, the same, because of us and because of our salvation begotten from the Virgin Mary, the *Theotokos*, as regards His manhood; one and the same Christ, Son, Lord, only-begotten, made known in two natures without confusion, without change, without division, without separation, the difference of the natures being by no means removed because of the union, but the property of each nature being preserved and coalescing in one *prosôpon* and one *hypostasis* — not parted or divided into two *prosôpa*, but one and the same Son, only-begotten, divine Word, the Lord Jesus Christ, as the prophets of old and Jesus Christ Himself have taught us about Him and the creed of our Fathers has handed down.[46]

The seeds of this teaching are already germinating in the New Testament itself, where the mysterious twofoldness yet unity of

---

[45]H. Bacht — A. Grillmeier, S. J., (eds.), *Das Konzil von Chalkedon* (Würzburg 1962²); W. Pannenberg, *Grundzüge der Christologie* (Gütersloh 1964); A. Grillmeier, S. J., *Christ in Christian Tradition* (London 1965); L. Bouyer, *Le Fils éternel* (Paris 1974); J. N. D. Kelly, *Early Christian Doctrines* (London 1977⁵), pp. 223-343.
[46]D.-S. 301-302.

the Lord is already affirmed. Jesus is both 'according to the flesh', and 'according to the Spirit'. In a Semitic culture, Christians contented themselves with pursuing a symbolic theology of the christological titles — Servant, Messiah, Lord, Son of Man, Son of God, offered in abundance in the Gospels and other New Testament writings and now added to by Jewish Christians through such images as 'Law', 'Covenant', 'Beginning', 'Day-Star', 'Angel', and so forth.[47] Such a symbolic Christology had the advantage of presenting the Word Incarnate as fulfiller of all the rich complexity of the Old Testament promise, but it also carried concomitant disadvantages. In avoiding a reflective presentation of the mystery of Jesus as simultaneously human and divine it left the way open to an implicit — or even explicit — denial of one or the other of those two dimensions. Docetism and Gnosticism took the first of these paths; Ebionitism and Adoptionism the second. When Irenaeus of Lyons, faced with these threats, declares repeatedly in his *Adversus Haereses* that Christ is 'one and the same', and that this single Jesus Christ is 'truly God and truly man' he sketches out in advance the portrait painted by the Fathers of Chalcedon.

Both Irenaeus and Ignatius of Antioch, while continuing to speak, with Paul and John, of Jesus Christ as the centre of an entire economy of salvation, as wide as the world, were obliged by the christological heresies of their day to refine their account of the person of the Saviour. For Ignatius, the unity of Christ as both God and man is so perfect that his letters can refer to the blood and the sufferings *of God*, who as Jesus was 'conceived by Mary'. At once fleshly and spiritual, born of Mary and of God, Christ's unity is that of a divine subject: 'God in man, true Life in death', the 'flesh-bearing Lord' (rather than a man carrying the divine presence). For Irenaeus, the single Lord Jesus Christ is, as the eternal Word the 'head' of the invisible creation, and, as the Word made flesh, the head likewise of the entire visible world. Increasingly indeed the Johannine formula 'The Word became flesh'[48] will control

---

[47]See on this J. Daniélou, *The Theology of Jewish Christianity* (Et London 1964).
[48]John 1, 14.

patristic thinking about the christological problem: for the violent contrast of the twin poles of that formula raise that problem in its most acute form, whereas the Pauline equivalent — 'according to the flesh, according to the Spirit[49] — leaves it simply tacit.

Twentieth century patristic scholars are accustomed to categorise the succeeding Christologies of the age of the Fathers into two kinds, '*Logos-sarx*' and '*Logos-anthrôpos*': both, as their names (Word-flesh, Word-man) imply, take their rise from St John's epoch-making gloss on the apostolic preaching. The first scheme, *Logos-sarx*, does justice to the unity of Christ as the God-man but at the price of underplaying his full humanity. 'Flesh' in the context of John's Prologue means the whole man in his moral condition, and not the body only. The second scheme, *Logos-anthrôpos*, renders well enough the duality of divinity and humanity in Christ, but obscures the unity of his personhood, insinuating that the union of divine and human factors in his life and destiny differs only qualitatively from the experience of prophets and saints.

The Logos concept of Greek culture at large could not in any case serve the Christian case without a re-baptism: its connotation of a lower grade divinity than the One, the truly divine, ensured that. For the Arians, whose thinking constituted the greatest challenge so far to the trinitarian and christological consciousness of the Church, it was natural to suppose, working as they did within the *Logos-sarx* framework, that a Word which in the flesh was subject to weakness and the passions could not be fully God. Athanasius, operating with the same concepts, came to a radically different conclusion: in order to redeem us the Word must really be God; if, as a consequence the attributes of humankind normally ascribed to the soul must be re-assigned to the flesh (the body), this was a price the great Alexandrian doctor was happy to pay.

Athanasius' theological engagement ensured that the later Church would not forget two specifically christological truths. First, over against the 'dividing' Christology of Paul of Samosata,

[49]Romans 1, 3.

and the thinking that would later crystallise as Nestorianism, Christ is, and must be, *one*: else he could not both save and be the first-fruits of salvation at the same time. Secondly, in the divine-human composite of the incarnate Word, it is the Word which is *to hegêmonikon*, the governing principle. Divine and human in Christ are asymmetrically arranged, with the Logos bearing the flesh, and not the other way round. Unfortunately, in leaving in shadow the *soul* of Christ, Athanasius unwittingly prepared the way for a second christological crisis in the fourth century Church: that centred around Apollinaris of Laodicea. For Apollinaris, since the Word, of one being with the Father, takes the place of a human mind in Christ, the Gospel accounts of the Lord's emotions, weakness, even ignorance cannot be allowed their face value. To this the Cappadocian Fathers replied that whatever has not been assumed has not been saved: a non-psychological, non-intellectual humanity of the Word would signify for us the non-salvation of our psyche and our intellect. The Church's conciliar response (362) in affirming that the Word took on in Jesus a rational soul also cleared the way for a better understanding of the Logos who is a saving mediator but not as such a 'middle being', mid-way between God and matter. Gradually, the *Logos-sarx* schema yields to its *Logos-anthrôpos* competitor — even if some, such as St Cyril, continue to use it with, however, an accompanying anti-Apollinarian intent.

The *Logos-anthrôpos* schema carried with it, though, its own peculiar disadvantages as first Theodore of Mopsuestia and then, more perspicuously, Nestorius soon proved. If extreme Cyrillians pressed the declining *Logos-sarx* terminology into heretical use as Monophysitism, where the divinity of the Word Incarnate totally absorbs his humanity, this was by reaction to extreme Antiochenism (for Theodore and Nestorius had their formation in that city) where the unity of subject in Christ, that vital feature of post-Athanasian orthodoxy, was neglected or even denied. In a Christology centred on the exemplary qualities of the Redeemer as man, the difficulty was to move from 'below' to 'above', to the positing of a transcendent subject of the redemptive action whose ethos the moral virtues of Jesus — to be sure — displayed. The suggestion that the

Gospel tradition knew two sons — the Son of David and the Son of God, and the scorn poured on the instinct of the faithful to address Mary as *Theotokos*, the Godbearer, revealed these defects in christological thinking.

Once the full reality of human ensoulment in Jesus was recognised, the question was how to maintain the unity of this divine-human person. Chalcedon profited from the debates between Cyrillians and Antiochenes. It also drew upon the concepts of *phusis*, nature, and *hypostasis* or *prosôpon*, person, introduced into the conciliar tradition by the Apollinarian controversy, as well as the idea of *ousia* already familiar from the trinitarian crisis associated with Arius, in order to underline that Jesus Christ is indeed one and the same, one single *hypostasis* or *prosôpon*, while by its famous quartet of adverts — 'without confusion', 'without change', 'without division', 'without separation' — presenting the union of *physeis*, 'natures', whereby he is *homoousios* both with the Father and with us, in such a way that no false inferences could be drawn about some supposed annihilation of the humanity by the divinity.

It is this foundational Chalcedonian conviction which Maximus inherits. Piret opens his account of Maximus' exposition of the mystery of Jesus by pointing out, helpfully enough, that Christ's hypostasis can be referred to in a variety of ways, all faithful to the teaching of Chalcedon. 'One of the Trinity' expresses the hypostatic identity of the two different *ousiai* in relation to the remaining two trinitarian hypostases. 'The Logos' expresses the numerical identity of the hypostasis and its divine *ousia* in relation to human *ousia*. 'The Son' expresses hypostatic identity in the mode of generation — by the Father according to the divine *ousia* and by blessed Mary for the human. 'The Lord Jesus Christ' expresses the identity of the hypostasis in his two *ousiai*, divine and human. The peculiar genius of the expression 'The Logos Incarnate' in Piret's eyes is that it has the virtue of bringing out the relation between the human *ousia* of Christ and his *hypostasis* in its divine *ousia*. After all, in the face of Arianism, Athanasius had favoured this title of Logos, Word, as accentuating *the numerical identity of the Son with the Father*, while Cyril, in the different circumstances of Nestorianism, had espoused the name of the Logos Incarnate as a lucid confession of *the numerical identity of the flesh with the Son.*[50]

Piret's exploration of Maximus' fundamental Christology, governed as this is by the theme of the Word Incarnate, takes the form of an interpretation of his fifteenth Letter,[51] and notably of its central section. Maximus begins by making two claims about Christ. First, in his own words:

> The Logos of God teaches us with precision that he exists in perfection, according to that *ousia* and nature whereby he is identical and *homoousios* with the Father and the Spirit, and according to that person and hypostasis whereby he is posited as other in relation to the Father and the Spirit, safeguarding without mixture the personal difference ...

But secondly, that Word of God also teaches that

> he has taken flesh of the Holy Spirit and the holy Mother of God and ever-virgin Mary, and has become man in perfection.[52]

In the first of these two statements, as Piret understands them, there is not only confession of the Nicene faith that the Father is the origin of the hypostasis and *ousia* of the Son. Further, filiation designates here the 'fact of existing by relation to the Father, in an originated way'. The Son, the Originated One, is, then, at the personal origin of his relation to Father and to the Spirit. And the significance of this is that it prepares the way for Maximus' second statement by showing that the Son is of himself, in person, *at the origin of his own Incarnation.* In that second statement, Maximus proposes that the Incarnation of the divine Logos is the union of his human *ousia* with his hypostasis in its divine *ousia* by means of the Spirit who is

---

[50]P. Piret, *Le Christ et la Trinité selon Maxime le Confesseur*, op. cit., p. 157.
[51]*Epistle* 15 (PG 91, 544D-576B).
[52]PG 91, 553D.

himself the final hypostasis in the trinitarian *homousia*. While the union of Son and Spirit in terms of the common divine *ousia* is their difference in terms of trinitarian hypostasis, the difference of Son and Spirit in the human *ousia* proper to the Son is their union by way of a hypostasis in human nature: namely, the Virgin Mary.

Yet despite the vital rôles of the Holy Spirit and of the *Theotokos*, as hypostatic terms of the Incarnation according to, respectively, the divine and the human *ousiai* of Christ, nevertheless the union of those two *ousiai* is of course proper to the *hypostasis* of the Son, who became perfectly human, that is, as Maximus now explains:

> according to the taking of flesh, possessing a thinking and rational soul, taking into himself nature and hypostasis.[53]

To some degree Maximus is simply repeating here the conciliar formulae. Chalcedon had already spoken of the Saviour's perfect humanity in terms of a rational soul and a body, while the Second Council of Constantinople had added 'flesh animated by a rational and thinking soul'. The phrase 'taking (or assumption) of flesh' is not so much conciliar as simply theological — from the school of Antioch, which liked the term *proslêpsis*. What is more interesting, indeed arresting, is that Maximus should go on to assert that the divine Logos assumed humanity in its proper constitution, that is according to both nature and *hypostasis*. As Piret points out, such an affirmation seems in flagrant contradiction with the Chalcedonian teaching that the two natures in Christ are united according to one only hypostasis — which Justinian's Council of Constantinople went on to identify with that of the divine personhood of the Son. In this passage, Maximus defines nature in terms of being, *to einai*, the sheer fact of existing in the order of *ousia*; and he understands hypostasis as the subsisting, *huphestanai*, of what exists: as Piret paraphrases, the support and maintenance of its existing. Now we know from elsewhere in this lengthy christological epistle that

---

[53]Epistle 15 (PG 91 553D).

Maximus had given just this point considerable attention, by way of considering the viewpoints of two predecessors, the so-called 'Neo-Chalcedonian' theologians Leontius of Byzantium and Leontius of Jerusalem. If Piret is right, then Maximus had spotted a weakness in each of the two Leontii. For Leontius of Byzantium, hypostasis is when someone subsists by or according to themselves, *kath' heauto*, but the Byzantine Leontius had gone on to speak of such personhood as circumscribed by its individuality and properties. If true, this would render impossible the affirmation of particular humanity for the Chalcedonian Saviour: his human *ousia* would have to be simply humanity at large. For Leontius of Jerusalem, hypostasis is a nature with its properties. Were the Jerusalemite Leontius correct, and hypostasis only a further specification of *ousia* — a particular *ousia*, in fact — then Christ's humanity would have to be identified with a human hypostasis — which was presumably not the meaning of Chalcedon, and manifestly not that of Constantinople II. Maximus' response is to marry elements of these two accounts: hypostasis is self-subsistence but not in such a way that the *ousia* is sundered from its properties. The human existence of Jesus Christ *subsists*: but it does so — and here Maximus' Chalcedonian and Second Constantinopolitan orthodoxy is saved — enhypostatised in the Logos[54]. And as Piret insists, in Maximus' version of the *enhypostaton* idea, itself authorised by Leontius of Byzantium, enhypostasia is not a really existing intermediary between the hypostasis and its *ousia*; rather does it locate the being and subsisting in question *in* the relationship of the *ousia* to its hypostasis. Christ is not a 'composed nature' of two hypostases, but he is a 'composed hypostasis', as Maximus' Letter 13 maintains:[55] for his own hypostasis is the composition of human *ousia* with the divine.

From this certain wider consequences follow. First, the relation of Christ's particular human *ousia* to that of other human beings is the same as the relation of the Logos to all

---

[54] Cf. St Thomas' account of this as described in A. Hastings, 'Christ's Act of Existence,' *Downside Review* 73.232 (April 1955), ff. 139-159.

[55] *Epistle* 13 (PG 91, 517C).

humanity: this relation has the properties of the Logos himself, in his divine *ousia* and his trinitarian hypostasis. Secondly, the relation of humanity to the Logos is the relation of his created being to the Creator. On the basis of a theological cosmology and anthropology, Maximus held that created human nature is in movement of a self-transcending sort towards the Logos. But now, with the Incarnation of the Word, something even more extraordinary can be said. In Piret's words:

> The human nature proper to the Logos, which is also common to human hypostases, is united to the Cause of this movement. As term of this movement, the Incarnate Logos is equally the movement's human and divine, natural and hypostatic, principle. He is its principle and its term, in a way both proper to his hypostasis and common to the Trinity inasmuch as the divine *ousia* of the Logos is common to the trinitarian hypostases.[56]

Turning a fresh page of his christological story, Maximus now goes on to assert that the flesh assumed was conceived *in the moment of its union* with the Logos. Deriving from John the Grammarian, this thesis provoked dissent as well as grateful acceptance from the divines of the sixth century. For Maximus it is a point of some importance: the temporal simultaneity of the conception and divine assumption of the human nature of Jesus signifies the real identity between the Logos as origin of the Incarnation and his incarnate being as its term. As human temporality and divine eternity are different, their compenetration in the moment of the hypostatic union constitutes the distinctive mode of existing, *tropos tês huparxeôs*, of the Son made man.[57] In this connexion, we can note that Felix Heinzer, in his study *Gottes Sohn als Mensch*, has seized on the importance of Maximus' couplet *logos-tropos*, already touched on here in considering his fundamental theology and also vital, as we shall see, in his cosmology, anthropology and soteriology as well. Heinzer remarked:

---

[56]P. Piret, *Le Christ et la Trinité selon Maxime le Confesseur*, op. cit., pp. 175-176.
[57]Ibid., p. 178.

It seems indeed that Maximus found here an instrument which allowed him to express the specific (divine) quality with which the humanity of Christ is furnished in the perspective of the 'how' or mode of its existence without taking away the concordance of that humanity with our own in the perspective of its 'what', its essential (human) constitution, and without, therefore, injuring his full and genuine humanity.[58]

This is not, however, the line taken by Piret who prefers to turn his attention, rather, to the query addressed to Maximus' shade by Hans Urs von Balthasar in his *Kosmische Liturgie*. Balthasar's question was, How can the uncomposed divine hypostasis of the Logos be identically the composing and composed hypostasis of the two natures? How can the Logos, the subject of this synthesis, be also its result?[59] Piret's answer on Maximus' behalf is that the origin and the term of the Incarnation, according to both divine and human *ousiai*, can be found in the relation of the Son to Father and Spirit. Nor is this all. By dint of the fact that the human nature assumed by the Word is the human *enhypostasia* of his divine personhood, the Logos is his own human *enousia*: a term which, Piret points out, both Leontius of Byzantium and Maximus regard as the inseparable pair of *enhypostasia*. And in any case, Piret goes on, the human *enhypostasia* of the Logos is only symmetrical with his divine *enhypostasia*, a theme which will lead him to the next section of his study, that of the two natures. As he writes:

The divine *enhypostasia*, namely, the interiority of the *ousia* to the hypostases, is identically the trinitarian *enousia*, the interiority of the hypostases to the *ousia*. The christological *enhypostasia*, that is, the interiority of the divine and human *ousiai* to the hypostasis of the Incarnate Son, is equally that hypostasis' double *enousia*: the Incarnate Son is and subsists in two natures.[60]

[58]F. Heinzer, *Gottes Sohn als Mensch. Die Struktur des Menschseins Christi bei Maximus Confessor* (Freiburg in der Schweiz 1980), p. 25.
[59]H. U. von Balthasar, *Kosmische Liturgie*, op. cit., p. 184.
[60]P. Piret, *Le Christ et la Trinité selon Maxime le Confesseur*, op. cit., p. 183.

And in a formulation entirely his own, Maximus feels justified in speaking of Christ's two natures 'which he is'.[61]

And the reason why Maximus can claim *this* is that the union of the divine and human *ousiai* in their difference implies the relation of the Incarnate Son to Father and to Spirit. No more rigorous correspondence between trinitarian theology and christology can be imagined. Yet, as Piret notes, even this, basic as it is, has a deeper foundation — the loving plan of God whereby the Logos, faithful to the trinitarian counsel, realised through philanthropy the hypostatic union: the correspondence between Triadology and Christology itself depends on the will and operation of the Father's Son, a glance ahead to the issue, so central to Maximus' life and struggles, of Monothelitism and Monoenergism.

The Two Natures

Maximus' most common formulae for the two natures of the Word Incarnate are slight variants on a single phrase: 'the natures from which and in which Christ is, and which he is'.[62] While the third phrase is, as we have just seen, Maximus' own, the idea of putting together Cyril's phrase 'of two natures', *ek duo phuseôn* (from the 433 reconciliation with the Antiochene party) and Chalcedon's *en duo phusesin*, 'in two natures', had already occurred to the theologians of the sixth century.

Piret concentrates initially on Ambigua 27, where Maximus is commenting a text of Gregory Nazianzen in the *Fourth Theological Oration*, itself a meditation, in part, on the words of the risen Christ to Mary Magdalen in the Fourth Gospel, 'I am ascending to my Father and your Father, to my God and your God'.[63] The Cappadocian doctor had pointed out that the names 'Father' and 'God' here are at once interchangeable but unconfused, thanks to the union of the two natures in Christ. Now for Maximus the simultaneous evocation of the natures is equivalent to invoking Christ's hypostasis. More

---

[61]*Epistle* 15 (PG 91, 573A).

[62]E.g. I *Ambigua* 5, 1 (PG 91, 1052D).

[63]John 20, 17; cited in Gregory Nazianzen, *Discourse* 30 (PG 36, 113B), itself quoted in II *Ambigua* 27 (PG 91, 1268C-1272A).

widely, then, through the single hypostasis, what one nature possesses naturally is given in exchange to the other.

In *Ambigua* 5, Maximus acts on his own statement. The relation of Christ to his natures allows, on the one hand, the ascription to the Logos of the movement and activity proper to human *ousia*, and, on the other, the attributing to that human *ousia* of the genesis and engendering of which God is the origin. God the Word can thus be named as the principle of that movement of becoming which is the created *logos*, or essence, of human nature, while the *tropos* or mode of existing proper to the hypostasis of the divine Son can now be spoken of as inscribed in human nature itself.[64]

A more substantial text already investigated by Piret, Letter 15, ends with a 'confession of the faith according to the Fathers', whose materials fall into two connected sections, a commentary on, respectively, Cyril's '*from* two natures' and Chalcedon's '*in* two natures'. In the first, Maximus insists that the 'natural union', *phusikê henôsis*, of which Cyril had spoken, means simply a true and real union, and not that Christ has one 'composed nature', as the Severans maintained. For Maximus, in fact, the formula *ek duo phuseôn* means precisely that because the natures are different, their union can only be in terms of the hypostasis. It is from, *ek*, Christ's *heterocusia*, starting from his two naturally different natures, that we recognise his *homohypostasia*. Moving on to the Chalcedonian *en duo phusesin*, Maximus interprets this phrase, originally found in Leo the Great's *Tome*, in a way which picks up the great pope's own emphasis on the actions of Christ in his two natures. As Maximus understands things, each nature is the hypostasis whilst not being the other nature. But more than this, as Piret sums up:

> Each nature, in manifesting the hypostasis in a direct fashion, manifests indirectly the other nature which it is not, equally identical with the hypostasis. And so each nature manifests its communion with the other, a

---

[64] I *Ambigua* 5 (PG 91, 1052D).

communion which comes about from the single hypostasis common to both. For the hypostasis is in both natures.[65]

However, Maximus only really confronts the Monoenergist position that the Incarnate Word has thereby but a single (theandric) activity when he recalls that a nature is not without existence, and therefore not without activity. Divinity and humanity each have their proper operation, even though, thanks to the interiority of the hypostasis to each of the natures, Christ works 'divine things carnally ..., and human things divinely'. The topic of Christ's actions leads Maximus to refer to the chief events of his Life, Death and Resurrection. Placed in the context of this thorough-goingly ontological Christology, how do these appear? In Piret's words, the Cross, Death and Burial manifest, in the saving economy, the extreme otherness of the human *ousia* vis-à-vis its divine counterpart. But, since that human *ousia* remains, even in these most negative events, identical with the divine hypostasis, those happenings also disclose the supreme identity of the human *ousia* with that hypostasis in its divine being. It is in the Death and Burial, Piret concludes, that the Son's human *ousia* has *become* his relation to Father and Spirit in their divine one. What then of the Resurrection? As relation of the flesh of the Son to the *Spirit,* the Resurrection is the definitive subsisting of the human *ousia* in its origin, while the Ascension, the closing moment of Christ's glorification is, as relation of the Son's flesh to the *Father,* the definitive subsisting of that same human *ousia* in its term. This is, at any rate, how Piret's interprets Maximus' words, 'According to the Economy, the world of the flesh of the Logos happens with the Father' — a citation not from the letters but from the *Ambigua.*[66]

It remains to consider the two wills of Christ and his two operations. But first we must discover how the move is made from talk of the two natures to these other aspects, central as they were to the problematic of the period. Maximus'

[65]P. Piret, *Le Christ et la Trinité selon Maxime le Confesseur,* op. cit., p. 214, with reference to *Epistle* 15 (PG 91, 573AC).
[66]II *Ambigua* 60 (PG 91, 1385B).

fundamental statement of position is that will and operation are determinations of nature. Yet he adds at once that the difference between human and divine will and operation is not *opposition*; they are not counterposed to each other by contrariety, *enantiôsis*.[67] Above all, the divine will and operation in Christ to work our salvation is in no way crossed, but on the contrary served, by his human will and operation, which Maximus sums up, with reference to the Philippians hymn, in Jesus' *obedience* as the Servant.

Elsewhere in the *Opuscula theologica et polemica* Maximus insists that it is on the basis of his divine and human activities that we know Jesus Christ to be God and man;[68] and that, *pace*, perhaps, the anxieties of the critics of Leonine Christology, to say of Christ that his natures are 'not incapable of operation', *anenergêtoi*, is not to turn them into hypostases or operating subjects, *energountai*, but to confess in an orthodox way the essential and natural character of his 'existences and operations'.[69] Christ's action and willing, though determined by the hypostatic identity of his different natures, are not themselves a new determination of that hypostatic identity — which would make three activities, three wills.[70]

The Two Wills

It is time to look more closely at the question of the two wills — a topic which Maximus approaches, above all, via the mystery of the Saviour's Agony in the Garden. Nor is that surprising, insofar as reflection on that event in the Passion narrative seems to have played a part in the making of the main monument of Monothelite teaching — the *Psêphos* or solemn declaration sent by the patriarch Sergius of Constantinople to his new opposite number at Alexandria, Cyrus of Phasis. Following Piret's analysis of that document: Sergius had opened by rejection the expression 'one activity' of the Word Incarnate

---

[67] *Opuscula theologica et polemica* 6 (PG 91, 68A).
[68] Ibid., 7 (PG 91, 80B).
[69] Ibid., 16 (PG 91, 205B).
[70] Ibid., 9 (PG 91, 117CD).

on the grounds that it undermines the Chalcedonian
affirmation of two natures hypostatically united. But then
Sergius goes on immediately to rule out 'two activities' also,
since that could imply two wills set in contrary directions
(*enantiôs*), the one to the other: as if, whereas the Word had
willed to accomplish the saving Passion, the humanity he had
assumed opposed its will to his divine decision.[71] As Piret points
out, Sergius here identifies the idea of 'contrariness' or
'opposition', *contrariété*, with that of 'otherness', *altérité*. To
affirm two wills would seem to imply affirming two contrary
subjects or objects of will. Rather, the Redeemer is 'one single
self-identical subject', *hupokeimenon*, of willing, and the saving
Passion is the unique reality willed by him. As Piret writes:

> The cup cannot be, in this selfsame moment of the Agony,
> simultaneously refused and accepted by 'one single self-
> identical' willing subject. From consideration of the Agony
> of Christ, Sergius disengaged a general principle of 'non-
> contradiction', which is the explicit negation of the two
> wills of the Lord.[72]

But the price paid is that of representing the human *ousia* of
Christ as in a condition of unstable exteriority vis-à-vis his
divine person. In *Opuscula theologica et polemica* 6, Maximus
invites his interlocutor to consider the saying of Jesus in his
Agony, 'My Father, if it be possible, let this cup pass from me'.[73]
Gregory Nazianzen, whose own comment on this text in the
Fourth Theological Oration Maximus cites, had thought that,
were these words pronounced by a human being, they would
indeed imply a contrariety of human willing and divine. They
were not, though, pronounced by a man as we are or even
through the humanity assumed by the Son, but by the assuming

---

[71]The *Psêphos* is found in Mansi XI, 533C-536A for the proposal that the Agony
scene lies behind the *Psêphos* at this point, see P. Piret, *Le Christ et la Trinité selon
Maxime le Confesseur*, op. cit., p. 243.

[72]Ibid., p. 245.

[73]Matthew 26, 39, cited in *Opuscula theologica et polemica* 6 (PG 91, 65A-68D).

Son himself. As François-Marie Léthel put it in his study of the Agony in the Garden in Maximus' thought:

> Because he does not distinguish the moral problem of contrariety from the physical problem of otherness, Gregory cannot think of a will as being at once other and non-contrary. The hypothesis of a human will in Christ not running counter to the divine will lies totally outside his perspective.[74]

For Gregory, the Son has no will other than the Father's: a point essential to him in his anti-Arian writing, where the recognition of the common, indeed identical, will of Father and Son was vital to the defence of the *homoousion* between them.[75] In Sergius' Monothelite interpretation both of the Gospel text and of Gregory's commentary thereon, the Lord Jesus, by his own divine will, which is that of the Father, while recognising the reality of the movement of revulsion against the Passion and Death in his human flesh, denies the existence of a human will in him contrary to that uncreated one: 'not as I will, but as thou wilt'. Maximus, by contrast, understands these words, — in his paraphrase (following Gregory) 'not what I will but that thy will may triumph' — as *prayer made to the Father*, a prayer in which the Son gives himself to the Father, in perfect concord and consent. Such a *movement* towards God as Father is, for Maximus, a characteristic of the human will of the Saviour, whereas the divine will common to Father, Son and Holy Spirit constitutes, rather, its own *stasis*, stability. The concord of Christ's will with the Father is a matter, then, of his *human* willing. But man's salvation, which is thus willed by Christ's human will, as well as by his divine one, manifests the accord of the two wills of the willing subject, the Saviour. At the same time, by confessing the accord of the two wills whilst safeguarding their natural difference, Maximus also affirms

---

[74]F.-M. Léthel, *Théologie de l'Agonie du Christ. La liberté humaine du Fils de Dieu et son importance sotériologique mises en lumière par Saint Maxime le Confesseur* (Paris 1979), p. 33.

[75]*Discourse* 30, 12 (PG 36, 117C-120B).

the communion of the two activities of Christ in their natural distinction also.

Elsewhere in the *Opuscula theologica et polemica* Maximus points out that while the absence of human contrariety to God does not of itself imply the union of natures in Christ, such union certainly implies the absence of human contrariety. And so he distinguishes *difference* from *opposition*: difference is preserved in that union which is opposition's absence. Human nature is not as such contrary to God: that is not where contrariety takes its rise.[76] But if the *logos* of human nature in no way founds an opposition of man's will to God's, the same is not true of the *tropos* of the will's movement, which can be either in or out of conformity with man's natural *logos*. And here Maximus distinguishes three kinds of *tropoi*. Sin, as the opposition of human willing to God, is a *tropos* which is contrary to nature. Virtue, the accord of human willing with God, is a *tropos* in conformity to nature. And lastly the union of the human will of Christ with the divine will is a *tropos* higher than human nature, being nothing other than the hypostatic identity of the Incarnate Son. In terms of these three *tropoi*, it is clear that opposition to the divine will typifies only *sinful* man. Accord with the divine will is common both to Christ and to humanity as such when the latter's movement or *élan* is not distorted by sin. What is specific to Christ is the hypostatic union of human willing and divine, the foundation of his 'impeccability'. Nazianzen had spoken of the Saviour's will as 'altogether divinised', and this Maximus can understand, then, in terms of the *tropos* of the hypostatic union, the basis of Christ's incapacity to sin as of his human virtue. Yet within that union, as a union of natures 'without confusion and without mixture' (as well as 'without separation and without division'), the permanence of the human *logos* in its entirety is of course not only presupposed but also here affirmed. *Tropos* so far from replacing *logos* is unthinkable without it, being as it is the 'how' of the 'what' that exists.

---

[76] *Opuscula theologica et polemica* 20 (PG 91, 236A-237C).

But this analysis obliges Maximus to confront the question of how Christ is related to that concrete human nature of fallen humanity whose *tropos* is sin. On this Maximus writes:

> The blameworthy things which are contrary to nature and reason are appropriated by him as the Head of the body in the same way that a doctor appropriates the sufferings of a sick person, until he frees us from them, destroying them totally by the power of the incorporation which he accomplishes in himself, he who is God become man for us.[77]

And here Maximus distinguishes between, on the one hand, that *logos* or pattern of emotional life which is proper to human nature as created by God — and to the passions in this sense he applies the name 'the *logos* of "dignity"', *epitimia* — and, on the other hand, that pattern of emotional life which distorts created human nature, to which he gives the phrase 'the *logos* of "indignity"', *atimia*. What the Word made flesh assumes is the *logos* of dignity, that dignity which itself manifests the integrity of human nature. In assuming this, the Word divinely guarantees it for the future, thus wiping out the notice of condemnation served on man on account of sin. Faced with the *tropos* of disobedience, which manifests rather the indignity of human sinfulness, the *tropos* of Christ's voluntary obedience to God reveals the *logos* of human nature as made for a life of concord with its Creator. At the same time, as we have already seen, Maximus can speak of the Incarnate Son as taking on also our disordered passions — something Maximus describes in the vocabulary of 'appropriation', *oikeiôsis*, not of assumption, *proslêpsis*. He takes on the *logos* of indignity, proper to us as fallen human beings, so as to destroy it, meanwhile communicating to us what is proper to himself, to the benefit of that human nature of ours which he has made his own. And so he at once restores the interrupted movement of human

---

[77]Ibid., at PG 237AB.

nature towards God and unites the human nature thus restored
to the divine nature.[78]

But does this account, happy as it is in terms of saving the
Chalcedonian Christology, really do justice to the drama — the
elements of struggle and conflict — which the Gospels so
graphically convey? It may be good doctrine; but is it convincing
exegesis? In the *Disputation with Pyrrhus*, Maximus has more to
say about what in the *Opuscula theologica et polemica* he had
called the 'appearance of repulsion', *emphasis tês sustolês*, given
by Christ in the Garden when confronted with the imminent
prospect of his Passion. Maximus proposes, not without support
from such earlier Fathers as Cyril of Alexandria and John
Chrysostom, that Christ's first movement of will at Gethsemane
was indeed one of resistance — not, however, of resistance to
the Father's saving plan, but of *resistance to death*. The Incarnate
Word, in assuming human *ousia*, also took up what Maximus
calls the 'power of beings to attach themselves to being and not
to non-being'. Through that power every creature tends to
what preserves it in being, and experiences repugnance at
what can destroy it. It was by this natural power of his humanity
that the Word at first resisted his own approaching human
dying.[79] Here, in the context of his prayer to the Father, the Son
manifested his humanity voluntarily, with goodness, and in
humility. But in going on to pray, not now that the cup might
pass, but that the Father's will should triumph, the Saviour
manifests that same human will not this time in the *logos* of
human nature but in the *tropos* of the union. His human will,
consenting to the divine will of the Father that the Son might
carry out man's salvation, accepts the Passion. Or, in an
alternative interpretation of this Maximian text suggested by
Piret, by means of the *tropos* of hypostatic union the Incarnate
Son wills that this human power through which he, though
God, fears death, should be the means through which man's
salvation is achieved. On this second view, right from the
beginning of his two-stage prayer, the Saviour in the Garden
willed our redemption in and through his very human fear

---

[78]P. Piret, *Le Christ et la Trinité selon Maxime le Confesseur*, op. cit., p. 271.
[79]*Disputatio cum Pyrrho* (PG 91, 297A-300A).

itself.[80] His tendency to conserve his own being, and his fear of dying were different in their mode, their *tropos*, from ours, though the same in their root, their *logos*. We corrupt our tendency to being by a selfish egoism, *philautia*, which turns us from God and our neighbour, and our fear of death becomes, by the same sinful *tropos*, a reprehensible fear. In his opening prayer, the Redeemer willed to safeguard the human nature which is his and ours, but he also willed to save it from the sinful *tropos* which turns it from God. At the conclusion of the prayer in the Garden, therefore, he willed his Passion in order to destroy utterly the sinful *tropos* which our death sanctions. He did so, incorporating us definitively in God, in his *tropos* of union with the Father, into whose hands he committed his human life and work, so that we might be forgiven and redeemed. Hilaire Belloc, the English Catholic man of letters, put it well in a letter. Speaking of death's domain as 'a curtain of Iron, a gulf impassable, an impenetrable darkness, and a distance as it were limitless, infinite', Belloc remarks of the Agony in the Garden:

> The miracle whereby such an enormity coming upon immortal souls does not breed despair, is the chief miracle of the Incarnation — and to work that miracle, the Incarnate — with what a supreme energy — accepted our pain, almost refused it, but accepted it; and it was greater than any pain of ours: physically beyond endurance and in the spirit a descent into Hell.

'Olivet', for Belloc, is the holiest place on earth for those who 'know the significance of Christendom', since there God himself feared death.

> Not that God himself can suffer, but that God was so intensely, so intimately Man in the Incarnation, that the memories and experience of Divinity and Humanity are united therein: and through it, the worst pain of the

---

[80]P. Piret, *Le Christ et la Trinité selon Maxime le Confesseur*, op. cit., p. 281.

creature is *known*, by actual experience of our own kind, by the Creator.[81]

We should not expect of a literary artist the same care in doctrinal formulation as we expect of a Byzantine doctor — to whom we can look, with Piret's help, for a more exact account of this mystery whose depth Belloc here plumbs.

So far, however, Piret has said nothing about the *divine* will of the Redeemer. Where does *that* fit into the picture? Maximus ascribes the negative qualification made by the Saviour in his Garden prayer through the words 'not what I will' to the 'unoriginated divinity of the Only-begotten' — that is, to the Son's divine *ousia*. This negative clause in the Lord's praying signifies to Maximus that the Son wills nothing separately from the Father: the will of Father and Son is one and identical thanks to their *homousion*.[82] But basically, for Maximus, the identity of nature, and so of will and operation, possessed by Father, Son and Spirit is not *directly* shown forth by the Gospel accounts of the Agony. Piret indeed contributes the comment that the Agony and Passion of the Incarnate Son, in manifesting the Son's obedience, in his human will, to the Father, actually signify the *difference* of his hypostasis from that of the Father ('heterohypostasia'), whereas it is the Resurrection and Ascension, constituting as these do the communion of the Son's humanity with the Father in the Holy Spirit, that testify to the identity of nature ('homoousia') of all three trinitarian persons.[83]

The Two Operations

Father John Meyendorff, in his study *Le Christ dans la théologie byzantine*, had proposed that for Maximus, as for the earlier Greek patristic tradition, 'operation', *energeia*, is largely synonymous with 'will, *thelêma*.[84] However, following Piret and

---

[81]Cited A. N. Wilson, *Hilaire Belloc* (London 1984), pp. 389-339.

[82]*Opuscula theologica et polemica* 6 (PG 91, 68AD).

[83]P. Piret, *Le Christ et la Trinité selon Maxime le Confesseur*, op. cit., p. 296.

[84]J. Meyendorff, *Le Christ dans la théologie byzantine* (Paris 1968).

his source in this regard, an unpublished dissertation on the *Disputation with Pyrrhus*, Maximus' habitual mention of 'two wills' and 'two operations', distinctly and in that order, is by no means an unheralded linguistic redundancy.[85]

For Maximus, *nous*, the spiritual determination of the human soul, symbolises the rational and volitional life of man, where reasoning activity and desire or appetition form one reality. Will, *hê thelêsis*, is in fact *orexis logikê*, rational appetition, something rooted in human nature and therefore itself 'natural', *phusikê*.[86] Further, in the *Disputatio cum Pyrrho*, Maximus, distinguishes between the willer, *ho thelôn*, the volitional power, *thelêsis* or *thelêma*, and the object willed, *to thelêton*. *Thelêsis* and *thelêma* are distinguished by a subtle difference which can only be brought out periphrastically in English. As a Francophone Catholic author, Piret turns unsurprisingly, but illuminatingly, to the early twentieth century French philosopher of 'action', Maurice Blondel, for guidance. *Thelêsis* stands for the power of will, considered as immanent to the personal subject who does the willing, what Blondel in his analysis of human action called *la volonté voulante*. *Thelêma*, by contrast, signifies the relationship between the volitional power and its object — what Blondel terms *la volonté voulue* — while at the same time indicating also the immanence of this power in its subject. And here Piret tries to bring out the broader character of *thelêma*, in Maximus' usage, by calling it, simply, 'will', and reserving to *thelêsis* the term 'volition'.[87] Whereas the Monothelites regarded Christ's single willing activity as a simple transition from the willing subject, *ho thelôn*, to what he willed, *to thelêton*, Maximus insists that willing subject and reality willed must not be separated from the nature which is 'of itself volitional,' *thelêtikê heautês*, and, thanks to will, 'mistress of itself', *autexousios*.[88]

[85]M. Doucet, 'Dispute de Maxime le Confesseur avec Pyrrhus' (Thesis, Montreal 1972).

[86]*Opuscula theologica et polemica* 1 (PG 91, 12C).

[87]P. Piret, *Le Christ et la Trinité selon Maxime le Confesseur*, op. cit., p. 307, by way of comment on *Disputatio cum Pyrrho* (PG 91, 292C).

[88]*Opuscula theologica et polemica* 1 (PG 91, 12c-13A); *Disputatio cum Pyrrho* (PG 91, 301C).

This, however, does not exhaust Maximus' vocabulary or concepts where willing is concerned. Most importantly, there is also our disposition towards our own will, an appetition consisting of inward disposition, termed by Maximus *gnomê*. Piret, helpfully, understands this as the personal temperament or character which, by way of seeking and deliberating on possible objects of volition, comes to expression in the individual's appetition and his or her particular choices. While 'natural will' is the concrete form of simply willing, 'gnomic will' is the concrete form of the manner in which we will, *to pôs thelein*: our personal habitual way of exercising rational and spiritual self-mastery.[89] For good or ill, our gnomic will is a reality both moral and psychological, and psychological because moral.

There are two further terms, or ideas, which Maximus works with in this context, *prohairêsis*, 'choice', and *boulêsis*, 'decision'. While *prohairêsis*, the choice for which the will decides, is unproblematic, the concept of *boulêsis* is more complex: in Maximus' use it comprises both the first moment of the willing process which may lead to choice, and the last end for which we choose, decidedly, some means. By *boulêsis*, we wish for various goods, not all of which, such as health and immortality, depend on our decision. The significance of *boulêsis* in Maximus' scheme is that it joins *thelêma phusikon* to its own infinite object, God, an infinitude which is at one and the same time both possible to it and impossible.

But the point of this analysis is not ultimately anthropological but christological: how does this throw light, then, on the mystery of Christ?

From the very beginning of the *Disputatio cum Pyrrho* the former patriarch objects to Dyothelitism that the unity of Christ presupposes the unity of Christ's will. But to this Maximus replies that Christ's hypostasis cannot be the sole principle of his willing, which is, then, not 'monadic'. Were Christ's will monadic, the hypostasis of the Saviour would be really distinct, in his willing, from his two natures and their natural powers. The union, safeguarding the difference of the two natural

---

[89]P. Piret, *Le Christ et la Trinité selon Maxime le Confesseur*, op. cit., pp. 311-312.

realities, as taught by Chalcedon, would no longer be the identity of the hypostasis with its natures. Maximus, by contrast, affirms that only the twofold natural principle of willing can do justice to the singleness, the unicity, of *this* willer, Jesus Christ. Because Christ's hypostasis is the union of two differing *ousiai*, the unique singularity of his will must be intrinsically related to his twofold *homoousia*.

In Christ, according to Maximus, there is a normal human will, but *not* a gnomic will.[90] *Gnomê* and *prohairêsis*, which are varying orientations and decisions, respectively, of individual human beings vis-á-vis their own end, cannot be attributed to the Word Incarnate. As Maximus points out in *Quaestiones ad Thalassium* 42, the Lord's human will remained unchangeably oriented towards the good.[91] In the first of the *Opuscula theologica et polemica*, Maximus remarks that, whereas our humanity is in movement — both by nature and by the kind of choices that bring salvation — towards God as its term, where alone it will find its stability, Christ's humanity is not moved in terms of choices leading to such an end, for its stability lies in its union with the Word of God. Nevertheless, though without *prohairêsis*, the humanity joined to the Logos retains all its natural appetition, its *thelêsis*.[92] Nor can one speak of *gnomê* in the case of Christ. Choice belongs to a movement oriented by gnomic will, which turns to the one side or the other as personal character suggests. *Gnomê*, belonging as it does to a merely human hypostasis, cannot be ascribed to the hypostasis of the Logos Incarnate. What in our case is the term of our willing — definitive communion with God — is in Christ's case not only its term but also its origin, since he is, in his hypostasis, united with the Father and the Holy Spirit.[93] Yet once again this must be without prejudice to the reality of Christ's human willing: for just as God, man's archetype, is by nature *autexousios*, 'self-mastering', so man, the image of God, must be of a volitional nature. But in the Redeemer, the archetype has

---

[90]Ibid., pp. 321-325.
[91]*Quaestiones ad Thalassium* 42 (PG 91, 405C-408B).
[92]*Opuscula theologica et polemica* 1 (PG 91, 29D).
[93]P. Piret, *Le Christ et la Trinité selon Maxime le Confesseur*, op. cit., p. 325.

become the image, and so is doubly willing, in his humanity as in his divinity.[94]

Understandably enough, what Maximus is especially concerned to emphasis, in his reply to Pyrrhus, is the absence of contrariety between the two wills of Christ. Such contrariety as Monothelites suspect, once a two wills doctrine be accepted, is illusory. There is no sin in God Incarnate, nor is human will of its nature counterposed to God, for God has not created opposition to God.[95] Though Christ's two wills remain different, their difference is simply that which characterises their natures. In Jesus Christ divine self-mastery and human self-mastery are united, in the identity of the single hypostasis, which is why, as Maximus puts it, he 'wills to, and can, save us perfectly'.[96] And in any case, Maximus could, and did, add here for Pyrrhus' benefit a reference to the already traditional patristic notion of the *communicatio idiomatum*, that mutual communication of properties which Maximus calls *hê antidosis*, 'the exchange'. Though Pyrrhus, as a Chalcedonian, accepts in principle the mutual communication of natures, he does not draw the necessary inference: for how could one recognise such an exchange in Christ without affirming the rational and spiritual properties of the natures in question, and notably, therefore, the two-fold will? Or as Piret sums up Maximus' thought in the *Disputation:*

> The mutual communication discloses to us the accord, *sumphuia*, of the two wills and the consent, *sunneusis*, of the human will to the divine will of the Father, who is the primordial source of the Incarnation and the final term of the paschal mystery.[97]

But what, then, of the two *operations* in relation to the two wills whose reality Maximus now believes himself to have vindicated? In ascribing the single will of Christ to his hypostasis,

---

[94]*Disputatio cum Pyrrho* (PG 91, 324D).

[95]Ibid., at 292AB.

[96]Ibid., at 325B.

[97]P. Piret, *Le Christ et la Trinité selon Maxime le Confesseur*, op. cit., p. 331.

the *Psêphos* had claimed to resolve the problem of Christ's operation or activity. The flesh of Christ, animated by a rational soul, brought about his natural movement when God the Word willed it, as he willed it, and as often as he willed it. Thanks to the one hypostatic will of the Saviour, the divine activity directs the human in Christ. Maximus reminds Pyrrhus, the inheritor of the Monoenergist teaching of his predecessor Sergius, that the various movements or operations which one might ascribe to the body or the soul are, as human activities, the work of a single human nature.

But how does Maximus substantiate this case that a created *ousia* must have its own *energeia*, its own distinctive operation? For Maximus, *energiea* is the movement, *kinêsis*, of a specific created *ousia* towards its own end or goal. As he affirms in *Ambigua* 7, all created things are, by their *logoi*, in some way mobile. By a power contained in their nature, *dunamis phusikê*, they press on towards their *telos*, their goal, by an activity, *energeia*, which comes to rest only in an 'end' which is their ultimate finality, *to autoteles*.[98] However, as Piret stresses, Maximus does not regard the trilogy of terms — nature, power, operation — as identifying merely an order of succession: a beginning, middle and end (in the sense of chronological terminus). Rather, as *Ambigua* 5 would show, does he see these three elements as compenetrating to form a single 'specifying movement' of the creature in question.[99] As Maximus writes:

> The sole true demonstration of the *ousia* lies in its constitutive power, *sustatikê dunamis*, which can also rightly be called its natural operation, *phusikê energeia*. That marks out *ousia* primordially and directly, because it is a specifying movement, *eidopoios kinêsis*, the most general of all comprehensive properties, outside of which there is only non-being — that non-being of which the great doctor [Denys] says that 'it possesses neither existence nor movement'.[100]

[98]II *Ambigua* 7 (PG 91, 1072AB).
[99]P. Piret, *Le Christ et la Trinité selon Maxime le Confesseur*, op. cit., p. 338.
[100]I *Ambigua* 5 (PG 91, 1048A).

Although Maximus would not ascribe movement to God, in all other respects the elements of this description can be, and are, applied by him to the Creator likewise. The compenetration of *ousia* and *energeia* is as much a reality in God as in creatures, although in a mode which is utterly different from theirs. As the same section of the *Book of Ambiguities* puts it, the 'delimitation', *horos*, of every nature is established through the *logos*, (the pattern), of its essential operation.[101]

These convictions typify Maximus' approach to Monoenergism from the outset. But in the course of his reflections on will as a power of nature, stimulated by the Monothelite debate from 640 onwards, he tends to replace the middle term of the trio 'nature, power, operation' by the word 'will'. In personal beings, *energeia* is not just the actualisation of some indeterminate power of the *ousia* in question. Instead it is, rather, the operation of, precisely, will — rational, voluntary action. A willing nature may be without achievements, *erga*, but should it lack that operation which is distinctively its own, it can neither be, nor be known.[102] Both will and operation are intrinsic to (spiritual) nature's constitutive structure where all three factors — nature, will, operation — are simultaneously present and inter-active.

Vis-à-vis Pyrrhus, just as earlier Maximus had argued that the principle of Christ's willing must be sought both in the two natures and the single hypostasis, so now he does the same for Christ's 'operation'. First, Maximus proposes that nature shares the unifying power of the hypostasis: if 'operations' are not unified by *ousia* — of which the hypostasis is the act of subsisting, then those operations, in their very multiplicity, would multiply the hypostases. To this he adds, secondly, that, if the *ousia* is not the 'be-ing' of the operation, then the acting subject, which is the act of subsisting of the *ousia* in its operation, would be excluded from being — Christ's person would be suppressed.[103] The unicity, the singularity, of Jesus Christ is his

---

[101]Ibid. as 1057B.

[102]*Disputatio cum Pyrrho* (PG 91, 341C).

[103]P. Piret, *Le Christ et la Trinité selon Maxime le Confesseur*, op. cit., pp. 345-346.

hypostasis, and his hypostasis is the union of his two operating natures, divine and human.[104] As for Denys' 'new theandric operation', *kainê theandrikê energeia*, Maximus takes the crucial word there to be *kainos*, 'new': and novelty, as a quality, is not to be counted, unlike the realities which it qualifies, realities which are, in fact, the two natural operations of Christ.[105]

However, Maximus is willing to go rather further. There is in Christ a real *perichôrêsis* between the divine nature and the human, that is, a genuine reciprocal penetration of them. For G. L. Prestige, indeed, Maximus was the first to use the noun 'perichoresis' in Christology, even if Gregory Nazianzen did centuries before employ the verb.[106] And if, on the one hand, Maximus ascribes the *perichôrêis* of the natures of Christ to their 'mode of reciprocal communication [or exchange] according to the union', *ho tropos tês kata tên henôsin antidoseôs*, on the other hand he is also willing to refer it to the 'mode of manifestation of the natural operations', *ho tropos tês tôn phusikôn energeiôn ekphanseôs.*[107] At the same time, Maximus can speak of the unity of Christ's human activity with his divine as being owed not only to the *perichôrêsis* but also to the *sumphuia*, the accord, between his human will and his divine.[108] As Piret concludes, the human and divine wills of Christ in their common accord are 'exchanged' in giving themselves one to the other, and that union is manifested by the circumincession of the divine and human operations which shows at once that these operations are natural and that the natures, divine and human, are operative.[109] Here Maximus anticipates in fact the teaching of the Lateran synod of 649, for whose participants 'the only and self-same Christ our God' possesses 'two natures, two wills, two operations', and 'by both of his natures willed naturally and was operative naturally for our salvation'.[110]

---

[104]Ibid., pp. 346-347.
[105]*Disputatio cum Pyrrho* (PG 91, 345C-348A).
[106]G. L. Prestige, *God in Patristic Thought* (London 1936), p. 291.
[107]*Disputatio cum Pyrrho* at 345D-348A.
[108]*Opuscula theologica et polemica* 7 (PG 91, 85D-88A).
[109]P. Piret, *Le Christ et la Trinité selon Maxime le Confesseur*, p. 351.
[110]*Denzinger-Schönmetzer* 263-264.

In sum: for Maximus both will and operation are immanent in *ousia* which, indeed, defines itself by its own act: in the Thomist adage, *agere sequitur esse* — and so being reveals itself in activity. While will for Maximus is *autoexousia*, literally 'being itself from being', operation remains always inherent in such will. Though operation proceeds from will, the two realities compenetrate: the being in question operates by willing, and wills in operating. Moreover, just as human will is not of its nature in opposition to the divine will, so the operation which comes forth from it cannot be opposed by virtue of its nature to divine activity. That activity is in no way sundered from the divine *ousia*, and human operation too inheres in man's being. To Maximus' eyes, the incarnate Son must possess in integrity two wills and two operations, since he wills and operates our salvation in terms of the two natures from which and in which he is and, in fact, which he is. Both divine and human natures are willing and operative.[111] That mystery of the Word Incarnate, doubly active for our salvation, is summed up in the Blessed Virgin Mary; 'Maiden, yet a Mother,/Daughter of thy Son', in the words of Dante Alighieri, as translated by the late Mgr, Ronald Knox.[112] What form did Maximus' Marian understanding take? The question enables us to investigate a most fascinating text, in the chapter that follows.

[111]P. Piret, *Le Christ et la Trinité selon Maxime le Confesseur*, op. cit., pp. 358-359.

[112]*Paradiso*, canto XXXIII, 1; for Knox's translation, see *The Divine Office. The Liturgy of the Hours according to the Roman Rite* (Et London 1974), I., p. 561*.

4

Michel van Esbroeck on Maximus' Mariology

In the Byzantine *Life* of Maximus Confessor, which, though generally dated in its present form to the tenth century, some three hundred years after his death, is widely believed to incorporate much earlier materials, we find in chapter 31 a curious incident related to his trial. Soldiers accused him of having blasphemed the Mother of Christ; more specifically they charged him with not recognising as *Theotokos*, Mother of God, 'the blessed Virgin, our Queen'.[1] This is indeed a strange charge to bring against a Chalcedonian Christian, who in his ecclesiology always cites the authority of the six Councils — namely, the Lateran Council of 649 and the first five Ecumenical Councils, including, then, that of 431 at Ephesus where the title *Theotokos*, the God-bearer, was solemnly accorded to the Mother of Jesus. If we allow that in seventh century Constantinople, the level of theological culture enjoyed by members of the imperial army would in all likelihood be superior to what is the case today among, for example, the Royal Green Jackets, some kind of explanation can be offered. One of Maximus' favoured phrases for the Incarnation is to speak of Christ as 'from two natures, in two natures, and [himself being] two natures' — for the hypostasis of God the Word, his personhood, is interior to those natures, acts as those natures, and in this sense is not a different reality from those

---

[1]Cf. PG 90, 168D.

natures.[2] In order to press home the point, so crucial to his
doctrinal mission, that Jesus Christ enjoys the exercise both of
a divine will, or else he could not save us, and a human will, or
else he could not be the first-fruits of a salvation that is
genuinely ours, Maximus was obliged to stress the absolute
difference of the two natures, divine and human (though also
the communion between them), and so to present the
Incarnation as a continuing miracle, the most wonderful of all
miracles, the condescension of the whole Trinity that one of its
hypostases — the Logos — should become and remain man.
This Maximus presents as in every sense above nature — not
only above human nature, but also above divine nature, and
only made possible by the charity of the trinitarian Persons,
relatively distinct as these are from the simple divine nature
itself. Such a christological doctrine was wounding to the
Marian sensibilities of Monophysite Christians, for whom the
Word became, in the womb of Mary, one substance, one *phusis*,
one natural reality, with mankind.

Did Maximus ever attempt to clear himself of this charge of
impiety towards the Mother of our Redeemer? No treatise of
his on Mariology is known in the Greek church. However,
scholars working in the field of Caucasian studies have been
aware for most of this century of the existence of a number of
incomplete manuscripts, eleven in all, in the Georgian language,
which manuscripts, where 'cephalic' (headed by a title), declare
themselves in some version of this form:

> A canticle and glorification, eulogy and act of praise of
> our all-holy Queen, the immaculate and ever-blessed
> *Theotokos,* Mary, the ever-virgin, and a notice about her
> stainless and blessed life from her birth to her passing-
> over, written by our blessed Father Maximus the
> philosopher and confessor.[3]

---

[2]PG 91, 221B; cf. P. Piret, *Le Christ et la Trinité selon Maxime le Confesseur* (Paris
1983), pp. 203-240.

[3]Maxime le Confesseur, *Vie de la Vierge*, traduite par M.-J. van Esbroeck (Louvain
1986, = *Corpus Scriptorum Christianorum Orientalium* 479, *Scriptores Iberici* 22), p. 1.
Cited below as CSCO 479.

In 1986 the noted Belgian Orientalist Michel-Jean van Esbroeck, of the Society of Jesus, professor of the non-Greek Eastern Christian languages at the University of Vienna, collated these neglected fragments from the middle and late Byzantine periods, corresponding to the Western middle ages. Five were found in the capital of Soviet Georgia, Tbilisi, three in the library of the Jerusalem patriarchate; one is in the Museum of the Book at Odessa, one at the monastery of St Catherine's on Mount Sinai, and one, apparently the oldest, from the tenth century, was used to bind a sixteenth century Armenian prayer-book, now in private hands.[4] Van Esbroeck produced from these manuscripts, three of which are substantial, a single complete text, and declared it to be what it claims to be: namely, a mariological treatise of St Maximus, translated from the Greek on Mount Athos towards the end of the tenth century by the Georgian monastic writer Euthymius the Hagiorite. It is, he believes, a direct response to the charge of *disprezzo* towards the Virgin Mary brought against Maximus by his captors. Those circumstances, when combined with Maximus' own intellectual personality, philosophically gifted as that was, and even, to a degree, critical in the use of sources, give this *Vita Mariae* qualities which make it outstanding among its rivals in this genre of literature.

As the long title prefixed to the *Life* rightly suggests, its form is what may be called 'doxological biography', at once the praise of God and religious history. It is both devotional and doctrinal: simultaneously a testimony to warm personal feeling for, and identification with, the Mother of God, and an exposition of the significance of the principal events in the lives not only of Mary but also, and more fundamentally, of Jesus himself, since, as the author insists, it is from Christ and by him that 'the beatitude and glory of his immaculate Mother consist'.[5]

---

[4]Maxime le Confesseur, *Vie de la Vierge*, éditée par M.-J. van Esbroeck (Louvain 1986, = *Corpus Scriptorum Christianorum Orientalium* 478, *Scriptores Iberici* 21), pp. vi-xi.

[5]CSCO 479, p. 2.

Some comment on the early Church background to Marian doctrine and devotion may be in order here. The references of the Gospels to Mary's rôle in the Lord's infancy, his ministry (especially at the marriage-feast at Cana, for St John the first 'sign' whereby he revealed his glory); his Passion and Death and (in Acts) the descent of his Spirit were set within their wider biblical context by a variety of early ecclesiastical writers. For Justin Martyr, Mary is the New Eve, who reverses the fate of the first 'mother of all the living': the one brought death by disobedience, the other by obedience life.[6] Irenaeus of Lyons accordingly, makes Mary the cause of salvation for herself and for humankind at large, hinting moreover at her universal motherhood and co-operation in Christ's saving work.[7] Though these contributions by individual doctors were important, the chief stimulus to the high and later patristic efflorescence of Mariology was the conciliar debate over the person of Christ in the mid-fifth century Church — we have already traced its outlines in connexion with Piret's presentation of Maximus' Christology. As the Oxford patristic scholar J. N. D. Kelly remarked in his magisterial *Early Christian Doctrines*:

> The Christological debates of the mid-fifth century, with the councils of Ephesus and Chalcedon in which they culminated, marked the climax of Mariological development in the classic patristic period. It was not their concern, of course, to do honour to the Blessed Virgin, but rather to clarify and define the union of divine and human in the incarnate Lord. But the generally agreed conclusion that this could only be achieved by recognising that Mary was in a real sense *Theotokos*, mother of God, finally brought out the full significance of her role, and in doing so inevitably enhanced her status, integrating Mariology firmly with Christology.[8]

---

[6]*Dialogue with Trypho*, 100.
[7]*Against the Heresies* III. 22, 4; IV. 33, 1.
[8]J. N. D. Kelly, *Early Christian Doctrines* (London 1977⁵), p. 498.

At the same time, however, we should recognise the rôle of a more popular movement of piety not only in the great Hellenistic cities but also, and more particularly, in circles where remembrance of the traditions of the Jewish-Christian communities of early times was still lively. A series of 'apocrypha', some of which may contain genuine memories passed down in the 'Church from the Circumcision', came to exert a powerful influence on mariological feeling and belief. Here the most potent text was undoubtedly the *Protoevangelium* of James — and not least, as we shall see, for Maximus.

The work re-assigned to him by van Esbroeck opens with a poetic acclamation, calling on peoples and nations to honour the Virgin Mother, whom the writer describes as 'our hope and our intercession'.[9] It states its source: Scripture; the Fathers, notably Gregory of Neo-Caesarea (the 'Thaumaturge'), Athanasius of Alexandria, Gregory of Nyssa, and Denys the Areopagite — though actually the Marian homilies ascribed to the first two of these are fifth century works; and lastly, the apocrypha from which the writer proposes to draw certain elements, as he says, where these are accepted by the approved Fathers.

The substance of the narrative begins with an account of the marriage of Mary's parents, Joachim and Anna, which falls under this last rubric, since it echoes (with variations) the *Protoevangelium* of James. The same is true of the material on Mary's girlhood, though the author lays his emphasis resolutely on the development in Mary of the virtues, her inner glory, here interpreted in terms of the messianic wedding-psalm, psalm 44. One thinks in this connexion of Maximus' theology of the virtues as themselves a kind of incarnation of the Word of God. The author's biblical learning is equally apparent when he gathers up pieces of Zion theology from different parts of the Old Testament to bring out the significance of Mary's upbringing in Jerusalem, the Lord's chosen dwelling-place. Mary's betrothal to Joseph, and the episode of the Annunciation gives the writer the opportunity to expound his Christology which is to say the least compatible with Maximus'

[9]CSCO 479, p. 2.

own. To this he adds some reflections on Mary's blessedness, as attested by the Magnificat, and the inversion of power and dignity prophesied in that canticle, which the author understands as fulfilled in the apostolic preaching when the mysteries of God are made known to the poor, and also to pagans.

Then comes the Nativity where the writer stresses at one and the same time a number of points, all handled with considerable theological sensitivity. Notable among them are: the providential succession of the universalist Roman empire to the princes of Judah, though Christ's own kingdom is not only over the Romans but over all creatures; the marvellous abasement whereby the inaccessible and uncontainable Word of God was circumscribed by the cave of Bethlehem; the painlessness and joy of Mary's giving birth, interpreted in terms of the Deuteronomic canticle of Moses, 'May my speech distil as the dew' (Deut. 32, 2); the witness of the star followed by the magi, understood not as a natural occurrence, for the magi were to be, precisely, delivered from astrology, but as a phenomenon ordered rationally, for a specific divine end, by the Creator; the reversal of values represented by their adoration of the Christ-child who, rich king though he was as the Father's Word, on entering this world chose poverty and gave the poor dignity by that choice. Finally, the massacre of the Innocents is presented as a witness to the Word as the Light intelligible by those who had scarcely come to visible light, the light ephemeral.

On the presentation of Christ in the Temple, the author comments on Symeon's prophecy that the Child will be for the fall and the raising up of many: the divine will is for the life and divinisation of all, yet falling and being raised up again depend on the many — who either believe or do not. This Symeon told to Mary knowing that what touches the Son the Mother reckons as her own, but also because, as the Gospel of Luke records, a sword will pass through her soul, a prophecy of Mary's part in the Passion to which this *Vita* will devote considerable attention. The author reverts to the *Protoevangelium* of James for his account of the descent into Egypt, while using the Jewish historian Josephus to give an explanation of the political situation of the time in Judaea. Back at Nazareth, in the house of the holy family, the Incarnate Word, as man by human nature and hypostasis (here to be understood as 'subsistence' rather than as 'person') grows in the virtues thanks to his submission to the Mosaic Law, while his mother is gradually transformed from teacher, the mother of Wisdom, to disciple, Wisdom's daughter.

The account of the public ministry has three pillars: the Baptism, which in Maximus regains its earlier importance in ante-Nicene Christology; the miracles and teaching of the Lord; and the discipleship of women whom the author treats genially as especially accredited to Mary who acted as their guide and mediatrix with her Son. This involved no second class citizenship, but the contrary: if the evangelists are at times confused about the names and identities of various women mentioned in the Gospels, especially at the Crucifixion, this is because the men were not always at par with the women, as the flight of the male disciples, John alone excepted, from Calvary demonstrates.

As to the Passion itself, the author is careful to situate Mary's rôle within a re-creation of the Passion narratives as a whole. In his own name, the author begins a threnody on the Passion, which, in its rhetorical use of clashing contrast is reminiscent of the early Greek paschal homilies, such as that of Melito of Sardis. By incorporating into this a reference to Mary at the foot of the Cross, 'lamenting bitterly the sufferings and wounds of her sweet King and Son and glorifying the patience and freedom of him who suffered and was crucified for us',[10] the text moves naturally into a re-creation of Mary's own attitude, comparable to the best of the Western *planctus Mariae* for its combination of emotional power with restraint, and its theological deployment of sensibility. The consignment of Mary to John is carefully handled: it is not that the dying Redeemer foreswore future care for his Mother, far from it, but that he consoled her with a visible consolation, while repaying John for his love and sincerity.

The author believes that Mary never left the tomb of the dead Christ and thus became, despite the silence of the

[10]Ibid., p. 69.

Gospels, the first witness of the Resurrection: not mentioned by the evangelists both because it was so certain as to make mention superfluous and because to appeal to a mother's witness might endanger credibility. Extending the reference in Acts (1, 4) to the apostles' assembling in prayer with Mary the Mother of Jesus, he speaks of her, in the post-Ascension period, as not only inspiring, as model, the religious life of the apostolic group but also as sending out disciples, over and above the apostles proper, from the house of John in Jerusalem and co-suffering with these missionaries in their privations just as she had with her Son at the Passion. She both leaves Jerusalem with John to show that she is not the apostles' inferior, and returns without him to show that she is in fact their superior, and point of reference.

The rest of the *Life* is occupied with Mary's Dormition, and depends here, for its account of the gathering of apostles and disciples at her falling-asleep, on Denys,[11] and for the christophany at that moment on the abundant *Transitus* literature of the Christian Orient, probably in a relatively primitive stage of that literature's development. For the writer, just as Mary

> eluded the pains of the Nativity by an inexpressible birth, so the pains of death did not touch her at the last, for the sovereign and Lord of natures was then as now the changer of natures.[12]

The laying to rest did not go off, however, without incident, thanks to an impious Jew manhandling her bier, only to be struck down but then cured at Peter's prayer to Mary. Though she was laid in a tomb, three days later, on the arrival of a belated apostle, the tomb was found empty. The body gone, her tunic and belt survived, re-discovered in a Jewish household by two princes converted from Arianism at the time of the emperor Leo I in the mid fifth century: these were the relics

---

[11]*De divinis nominibus* III. 2.
[12]CSCO 479, p. 96.

venerated in Maximus' time at the Constantinopolitan churches of the Blachernae, the imperial palace, and Chalkoprateia, near Hagia Sophia.

The *Life* concludes with a hymn of considerable lyrical versatility; a concise theology of the Assumption, presented as the confirmation of our ascension with Christ and our final incorruptibility; and an acclamation of Mary as mediatrix of graces 'more innumerable than the sands of the sea'.[13]

This *Vita Mariae* is the work of a scholar who knew his Josephus and the learned etymologies of Eusebius' *Onomasticon*. He had sifted the New Testament apocrypha, finding the Gospel of Thomas wanting but accepting at least in part the *Protoevangelium* of James. He credited the main lines of the *Transitus Mariae* story, and accepted the common aetiologies of relics connected with her, treating both these facets of inherited tradition, no doubt, as validated by the corporate memory of the Church. His exegetical sureness of touch and the coherence of his theology at large encourage us to accept van Esbroeck's identification of him with Maximus and to look with greater confidence at the Assumption mystery which is his climax, bearing in mind the words of the apostle to the Corinthian community:

We shall not all die, but we shall all be changed.[14]

That 'change' is, for Maximus both christological and pneumatological, the work of Christ and the Spirit of Christ. Yet as our investigation, with Piret, of Maximus' Christology suggests, Maximus' account of these realities, while governed by a reading of the economy of salvation where what has not been assumed remains unredeemed, also owes something to a fundamental metaphysics. It is to Maximus' cosmology and the difference which salvation makes to the world that we must now turn.

---

[13]Ibid., p. 117.
[14]I Corinthians 15, 51-52; cf. M. Jugie, A. A., *La Mort et l'Assomption de la sainte Vierge. Etude historico-doctrinale* (Vatican City 1944), p. 47.

5

Lars Thunberg and Alain Riou on World and Church in Maximus

In this section our task is to provide an overview of Maximus' cosmology, his account of the world, and to show how, through Christ, the world is renewed as the Church, by participation in the energies of the Atonement, the victorious inauguration of the Kingdom.

Cosmology

The Swedish Maximian scholar Lars Thunberg, in his study *Microcosm and Mediator*, devoted principally to Maximus' theological anthropology as this is, introduces the topic of cosmology, as we have done here, in the immediate aftermath of a treatment of Christology. He gives as reason for this arrangement that:

> the Christological combination of inseparable unity and preserved identity is, in Maximus' view, equally characteristic both of the relationship of God to creation and of the different entities of creation in relation to one another ...[1]

As these words may already indicate, we are dealing, in Maximus, with an austerely conceptual cosmologist, one who attempts to identify the fundamental structures and inner relationships of

---

[1] L. Thunberg, *Microcosm and Mediator. The Theological Anthropology of Maximus the Confessor* (Lund 1964), p. 51.

the things that constitute the world — rather than, for instance, a close observer of the world about us — which is how others of the Greek Fathers, in their *physikê thêôria*, or contemplation of nature, have struck modern scholars.[2]

Maximus would have been, in one sense, more at home with twentieth century scientific cosmologists, with the mathematically expressed conceptual speculations of physics, both astro- and sub-atomic, than with the natural historians, the observers and recorders, of the eighteenth century. And yet in another sense, his spiritual affinities *are* with that second group. For his metaphysical theology, born, as we have seen, of the marriage between Hellenism and the Gospel, gave him a confidence in the purposiveness of things, and the ultimate beneficence of their design, which is closer to Gilbert White of Selborne, further removed from Stephen Hawking of Cambridge. This adjudication depends crucially on Maximus' acceptance of the doctrine of *creation*.

Thunberg presents Maximus' account of creation under eight heads.

First, the creation takes place, as patristic tradition universally confesses, 'out of nothing', in which context Maximus stresses the aspects of distance and difference that distinguish Creator and creature. In the *Ambigua*, Maximus states firmly that God has established the visible and invisible creation out of non-being.[3] Thunberg also draws his readers' attention to Maximus' definition of *telos* (goal) as 'that for whose sake all things are, though itself for the sake of nothing', taken together with the simultaneous affirmation that this end is in God alone.

These statements show that for Maximus arguments of causality and teleology may serve together to underline the absolute superiority of God in relation to all else.[4]

---

[2]D. S. Wallace-Hadrill, *The Greek Patristic View of Nature* (Manchester 1968); but cf. pp. 66-79.

[3]*Ambigua* 7 (PG 91, 1080A).

[4]L. Thunberg, *Microcosm and Mediator*, op. cit., p. 53, in connexion with *Ambigua* 7 at PG 91, 1072C-1073B.

But of more immediate relevance to the theme of *creatio ex nihilo* is Maximus' insistence on the primordial abyss, *chasma*, which separates created from uncreated nature and which only God's creative will can overcome. In the effort to translate the witness of Scripture into theology, Maximus stresses at once that God is the *sovereign* God, yet the one Lord of a creation which, even in its multiplicity, is essentially *good*. More specifically, in the creative act God places over against himself a world altogether distinct from him, but a world, all the same, that he intends to bring into a union-without-confusion with himself. Such a cosmological postulate is, evidently, reminiscent of the conciliar Christology, and notably of the Chalcedonian Definition. Though there is at work here a more specifically *theo*logical postulate — for God is such that he can overcome distance without letting it disappear, and only he is so, nonetheless Maximus typically expresses these foundational convictions about the God-world relationship in terms that are at least allusively christological.

The first of these which Thunberg highlights is *diaphora*, 'difference'. The word enjoyed favour both in the Christology of Cyril of Alexandria and in the general ontology of Denys. Like Cyril, Maximus affirms that in the Word Incarnate, the *diaphora* between the two natures is 'saved' (*sôzesthai*) after the union, even though, thanks to the living relationship between human nature and divine in Christ it is then only a 'naked difference', *psilê diaphora*.[5] Like Denys, he also finds in the created world at large a principle whereby diversity in relation to others (*heterotês*) is preserved.[6] This *diaphora* Maximus describes as 'constitutive', *sustatikê*, and 'distinctive', *aphoristikê*—hence marking it out not only as ineradicable but also as expressive of God's purpose. And this Maximus contrasts with the individualising factor in created beings, *idiotês*, which is more partial, *merikê*, yet not without a positive value of its own.[7] How does all this relate to the creative Word of God himself, the divine Logos? Thunberg tells us in a masterly exposition of *Ambigua* 7:

---

[5] *Epistle* 12 (PG 91, 472D-473A).
[6] *Opuscula theologica et polemica* 14 (PG 91, 149D).
[7] Ibid., 21 (PG 91, 249C).

Difference (*diaphora*) and diversity (*poikilia*) are characteristic of the world of created beings, but manifest themselves in such a way that the one Logos is recognised as many *logoi* in the indivisible difference (*adiairetos diaphora*) of creation, because of the unconfused individuality (*asunchutos idiotês*) of all beings — though, on the other hand, the different *logoi* may be seen as the one Logos thanks to the relationship (*anaphora*) which exists between him and all that is unconfused (*asunchuton*).[8]

Less prominent in Maximus' work is the difference of mind and will, *diaphora gnômikê*, largely indicative, it would seem, of a breakdown of harmony. Yet insofar as Providence wisely allows a difference between individuals in terms of their 'lives and behaviour, minds and decisions, desires, understanding, needs, habits and ideas', here too there is a positive aspect: unity in diversity.[9]

A second crucial term is *diairesis*, 'division', with this time a distinctly negative charge to it. Just as in Christology the second Council of Constantinople (553) rejected *diairesis* in the person of the Redeemer, so in Maximus' cosmological use division is something to be abolished through man's restoration and deification in Christ. In his own Christology, Maximus follows the anti-Arian tradition of Gregory Nazianzen, for whom *diairesis* in Christ does not imply estrangement, *allotriôsis*, and the anti-Nestorian tradition of Cyril, who rejected a 'division of nature', *phusikê diairesis*, in the Incarnate Word. Nevertheless, Maximus can also speak of divisions in the creation which include what he would normally regard as simple differentiations: the solution seems to be that, to his way of thinking, man is called to annul divisions in the world morally not ontologically.[10]

(Even) more ambiguous in this same context are the concepts of *diastasis*, 'distance' and *diastêma*, 'separation'. Very likely in

[8]L. Thunberg, *Microcosm and Mediator*, op. cit., pp. 56-57, with reference to *Ambigua* 7 at PG 91, 1077C.
[9]Ibid., p. 57, with an internal citation of *Ambigua* 10 (PG 91, 1192D 1193A).
[10]Ibid., pp. 59-60.

conscious opposition to Origen, Maximus speaks of distance and separation, understood as characteristics of creation, by contrast with its Creator, as the positive starting-point for the natural movements of creatures. (Origen, contrariwise, had seen movement as a consequence of the Fall.) In releasing the flow of historical time, God has marked out a distance from himself — yet this distance is full of promise, for it is the presupposition of all Godward movement. Through the Incarnation, so Maximus declares in the *Capita 200 theologica et economica,* no *diastasis* will finally separate God from those who are worthy of him.[11] Since movement is goal-directed, *diastasis,* which is movement's point of departure, necessarily includes a reference to *stasis,* movement's quieting. In the eschatological repose, man shares with Christ the 'non-distanced character of his hypostatic union of distinguished but not separated natures, energies and wills'.[12]

A contrasted pair moving in the same conceptual space are *diastolê,* 'expansion', and *sustolê,* 'contraction'. All that partakes of created being moves in both these directions, though not indefinitely, since nothing is more particular, more differentiated, and in this sense more *expanded* than that which is made particular by the Creator; similarly, nothing is more universal, more general, and in this sense more *contracted,* than the fact that all is created.[13] And here too a christological motive is at work. The movement of *diastolê,* of God's condescension in creating, is not unrelated to that of the Incarnation, while the movement of *sustolê,* of expansion, can be linked to his gracious work of deifying rational creatures.[14]

It is time to move on to a second aspect of Maximus' overall cosmology: the notion that it is God's sovereign *will* (and nothing else) which caused him to create the world. The *logoi* or principles of differentiated creation Maximus regards as none other than God's 'intentions', *thelêmeta,* his 'willings'. They represent, in Thunberg's words, not only a 'defining and

[11] *Capitula 200 theologica et economica* II. 25 (PG 90, 1136BC).
[12] L. Thunberg, *Microcosm and Mediator,* op. cit., p. 62.
[13] Ibid., p. 63, with reference to *Ambigua* 10 (PG 91, 1177BC).
[14] Ibid., p. 63, in connexion with *Ambigua* 33 (PG 91, 1288A).

unifying factor', but also a 'divine purpose'.[15] The Pseudo-Denys had already spoken of the 'intentional' character of the *logoi* of creation,[16] but Maximus goes further in asserting that these reveal a divine *skopos*, 'purpose', pertaining chiefly to human beings: in all things God wills to effect the mystery of his Incarnation.[17]

A third dimension to Maximus' cosmology to which Thunberg draws attention is the notion of creation by divine benevolence. In effect, this phrase acts in Thunberg's study as a peg on which to hang the ideas of *pronoia*, providence, and *krisis*, judgment. Apart from the general currency attained by these terms through exegetical and (at any rate for the first of them) philosophical debate, they were peculiarly prominent in Evagrius' Origenising scheme, where *krisis* denoted the judgment of fallen minds entailed in the second, material creation, and *pronoia* the divine restoration of a primordial spiritual unity. Terminologically, Maximus' remarks are reminiscent of Origenism, for instance in the trio *monas, pronoia, krisis*.[18] But, as Dom Polycarp Sherwood showed, in Maximus' view Origen and Evagrius had confused moral considerations, in matters of providence and judgment, with strictly ontological ones. 'Preserving' (*suntêrêtikê*) providence concerns being itself, while 'convertive' (*epistreptikê*) and 'educative' or 'punitive' (*paideutikê*) providence are concerned rather with the moral order.[19] Moreover, Maximus places the *monas, pronoia, krisis* triad within an imaginative christological context all his own. On the Mount of the Transfiguration, the divine simplicity (*monas*) is disclosed for human understanding (*theologia*) by Christ as God's Word. Its witnesses are Moses, whom Maximus links to providence and contemplative insight (*gnôsis*), and Elijah, whom he connects with judgment and the

---

[15]Ibid., p. 68.

[16]I.-H. Dalmais, O.P., 'La théorie des *logoi* des créatures chez s. Maxime le Confesseur', *Revue des Sciences Philosophiques et Théologiques* 36 (1952), pp. 244-249.

[17]*Ambigua* 7 (PG 91, 1084CD).

[18]*Capita 200 theologica et oecumenica* II. 16 (PG 90, 1132B).

[19]P. Sherwood, *The Earlier 'Ambigua' of St Maximus the Confessor* (Rome 1955), pp. 36ff.

life of the virtues.[20] Again, in the *Quaestiones ad Thalassium* judgment and providence are called the eyes of the Word, whereby, even in his Passion, he keeps oversight over the world, and the wings on which, silently, he comes flying.[21]

And indeed, fourthly, for the Byzantine doctor creation is by means of the Word of God, as well as (though this is less emphasised) by the Holy Spirit.[22] Maximus took up, and took further, the notion of the divine Word as crucially related to the 'words', *logoi*, of creation familiar from Origen and to a lesser extent Athanasius. Combining the Stoic cosmological theme of the *logoi spermatikoi* with the Christian belief, first articulated by the Johannine prologue, in Christ as the consubstantial divine Word 'without whom was nothing made that was made', Origen regarded the creative archetypes as present in Christ, the Wisdom of God. In their sum they constitute the intelligible world, on which the sensuous realm is patterned, and define its aboriginal goodness — as affirmed in the Genesis creation account. For Athanasius, to avoid the dividedness of a world differentiated by individual *logoi*, God created the world in accordance with his own (single) Logos.[23] From Denys Maximus borrowed, as already mentioned in connexion with creation through the divine will, the more dynamic notion of the *logoi* as divine intentions: for him the most basic kind of creative-and-created word is *logos tou einai*: the 'word of being', the created existence of a thing as founded on God's will that it should be. Thunberg states that, for Maximus, the *logoi*, indeed, define 'not only the essence (*ousia*) but also the coming into existence (*genesis*) of things'.[24]

Nevertheless, the pre-existence and unity of the *logoi* in God does not rule out a genuine independence and individuality of existence for the created world whose constitutive beings are not only differentiated but also mobile. Beings are summoned, in their free mobile condition, to approximate more closely to

---

[20]See note 18 above.

[21]*Quaestiones ad Thalassium* 53 (PG 90, 501C); ibid. 54 (PG 90, 517D).

[22]Ibid., 28 (PG 90, 364A).

[23]L. Thunberg, *Microcosm and Mediator*, op. cit., p. 77.

[24]Ibid., p. 78; cf. *Ambigua* 7 (PG 91, 1081B).

their own *logos*, which represents God's will not only for some particular being but for the entire created order to which it makes a contribution.

> Thus beings may be in or out of harmony with their *logos*, but at least if they are in harmony with it, they will also move according to a fixed purpose of God (*prothesis*).[25]

Maximus' approach rules out a naturalistic mysticism of the kind offered (in part) by Evagrius. In this world, the everlasting being of the Logos is to be perceived in the *logoi* only by faith, and in the light of Christology; it will not, in any case, be fully realised until the end of time. The *logoi* of creation are, as Thunberg puts it, 'intimately connected with' the *logoi* of the saving Economy, ordered as that is to the Incarnation of the Word and its consequences for the world.[26] With Croce's help, we have already seen how, in Maximus' fundamental theology, the Word holds together creation, revelation (or illumination) and salvation. Through the *logoi*, those whom the Spirit hallows gain spiritual contemplation of the divine Logos in his world. The same living Lord is also found in the *logoi* of Scripture, where he must illuminate the deepest sense of the biblical word, as once he did the words of the Hebrew Bible for the disciples on the road to Emmaus. And this Lord Christ is, finally, the substance of all the virtues; for those who partake of the virtues, on the way to salvation, share in the life of God himself.[27] As Thunberg concludes:

> Creation by the Word thus implies to Maximus not only a positive evaluation of creation but the inclusion of the latter in a purpose of universal unification, on the basis of

---

[25]Ibid., p. 79.

[26]Ibid., p. 81.

[27]*Ambigua* 33 (PG 91, 1285C-1288A); cf. H. U. von Balthasar, *Kosmische Liturgie*, op. cit., pp. 289ff. For the close inter-connexion of the *logoi* and conduct according to the virtues, see *Quaestiones ad Thalassium* 22 (PG 90, 321B); H. U. von Balthasar, *Kosmische Liturgie*, op. cit., p. 638.

the Incarnation by grace of the Logos, in which all the *logoi* of things abide.[28]

The Swedish patrologist touches more briefly on a fifth and sixth aspect of Maximus' cosmology: creation by God's prudence, *phronêsis*, and creation as an act of divine condescension. According to Thunberg, by his affirmation that it is God's prudence which has brought the world so wonderfully to be in its complex ordering Maximus is underlining the inscrutable character of the creative act. As an expression of God's 'practical reason' (a concept drawn from Aristotle), the source of that act is, quite properly, unsearchable.[29] Creation as an act of condescension turns on the fact that, in creating, the immovable God deigned to express his creative power in movement: for his world is to develop towards a unifying end, established by him in creating it. Replacing the Origenistic triad of *monê, kinêsis, genesis* (monad, movement, becoming) by his own trio *genesis, kinêsis, stasis*, with the latter the final end of all motion and desire, Maximus 'breaks the spell of the Hellenic circle': it is *love* which brings man to the authentic *stasis* (coming to be, movement, rest), and that because its power is divine, not because it re-assembles beings which have had their *stasis* in God already, in their first beginning.[30]

The last but one facet of Maximian cosmology to be dealt with here is creation as a composite of substances with their accidents. For Maximus the term 'being', *ousia*, applies in the cosmological context to the creation: God is *huperousios*, 'above being'.[31] As creaturely, the reality of being or substance is limited, for example by the duality which counterposes it to accidents, and again by its presence in things which are themselves typified by *diaphora*, 'difference'. In *Ambigua* 65

---

[28]L. Thunberg, *Microcosm and Mediator*, op. cit., p. 84.

[29]Ibid., pp. 84-85; cf. *Centuriae de caritate* IV. 1.

[30]*Ambigua* 15 (PG 91, 1217D); P. Sherwood, *The Earlier Ambigua of St Maximus the Confessor*, op. cit., pp. 92-102; L. Thunberg, *Microcosm and Mediator*, op. cit., pp. 85-88.

[31]*Ambigua* 1 (PG 90, 1084A): with debts to both Denys and Gregory of Nyssa.

Maximus insists, moreover, that *ousia* needs to be realised in a passage from *dunamis*, potentiality, to *energeia*, full activity.[32] In rational creatures this happens through the working of mind and heart, whereby being becomes 'well-being' and, through the grace of God, 'ever-being': though at each of these stages *ousia* is always a sharing in what God gives the world from out of his own super-substantial 'being', wisdom and life. Maximus can and does also speak of 'natures', *phuseis*: being as common to many who share the same *eidos*, 'form' or 'species'. As Piret showed in the context of Maximus' Christology, Maximus regards a nature as manifested through its characteristic activity or energy.[33] By contrast, another ontological term which came to him from the christological tradition — *hypostasis* — denotes the principle of *personal* being, transcending the strict limits of nature though not in any way contrary to it. Indeed, this transcendence of personal (hypostatic) being over natural appears already indicated by nature itself. As Thunberg splendidly sums up, in full agreement on this vital point with the earlier investigations of von Balthasar:

> According to Maximus' Aristotelian principles, all movement moves towards an end (*telos*), but created things cannot be an end in themselves (only God is *autotelos*), and thus the end of the natural movement of creation must be outside nature itself. And the ultimate end of the whole of creation must be that for which all things are, and which itself is caused by nothing, that which is its own end, namely God. Now this aspect of transcendence cannot be grasped by any automatism of nature as such; rather it is an expression of personal existence, of decisive freedom.... The realisation of these powers remains entirely natural — the limitations of natural existence are preserved — but in relationship to the end man may experience the aspect of transcendence, a transcendence, in preservation of nature, effected for man in Christ as hypostasis of two natures, each with its

---

[32] *Ambigua* 65 (PG 91, 1392AB).
[33] Ibid., 5 (PG 91, 1057B). See above, p. 107.

130 *Byzantine Gospel*

own will and energy. We must conclude with von Balthasar, that a new perspective is opened up, where personal existence and the mystery of union in infinity are brought together on the basis of Christological insights into what was felt as the deepest secret of created life.[34]

And this brings us to the final aspect of Maximus' cosmology and that is what may be termed its qualitative or *modal* aspect. If the 'qualifying' element in nature is that which belongs to it as being moved and moving, then it is by this modality (*tropos*) of existence in the concrete that natural powers are actually realised. Following the Cappadocians, Amphilochius of Iconium and, perhaps, Leontius of Byzantium, Maximus contrasts the principle of nature, *logos physeôs*, with the modality of existence, *tropos hyparxeôs*: the abiding divine intention for a particular nature with its variable manners of realisation. The novelty which Christ introduces into the world concerns the mode in which the powers of nature are called forth, a new quality, *poiotês*, of existence produced in the fruits of the coming together of the Incarnate Word's two energies and wills. Sanctification and deification take place through the gift of a new modality to the powers of human nature. God becomes 'incarnate' in the virtues of believers, thanks ultimately to the *communicatio idiomatum* and the *perichôrêsis* which has taken place in Jesus Christ.[36]

Cosmos and Christ: the Economy as 'Event of the Theandric Mystery'

Owing to his acceptance of the doctrine of creation, Maximus is able to present the cosmos and its structures as linked to God by its very contingency and dependence, and so open to fresh influxes of the divine action. The world may become, by God's grace, a transfigured world — and as such its name is the *Church*. Père Alain Riou, in his study *Le monde et l'Eglise selon Maxime le Confesseur*, begins his account of the difference that

[34]L. Thunberg, *Microcosm and Mediator*, op. cit., p. 95.
[35]Ibid., pp. 96-99.

Christ makes to Maximian cosmology by drawing his readers' attention to the challenge posed to Maximus by one of his sources.[36] In *Ambigua* 31, Maximus essays a commentary on Gregory Nazianzen's sermon on the Nativity, the Cappadocian doctor's 38th *Oration*. There Nazianzen had pronounced the Incarnation the very dissolution of the natural order: 'The laws of nature are dissolved; the world on high must find its consummation'.[37] Here Maximus' confidence in nature and her laws is challenged head-on. He responds by distinguishing various senses of the term 'natural laws'. In the first place, the 'laws of nature' may signify man's present unhappy condition, pock-marked by sin, and symbolised by sexual generation. In this sense, the Virginal Conception of the Messiah in the womb of Mary is the restoration of a previous order of things: a renewal, repair, restitution of the earlier *régime* of nature. But in the second place, the 'laws of nature' can denote the *logoi*, the natures of things, which reasonable persons will recognise as both permanent and good. And here the 'dissolution' of those laws mentioned by Gregory can only mean the condescension of the Word of God who, without in any way changing his divine nature into our human one, united himself to human nature in his hypostasis. In this marvel of the Incarnation the laws of creation are indeed surpassed.[38]

In *Ambigua* 36, Maximus returns to the task. In creating man in the image of the divine splendour and breathing into him his Spirit, God already entered into communion with human nature. But as a result of the Incarnation, human nature is transformed in its mode. Though remaining in the *logos* of its created existence, *to einai*, it begins to subsist divinely in terms of the *logos* of its *pôs einai*, the 'how' of that existence.[39] Finally, in *Ambigua* 41, the charmed term of *tropos* at last appears,[40] being, so Riou insists, something that

[36] A. Riou, *Le monde et l'Eglise selon Maxime le Confesseur* (Paris 1973), pp. 75-77.
[37] *Oration* 38, 2 (PG 36, 313B).
[38] *Ambigua* 31 (PG 9 1276B, 1280C).
[39] *Ambigua* 36 (PG 90 1289BD).
[40] Ibid., 41 (PG 90, 1313C).

emerges gradually in the course of his [Maximus'] spiritual journey, in the midst of his ruminations on the theandric mystery of the Living One.[41]

Though an exhaustive lexical account of the patristic use of the word is lacking, Riou believes that it is only with Maximus that it attains both precision of sense and centrality of position, as a way of speaking of the Incarnation and its consequence for the world. For Riou, Maximus discovered by his own spiritual struggle and hard-pressed confession the irreducibility of the hypostatic order, the order of personhood, to that of nature. At the same time, the christological heresies of his day, Monoenergism and Monothelitism, encouraged him to deepen his expression of these two inseparable principles in the being of the Word Incarnate. In Riou's version, the simultaneously foundational status ('la co-originalité') of the principles of nature and hypostasis had been recognised ever since the Cappadocians, by way of the 'apophatic tension' between, on the one hand, the absolute difference of the trinitarian hypostases in their *tropos* of existing, and, on the other, their communion in the divine essence according to the *logos* of their nature. In the face of the Origenist threat, Maximus took up this distinction so as to salvage personal freedom from outright submission to the teleological dynamism of the order of nature — whether by a simple acquiescence in that dynamism or a straightforward rejection of it. No longer now would Christ's hypostasis risk being reduced to one of his natures. His personal action cannot be absorbed by a single 'energy', since this would compromise the reality of the union, of the *kenôsis* of the Word, and so of salvation itself.[42] In the order of *genesis,* 'coming to be', the Lord stooped to take on himself created human nature and its *logos*; in that of *gennesis,* 'birth', he took upon his hypostasis what the hymn in Paul's Letter to the Philippians had called the 'condition of a slave'.

---

[41]A. Riou, *Le monde et l'Eglise selon Maxime le Confesseur,* op. cit., p. 79.
[42]Ibid., pp. 82-83.

On the one hand, by his Coming to be, *genesis*, he was naturally led to identity with man according to the life-giving Breath whereby as man he received the image and preserved it without losing its freedom or staining its innocence. On the other hand, by his incarnate Birth, *gennesis*, he took on willingly, via the form of a slave, likeness to the man of corruption, and by his own will accepted subjection, almost as our own, to the same natural passions as we have, sin excepted, just as if he depended on them, he the Sinless One.[43]

Genesis, with a single *nu*, is linked, then, to *logos*, the principle of nature; *gennesis*, with a double *nu*, to *tropos*, the mode of hypostatic existence.

Having for our sake assumed the *logos* of Coming to be and the *tropos* of Birth, God has renewed nature, or, to speak more truly, has innovated upon it, and led it back to the ancient beauty of incorruptibility by that holy flesh endowed with rational soul which he took from us, and he has munificently granted it divinisation.[44]

By condescension and *kenôsis*, not of divine *nature* but of the Word's divine *Person*, God has brought about the renewal or innovation of his image in man. And so, as Riou puts it, the hypostatic order acquires a certain priority, to Maximus' eyes, in the initiative of salvation. Yet at the same time, this very salvation is the liberation of nature for the dynamism inscribed in the being of the image.[45] The Saviour made birth the salvation of *genesis* by renewing the incorruptibility of *genesis* by what was possible in birth. And Riou conjoins thus to *Ambigua* 42 Maximus' affirmation to the Monothelite deacon Theodore that Christ appropriated our passible, 'affectable', characteristics in two ways. According to essence, he took on

---

[43]*Ambigua* 42 (PG 90, 1316CD).

[44]Ibid., at 1320A.

[45]A. Riou, *Le monde et l'Eglise selon Maxime le Confesseur*, op. cit., p. 87.

those natural passions bound up with our nature — like sleep, hunger, thirst. By attachment, or 'economically', he also voluntarily assumed the passions that issue from sin, like ignorance or the sense of abandonment that he felt on the Cross.[46] This is the distinction between the *proslêpsis*, assumption, of worthy passions, and the *oikeiôsis*, appropriation, of unworthy ones, which we have already met, in Piret's company, two chapters ago.

So far this is mostly Christology. How does it relate to cosmology, the subject of this chapter? In Alain Riou's words:

> The discovery of the hypostatic principle does not allow only the innovation of natures in Christ and the deepening of Christology; in the New Adam, Christ, there opens up a new vision of the Economy, no longer as a natural teleology but as an eschatology for the world in the coming of the Last Adam... ., and in the revelation of his body, the Church, the world's eschatological matrix.[47]

More specifically: though Maximus keeps his favourite triad — being, well-being, ever-being, it ceases to be simply the ascetic transposition of a trio from Aristotelian ontology — essence, power, act. Henceforth it is referred to *the mysteries of the Christian Economy themselves*:

> By his Incarnation our Lord and God has honoured our threefold birth — that is to say, generally speaking, the modalities of our coming to be, coming to be well, and coming to be for ever. The first birth is from the body ... whereby we have our being; the second is from Baptism, whereby we receive well-being in abundance; and the third is from the Resurrection, and by that we are transformed through grace for the sake of ever-being.[48]

---

[46]Ibid., with reference to *Capita 200 theologica et oeconomica* 19-20 (PG 9, 220B-237BC).

[47]Ibid., pp. 88-89.

[48]*Ambigua* 42 (PG 91, 1325B).

And later in this text we find, Riou reports, that the theory of the *logoi* is no longer constructed in terms of the problem of the One and the Many, even in a version consciously corrected from the bold but defective sketch left by Origen, but in terms, rather, of the Pauline themes of the divine plan, *prothêsis*, and the divine counsel, *boulêsis*.[49]

For Maximus, starting from such New Testament texts as the prologue to the Letter to the Ephesians, the order of creation and nature is theologically preceded by that of the saving design of the Holy Trinity. The object, *skopos*, envisaged by this design is for him the Incarnation, the *perichôrêsis* in Christ of the divine and human natures. In chapter 60 of the *Quaestiones ad Thalassium*, Maximus offers his most celebrated statement of the hypostatic union as foundation of the goal of the cosmos itself. There he writes, in an often cited passage:

> By Christ, by, namely, the Mystery [of the hypostatic union of natures] in Christ, all the ages and what is contained in all the ages have taken in Christ the beginning of being and its end.[50]

The context for this superlatively christocentric statement is Paul's reference in the Letter to the Colossians (1, 26), to the mystery of Christ as being a mystery formerly 'hidden for ages and generations but now made manifest' to God's saints.

> There has been conceived before all ages a union of limit and limitless, of measure and measureless, of term and non-term, of Creator and creation, of stability and movement. This union came about in Christ, manifested in these last times, and giving full expression to the foreknown project of God.

This mystery, the Incarnation, is, Maximus declares, the 'most inward foundation', *puthmena*, 'of the Father's goodness'; in it

---

[49]A. Riou, *Le monde et l'Eglise selon Maxime le Confesseur*, op. cit., pp. 90-91, with reference to *Ambigua* 42 (PG 91, 1328BC).

[50]*Questiones ad Thalassium* 60 (PG 90, 621B).

is shown forth the purpose for which all creatures were given being.[51] Riou, sensitive to the criticisms of the traditional Hellenic-Christian ontology in the French philosophical milieu of the later twentieth century, glosses Maximus' text here by speaking of a Christian 'nihilism' emerging from the apophaticism of Chalcedon, a nihilism of a strange sort, for in Maximus' vision it is 'nothing but' charity which founds the universe. Or as Riou puts it even more daringly in a lengthy footnote: 'the eschatological statute of creation is founded on the nothingness (*néant*) of charity'.[52] Be this as it may (and it is difficult to suppose that the classical ontology can be so summarily disposed of), what is clear is that for Maximus the Incarnation prefigures in the Head, Christ, the completion of the whole divine plan: the recapitulation of all things in God by the union and *perichôrêsis* of the created and the Uncreated.

According to Riou, this 'structure' also provides the basis for how Maximus understands human awareness of the mystery, and the standing of theology which is its intellectual exploration. Maximus proposes in this same text two distinct paths in the knowledge of God. The first is laborious, requires the mediation of intelligence, and leads to God by way of contemplation of natural realities according to their *logoi* — even though this cannot be *merely* natural, since, owing to the insertion of all creatures into the trinitarian plan, this kind of knowledge presupposes faith in the triune Creator. The second differs from the first in being owed rather to a supernatural perception of an experiential kind — and Riou feels justified in explaining this further by re-introducing those two key Maximian terms, *tropos* and hypostasis. This is, he writes, a 'union according to the hypostasis, by "tropic" divinisation'.[53] It is not so much a knowledge of the provident God, active in his creation, as of the *perichôrêsis* of the divine hypostases and their economic

---

[51]Ibid., at 621AC.

[52]A. Riou, *Le monde et l'Eglise selon Maxime le Confesseur*, op. cit., p. 97. The background debate allusively referred to here can be consulted in J.-L. Marion, *Dieu sans Etre* (Paris 1982), and D. Dubarle, *Dieu avec l'Etre. De Parménide à S. Thomas. Essai d'ontologie théologale* (Paris 1986).

[53]Ibid., p. 99.

missions. As Maximus puts it in a passage rich, certainly, in trinitarian content:

> This mystery was foreknown before all ages by Father, Son and Holy Spirit; by the former according to a benevolent design (*eudokia*); by the second according to a self-accomplishment (*autourgia*); by the third according to a co-working (*sunergia*). For one is the knowledge of Father, Son and Spirit, because one too is their essence and power. Truly, the Father was not unaware of the Incarnation of the Son, any more than was the Holy Spirit: in the Son, himself altogether bringing about (*autourgôn*) the mystery of our salvation by the Incarnation, is the Father, whole and entire according to his essence, not incarnate but projecting in his benevolence (*eudokôn*) the Incarnation of the Son; and in the Son in his complete reality exists the Holy Spirit, also entire according to essence, not incarnate but co-operatively bringing about (*sunergôn*) with the Son the secret Incarnation on our behalf.[54]

However, Riou finds it disappointing that Maximus does not, in this same chapter of the *Ambigua*, connect the two modes of the knowledge of God to that vital distinction between nature and hypostasis in any very explicit fashion. He is consoled by finding a happier text in this regard, the little studied *Ambigua* 10, concerned as this is with the episode of Christ's Transfiguration. This is a text we have already encountered, with Croce's help, in the context of Maximus' theological method.[55] Here, in the context of the difference Christ makes to the cosmos, it will detain us longer.

The drama of the Transfiguration event suggests to Maximus' the two modes of 'theology'. The first, which he describes as 'simple and without cause', is content to confess the divine truth by way of apophasis, and to celebrate its excellence in a song without words (*aphasia*). The second, which Maximus

---

[54] *Quaestiones ad Thalassium* 60 (PG 91, 621BC).
[55] See above, pp. 57-58.

calls by contrast complex, *sunthetos*, confirms the witness of the first by way of cataphasis, through created effects. The emphasis in Maximus' account falls, however, on the *inter-relation* of these two kinds of divine understanding. A knowledge of God and divine matters through the enacted symbols of the Transfiguration drama, suited as these are to our human condition, leads us on by both these routes, apophatic and cataphatic. As Riou puts it:

> Apophasis and cataphasis are no longer presented here as two opposed and mutually exclusive kinds of knowledge. On the contrary, they appear as two complementary and concomitant modes, intimately inter-connected and involved with each other.[56]

Cataphasis issues from the very structure of the mystery; it is a reading of the relevant events as mighty acts of God, where God is called 'cause', *aitia*, and his wonders 'effects', *aitiata*, by reference to that gratuitous loving Providence which has brought all things from nothing. At the same time, such cataphatic understanding constitutes just a first, provisional stage in the knowledge of God, being ordered as it is to apophasis. Yet we are not dealing here (to cite Riou again) with

> a regional demarcation between an ontological domain of creation and a transcendent one of divinity, at which latter one would arrive by a metaphorical *dépassement* of the former. Rather this distinction [between cataphasis and apophasis] is the interpenetration of two symbolic modes whereby creation 'is conjugated' in terms of, respectively, its *logos* of nature and its *tropos*, called as that is to a new condition in Christ.[57]

Such compenetration of the positive and negative approaches to the knowledge of God Maximus finds disclosed in the

[56]A. Riou, *Le monde et l'Eglise selon Maxime le Confesseur*, op. cit., p. 106.
[57]Ibid., p. 107.

Transfiguration, revealing as that episode does the mystery of the hypostatic union and the *perichôrêsis* of the two natures. In this light, apophasis is not just a negative moment in theology but relates — in a supremely positive way — to the reality intended by the key adverbs, at once privative and plenary, of the Chalcedonian Definition. The Lord's personhood is found one and the same in the two natures 'without mixing', *asunchutôs*; 'without change', *atreptôs*; 'without division', *adiairetôs*; 'without separation', *achôristôs*. The two natures are not synthesised in anything other than the 'antinomic tension of the hypostasis'.[58]

As Maximus himself puts it, in his transfigured humanity the Lord has become 'the type and symbol of himself'.[59] In his hypostasis he is

at once the Father's beloved Son, turned toward the intimacy of the trinitarian Persons and the inconceivable infinitude of the divine life, and also he who, for love of men, became a creature in order to manifest and fulfil the benevolent design [of God].[60]

And Riou here identifies the mystery of the hypostatic union with the mysteriousness of a philanthropy which allowed Christ to hold together the two modalities of which his being was composed — compared by this French scholar with the root meaning of the word 'symbol', *symbolon*, the fitting together of the constituent parts of a ring or a tablet.

The two modalities of the being of the Saviour are made explicit by Maximus in the lines that follow. In the first place, the divine Person of the Son remains hidden when considered in the modality of its divine *ousia*, its possession of the inner-trinitarian life. The *light* of the Lord's face on Thabor, a radiance which, Maximus remarks, the apostles found to surpass human happiness, belongs with apophatic theology. As he writes:

---

[58]A. Riou, *Le monde et l'Eglise selon Maxime le Confesseur*, op. cit., p. 108.
[59]*Ambigua* 10 (PG 90, 1165D).
[60]A. Riou, *Le monde et l'Eglise selon Maxime le Confesseur*, op. cit., p. 109.

The blessed and holy Godhead is by essence beyond the unspeakable and unknowable and infinitely exceeds all infinity. It has bestowed absolutely no trace — not the slightest — of understanding to those who were with it, nor has it allowed a single being to conceive how and in what fashion it is at once Unity and Trinity, since it is of the nature of the created not to contain the Uncreated and of the Infinite not to be grasped by finite beings.[61]

As Riou comments, the 'trihypostatic mode of the Trinity ... remains present and hidden in the *prosôpon*', which, he reminds his readers, in Greek signifies both face and person.[62] But in the second place, this same Person *is* manifested to creatures in his three-fold embodiment or Incarnation; in the *logoi* of creaturely essences, in the words of Scripture and in our human flesh. The hypostasis of the Son is revealed when considered in the modality of the divine activity whereby Jesus carries out the loving plan of God, recapitulating in himself the entire Economy of salvation. The shining vestments of the Saviour on Thabor are these created *logoi* sparkling with the divine light of his face and the glory of his Person, since in his loving-kindness towards men he has assumed creaturely being into his own hypostasis, thereby founding the possibility of cataphatic theology. As Maximus puts it:

> The cataphatic mode concerns him who determines according to operation both providence and judgment. This modality according to activity, indicating and manifesting from the beauty and grandeur of creatures that God is Creator of all things, is shown in the Lord's shining garments which the Word, taking them up in advance, has presented in the visible creatures.[63]

The hidden and the visible are united in the 'himself', the single face and Person of the Lord in his two natures.

---

[61] *Ambigua* 10 (PG 90, 1168A).
[62] A. Riou, *Le monde et l'Eglise selon* Maxime le *Confesseur*, op. cit., p. 110.
[63] *Ambigua* 10 (PG 91, 1168B).

Maximus does not, however, according to Riou, treat the 'transparency' of the Transfiguration moment as an end in itself. Rather is it a prefiguration of the Cross and Resurrection, for it is in the Easter mystery that the passage from the visible to the invisible is 'sealed'.[64] The saving work of Christ in the flesh is the eschatological movement of the world in Christ, its paschal leading into Glory. In his exegesis of the Transfiguration episode, Maximus makes Moses and Elijah represent respectively divine providence and divine judgment. As Thunberg had noted, Maximus thus draws back these key concepts of Origenist ontology into the ambience of the Bible.[65] By both, 'all has proceeded in good order towards the end known by God alone'.[66] By their conversation with the Saviour on Thabor Moses and Elijah learn of the final issue, *ekbasis*, of history, which will be presented in the Passion, with its cry 'It is consummated' on the Cross. They also learn what no creature can understand, namely the term, *peiras*, of God's plan for all divine ways of guiding the world, all the 'divine Economies'. *Askêsis* and the purification of the mind by the virtues opens to these saints of the Old Covenant, on the Mount of the Transfiguration, a knowledge of the existence which is to come, and this Maximus presents in explicitly cosmic terms. They perceive that created things in their entirety, *katholou*, their 'catholicity', are turned towards the final condition prefigured and inaugurated by the Redeemer on the Cross.

From this difficult text and also from others — notably Maximus' commentary on the *Our Father* and *Ambigua* 60, Riou draws the following conclusions about transformation of the world in Christ, according to Maximian thought. First, the Cross of Christ, recapitulating as it does the length and breadth, height and depth of the divine love, proclaims that all creation — all the *logoi* of providence and judgment — is summed up and taken up, in a filial *tropos* or way, in the Person of the beloved Son. In his saving Passion Christ has opened up a

---

[64] A. Riou, *Le monde et l'Eglise selon Maxime le Confesseur*, op. cit., p. 115.
[65] See above, pp. 125-126.
[66] *Ambigua* 10 (PG 91, 1168D-1169A).

passage from the created to the Uncreated, from natural contemplation to perception of the divine Glory. Secondly, this filial *tropos* is eschatological. The world is turned towards an ultimate goal foreseen in the divine counsel. The Cross reveals that, though the natural order has its own consistency, that present consistency of the world is in fact tributary to an imminent end, when the current ordering of things will be dissolved and a new creation brought to be. Thirdly, on the Cross, when the dying Son gives the Spirit into the hands of his Father he also transmits the Spirit to human beings, and, above all, to the Church born from his pierced side. And here we enter the *pneumatological* dimension of eschatology, which, in Riou's presentation of Maximus' thought, is also inseparably its *ecclesiological* aspect. The Holy Spirit, the Church and the End of all things are intimately inter-connected in what he calls the economy as 'renewal of the world in the Easter of the Church'.[67]

Cosmos and the Spirit: The Economy as 'Renewal of the World in the Easter of the Church'

In his Easter gift of the Spirit, Christ as new Adam restores to humanity the sonship, symbolised by the divine inbreathing of the Spirit, offered to the first Adam at the beginning. But Christ is not only the Alpha, the primordial archetype of this configuration of human beings to God the Son's 'form' and 'mode' of being. He is also the Omega, the Last Adam inaugurating the recapitulation of the whole creation in the bosom of his Father.

According to Maximus, the divine Son, in willing to restore the filiation we lost by Adam's sin, did not simply take on our nature, when the Spirit over-shadowed Mary at the Annunciation. Additionally, at his Baptism in the Jordan he took on the filial *tropos* which at the beginning had been bestowed on the first Adam, so as both to restore that way of being human and to carry it to its completion. As Maximus writes in *Ambigua* 42:

[67]A. Riou, *Le monde et l'Eglise selon Maxime le Confesseur*, op. cit., pp. 119-121.

Wanting to liberate man and to bring him back to a happy
destiny in God, the Word — the Creator of human nature
— became truly man from man and was born in the body
but without sin, for man's sake. He who was God by
essence and Son of God by nature was, moreover, baptised,
entering by his own will into a birth for spiritual sonship,
so as to suppress a birth that was merely bodily ... Adam,
having by his own will abandoned the birth from the Holy
Spirit for divinisation, was condemned to a corporeal
birth for corruption. That is why he who is good and the
Friend of men, chose to become man with us in our Fall,
and was himself condemned with us voluntarily, he who
alone is free and without sin, and having accepted to be
born by a merely bodily birth, in which lay the force of our
condemnation, he re-established by his mysteries the
birth in the Spirit. Untying in himself on our behalf the
chains of bodily birth, he gave us, by the voluntary birth
according to the Spirit, the power to become children of
God in the place of children of flesh and blood, we who
believe in his name.[68]

Christ's Baptism began the restoration of birth in the Holy
Spirit which was fully realised in the 'baptism' of the Cross.[69]
That is why we in our turn must be re-created through Baptism.
The new birth in the Spirit by Baptism is, Maximus remarks,
'for my salvation by grace and for my recall, or, to speak more
clearly, for my re-creation', *anaplasis.*[70] Riou, accepting the
Orthodox dogmatician Vladimir Lossky's statement that
'eschatology appears in the moment when man becomes
capable of collaborating with the divine plan', speaks in this
baptismal context of the Economy, seen as the development of
a scenario already given, in principle, with our creation,
yielding place to a *ceaseless* renewal of human freedom until

[68]*Ambigua* 42 (PG 91, 1348AB).
[69]Luke 12, 50.
[70]*Ambigua* 42 (PG 91, 1348D).

divine likeness comes about in us.[71] Here Riou can invoke the
Questiones ad Thalassium:

> For the Spirit does not engender a power of free choice
> devoid of will but in shaping it he gives it will with a view
> to divinisation ... And so, if we carry the Spirit of filiation,
> as a seed giving to those who are engendered a form like
> that of what has seeded them, we do not for all that offer
> him a power of free choice unaffected by attraction and
> disposition towards some other thing: while nevertheless
> engendered by water and the Spirit, we sin voluntarily.
> But if we prepare the power of free choice to receive with
> understanding their energy — I mean that of water and
> the Spirit — then by the practical life the mystic water will
> purify our conscience, and the Spirit, life-giving in this
> experiential awareness, will work in us the unchangeable
> perfection of the good.[72]

The image of the new Adam, given us *in nuce* with Baptism, can
be made manifest in the novel mode of likeness.

This re-creation is not offered, however, to individuals
atomistically and alone. It is ecclesial: as the *Mystagogia* makes
clear, we are re-created via the new creation of the Church
born from the water and blood issuing from Christ's pierced
side, the Church which gives us entry to the theandric mystery
of sonship in Christ. The Church gives to the diversity of
human persons a profound unity in the Son and in this way
shows forth the source of this gift of sonship as the Spirit in
person. Riou draws attention here to the relevance to Maximus'
thought of a line of speculation in contemporary Eastern
Orthodox dogmatics, which descends from Sergei Bulgakov,
through Vladimir Lossky to Olivier Clément: just as the Person
of the Son, stripped of his divine form in the *kenôsis* of the
Incarnation, was manifested in the form of a servant, so the
Person of the Holy Spirit, by a *kenôsis* all his own, remains

---

[71]A. Riou, *Le monde et l'Eglise selon Maxime le Confesseur*, op. cit., p. 129, with
reference to V. Lossky, *A l'image et à la ressemblance de Dieu* (Paris 1967), p. 221.
[72]*Quaestiones ad Thalassium* 6 (PG 90, 281B).

hidden in his secret hypostasis in the very act of uniting himself to each created hypostasis of the baptised, giving them new birth, a new humanity, so as to provide for Christ a multitude of brothers and sisters in his image.[73] As the opening chapter of the *Mystagogia* indicates, the Church is the unifying *tropos* joining God and the world, no longer by some 'external means', the imposition of an omnipotent causality, but from within the world, from its heart, in man himself[74]. As Riou, again, comments:

> Whereas in the fallen creation God is present by way of natural causality, the Church is henceforward the hypostatic, iconic presence of God in the world, no longer a dominating and constraining presence, but discreet and hidden, as befits the free play of his *kenôsis*, a presence imperceptible to natural or scientific investigation but how much more potent and necessary than the power and necessity of causation![75]

Here, for Riou, Maximus turns definitively away from any Neoplatonist cosmological scheme. Bearing within her as she does the christic *perichôrêsis* of God and man, the Church re-orients all things. The goal is no longer the summit of a pyramidal hierarchy of essences — as in a vision of the world based on the notion of inferior reality's ever-deficient participation in superior. Instead, the true orientation of the world is a unifying centre for all beings, one that consists in the goodness of God. The Pauline image of Christ as the Head of the body enables Maximus to present this not in terms of procession from and return to 'the One', but in terms, rather, of God's plan for taking up the natural differences of his creatures into a unity by the mystery of sonship in Christ and the Church.[76]

---

[73]A. Riou, *Le Monde et l'Eglise selon Maxime le Confesseur*, op. cit., p. 127.
[74]*Mystagogia* 1 (PG 91, 665C-668B).
[75]A. Riou, *Le monde et l'Eglise selon Maxime le Confesseur*, op. cit., p. 141.
[76]Ibid., pp. 142-143.

According to the *Mystagogia*, 'holy Church is an icon of God as accomplishing among believers the same union that God himself works'. The Church's being, then, is not of the order of nature: she is the restoration by Christ, in his hypostasis as Son, of the unconfused union of God and the creation, what Riou calls

> the paschal and eschatological 'exodus' of the Mystery into the world, and of the world into the Mystery.[77]

She is in herself, then, *the* mystagogy *par excellence,* numbered neither with God nor with the creation but the mutual transparency of God's presence in the world, and the world's presence to God. That is why, indeed, Balthasar entitled his pioneering study of Maximus 'The Cosmic Liturgy': the Church realises, thanks to God's own energy, the recapitulation of creation in the divine *tropos* of sonship.

But if, for Maximus, the Church is the icon of the divine being in its activity, so is she also 'type and icon of the world', constituted as this is of 'essences both visible and invisible' and that because she 'admits the same union and the same diversity' as the world. Here a favoured theme in Thunberg presentation of Maximus' cosmology recurs in a new ecclesiological context. The Church is not divided by her component parts as a result of those parts' difference one from another, but is herself hypostatically united: *mia kata tên hypostasin,* and so one unified reality.[78]

In chapter 5 of the *Mystagogia*, Maximus describes *both* the marriage union of the human creation with God by Christ in the Spirit — the divinisation of man thanks to the unconfused union of the soul with God, and *also* the cosmic dimensions or implications of that union, disclosing as it does the profound unity of the *logoi* of creation in the divine Word, beyond all the divisions which man makes use of in the service of his own self-separation from God.

---

[77]Ibid., p. 146.
[78]*Mystagogia* 2 (PG 91, 669A).

When the soul has become unified in this way and is centred on itself and on God, there is no reason to divide it on purpose into numerous things because its head is crowned by the first and only and unique Word and God. It is in him as the Creator and Maker of beings that all the principles of things both are and subsist as one in an incomprehensible simplicity. Gazing with a simple understanding on him who is not outside but thoroughly in the whole of reality, it will itself understand the principles of beings and the causes why it was distracted by divisive pursuits before being espoused to the Word of God. It is by way of them that it is brought harmoniously, safe and sound, to him who creates and embraces all principles and causes.[79]

While in itself comparing man to the world is an unoriginal procedure, for this is a commonplace of ancient thought, Maximus takes the innovatory step of basing this comparison on the unifying and synthesising vocation of the new humanity in Christ. As he presents matters, so Riou concludes:

Man is destined, not to lose himself in a sacral nature at large, or to de-personalise himself in an impersonal divine realm — as the gnosticisms of every period and provenance have proposed, but on the contrary by love to bring the universe to that consummation foreknown in the trinitarian Counsel, by becoming, in the Church, the iconic, loving presence of God in the world.[80]

As chapter 7 of the *Mystagogia* affirms, this presence is paschal, eschatological, for the present order awaits its liberation in the 'exodus' of the second coming.

By kinship, the universal and unique mode of the invisible and unknowable presence in all things of the Cause which holds all things together by his existence in all things

[79]Ibid., 5 (PG 91, 681B).
[80]A. Riou, *Le monde et l'Eglise selon Maxime le Confesseur*, op. cit., p. 158.

renders them unmixed and undivided in themselves and in relation to each other. And it shows that they exist by the relationship which unites them to each other rather than to themselves, until such time as it pleases the One who bound them together to separate them in view of a greater and more mystical arrangement in the time of the expected universal consummation, when the world, as man, will die to its life of appearances and rise again renewed of its oldness in the Resurrection expected presently. At this time the man who is ourselves will rise with the world as a part with the whole and the small with the large, having obtained the power of not being subject to further corruption. Then the body will become like the soul and sensible things like intelligible things in dignity and glory, for the unique divine power will manifest itself in all things in a vivid and active presence proportioned to each one, and will by itself preserve unbroken for endless ages the bond of unity.[81]

Following straight on this chapter, Maximus comes to deal with the Eucharist, the liturgical celebration which renders God's presence actual or contemporary, recalling the first Parousia, and anticipating his second. For Maximus the Eucharist is 'the sacred *sunaxis*', and as Riou suggests, whereas this may simply have been the commonest name in his time for the Eucharistic 'assembly' or 'gathering', the choice may, alternatively, have been deliberate, the word pregnant. If chosen specially, the term would indicate the continuity which links the first seven chapters of the *Mystagogia*, on the Church's ontology, to the remaining chapters, on her 'ritual economy'.[82]

Maximus explains the Eucharistic liturgy in terms of the paschal mystery which occupies the time in between the two *parousiai*. When the bishop comes into church at the start of the celebration, and passes through it to take his seat in his throne, he does so, Maximus comments, as type and icon of Christ in his first Parousia, when as the Incarnate One he

---

[81] *Mystagogia* 7 (PG 91, 685C).
[82] A Riou, *Le monde et l'Eglise selon Maxime le Confesseur*, op. cit., p. 160.

entered the world to carry out his saving work, until his Ascension to the Father's right hand. The people, entering the church in the bishop's wake, symbolise the great mass of believers called to conversion and configuration to Christ.

> Entrance into the church signifies not only the conversion of infidels to the true and only God but also the amendment of each one of us who believe but yet violate the Lord's commandments ... When someone is entangled in any vice but ceases voluntarily to be held by its attention and deliberately to act according to it and changes his life for the better by preferring virtue to vice, such a person can be properly and truly considered and spoken of as entering with Christ our God and High Priest into virtue, which is understood as the Church according to the *tropos*.[83]

The highway of this entry into the Church by the mode of virtue is signposted in the biblical readings of the Liturgy of the Word. These lections

> reveal the divine and blessed desires and intentions of God most holy. Through them each one of us receives in proportion to the capacity which is in him the counsels by which he should act, and we learn the laws of the divine and blessed struggles in which by consistent fighting we will be judged worthy of the victorious crowns of Christ's kingdom.[84]

Meanwhile the liturgical chants symbolise in their beauty the fruits of such ascetic configuration to the Redeemer, the 'vivid delights of the divine blessings', while the wishes of peace before the readings ('Peace be with you all!') represent the grace of detachment which God gives the saints in return for their efforts at virtue. And so we come to the proclamation of the Gospel itself. Maximus understands this in two ways. In its individual signification, taken *idikôs*, that is, as applied to the

[83]*Mystagogia* 9 (PG 91, 689AB).
[84]Ibid., 10 (PG 91, 689B).

person, the reading of the Gospel stands for that 'suffering on behalf of the Word' which each of the faithful must undergo if he or she is to be led with the angels to the Father in the Holy Spirit. In its corporate signification, taken *genikôs*, that is, as applied to the creation in its generality, the Gospel reading stands for the truth of which the New Testament is the image — the consummation and judgment of the world in the second Parousia of the Word of God.[85] In thus connecting both the personal eschatology of the martyr and universal eschatology to the same liturgical rite, Maximus implies, according to Riou, that these are 'one single, unique mystery'.[86]

Riou places Maximus' account of the second part of the synaxis, the Liturgy of the Sacrifice, under the rubric 'The Sacramental and Mystic Anticipation of the Second Coming'.[87] After the ascetic struggle, there comes the spiritual ascent, a proleptic entry into Christ's return in glory. Thus the 'Great Entry', when the Eucharistic gifts, prepared but not consecrated, are brought into the nave of the church, 'commences and inaugurates the future unveiling of the mystery of our salvation which lies within the impenetrable divine secret'.[88] The kiss of peace 'prefigures and describes in advance' the future reconciliation of all rational beings in the one Logos, the 'Cause of every word and meaning'.[89] The recitation of the Creed 'signifies in advance', *prosêmainei*, the 'mystical thanksgiving' which will take place in the Age to come for the 'marvellous principles and modes of the all-wise providence of God towards us'.[90] So far, as Riou points out, this is a matter, however, of 'representations', rather than realisation of the 'Economy of the paschal and eschatological passover of the creation into God'.[91]

The next three chapters of the *Mystagogia*, numbers 19 to 21, by contrast, speak more boldly of the actual entry of the

[85] *Mystagogia* 14 (PG 91, 692D-693A).
[86] A. Riou, *Le monde et l'Eglise selon Maxime le Confesseur*, op. cit., p. 162.
[87] Ibid., p. 163.
[88] *Mystagogia* 16 (PG 91, 693C).
[89] Ibid., 17 (PG 91, 695A).
[90] Ibid., 18 (PG 91, 696AB).
[91] A. Riou, *Le monde et l'Eglise selon Maxime le Confesseur*, op. cit., p. 164.

creation into the divine intimacy. In chapter 19, the singing of the *Trisagion*, (the *Sanctus*,) places the Church in a state of anticipated concelebration with the Angels, introducing her to the praise of the 'single three-Personed God' and so to the knowledge which the heavenly powers enjoy of the holy Trinity. In chapter 20, Maximus presents the Lord's Prayer, the *Pater*, as opening the way for a heightened intimacy with God, proper to the state of sons: the filiation which will be bestowed 'according to hypostasis and existence' by the gift of the Holy Spirit. In chapter 21, where Maximus treats of the ancient Greek-Christian hymn 'One is Holy', sung just before the actual communion, he speaks of

> the gathering and union beyond reason and understanding which will take place between those who have been mystically and wisely initiated by God and the mysterious oneness of the divine simplicity

—which 'oneness', according to J.-M. Garrigues, is not only for Maximus an attribute of the divine essence common to the trinitarian Persons but also a matter of the mysterious indwelling of the Father in Son and Holy Spirit by his gift to them of the divine nature.[92] Then comes the actual distribution of the sacrament which, for those who share it worthily, makes the communicants 'gods by adoption through grace'.

In other words, Maximus passes over, in complete taciturnity, the anaphora, the Eucharistic Prayer, the heart of the Liturgy! René Bornert, in his account of the Byzantine liturgical commentaries of the patristic and mediaeval periods, can find no satisfactory explanation for this.[93] Possibly Maximus thought it appropriate only to comment on those parts of the rite seen or heard by the people, not least because, so Riou thinks, he was himself a non-ordained monk. Yet *résumés* of the anaphora appear to have been sung by the people during the secret

[92]Mystagogia 21, (PG 91, 6967D); J.-M. Garrigues, 'Théologie et monarchie', *Istina*, 4 (1970), pp. 458-462.
[93]R. Bornert, *Les commentaires byzantins de la divine liturgie du VIIe au XVe siècle* (Paris 1966), pp. 107-108.

prayers of the celebrant in, at any rate, the sixth century.[94] Riou therefore offers a more recondite, if theologically profound, explanation of Maximus' surprising omission:

> The true anaphora — the configuring *anamnêsis* and eschatological *epiklêsis*—of Christ is brought to its fulfilment only in the martyr himself: in this apophatic anaphora, the Christian and the Church silently communicate with and consummate the mystery of the paschal transparency.[95]

The *Mystagogia* closes with two lengthy chapters which sum up all that has gone before, first, in chapter 23, in relation to the three main stages of the spiritual life (practical philosophy or ethics, natural contemplation, mystical theology), and then, in chapter 24, by reference to the unfolding of the holy Liturgy. Passing swiftly in review the chief moments of the liturgical action, Maximus insists that the origin and goal of the cosmos, the Father, can be found only by becoming sons, through cooperation with the Holy Spirit, the Spirit who impresses on the heart of the believer likeness to the Son:

> Every Christian should be exhorted to frequent God's holy church and never to abandon the holy synaxis contained therein, because ... of the grace of the Holy Spirit which is always invisibly present, but in a special way at that time. This grace transforms and changes each person who is found there and in fact re-moulds him in proportion to what is more divine in him and leads him to what is revealed through the mysteries which are celebrated... .[96]

But ultimate likeness to the Son, divinisation in its consummate form, Maximus reserves for the *kenôsis* of charity whereby Christian and Church are identified with the poor and suffering Christ as Servant:

---

[94]P. Trembelas, 'L'audition de l'anaphore eucharistique par le peuple', in *l'Eglise et les Eglises. Mélanges Dom L. Bauduin* (Chevetogne 1955), II., pp. 207-220.

[95]A. Riou, *Le monde et l'Eglise selon Maxime le Confesseur*, op. cit., p. 165.

[96]*Mystagogia* 24 (PG 91, 701D-704A).

The clear proof of this grace is the voluntary disposition of good will towards those akin to us whereby the man who needs our help in any way becomes as much as possible our friend as God is and we do not leave him abandoned and forsaken but rather with fitting zeal show him in action the disposition which is alive in us with respect to God and our neighbour. For a work is proof of a disposition. Now nothing is either so fitting for justification or so apt for divinisation, if I can speak thus, and nearness to God as mercy offered with pleasure and joy from the soul to those who stand in need. For if the Word has shown that the one who is in need of having good done to him is God — for as long, he tells us, as you did it for one of these least ones, you did it for me (Matthew 24, 40-41) — on God's very Word, then, he will much more show that the one who can do good and who does it is truly God by grace and participation because he has taken on in happy imitation the energy and the characteristic feature of his own doing good. And if the poor man is 'God', it is because of God's condescension in becoming poor for us, in taking upon himself by his own suffering the sufferings of each one and, until the end of time, always suffering mystically out of goodness in proportion to each one's suffering. All the more reason, then, will that one be God who by loving men in imitation of God heals by himself in divine fashion the hurts of those who suffer and who shows that he has in his disposition, safeguarding all proportion, the same power of saving providence that God has.[97]

The genius of the *Mystagogia* lies, then, as Père Irénée-Henri Dalmais has shown, in its correction of the theurgic illumination of Denys — with its danger of a Christianity that was purely liturgical and intellectualist — by associating with the mystical and cosmic contemplation of the Liturgy the daily, concrete discipline of charity.[98] But whereas the *Mystagogia* — which

---

[97]*Mystagogia* 24 (PG 91, 713AB).

[98]I.-H. Dalmais, 'Place de la *Mystagogie* de saint Maxime le Confesseur dans la théologie liturgique byzantine', *Studia Patristica* V (Berlin 1962), pp. 281-283.

dates in all probability from the middle period of Maximus' life
before the publication of the *Ekthesis* which hurled him into
christological controversy and brought before him, for the first
time, the threat of martyrdom — presents what Riou calls 'the
Church's ontology as already accomplished, already posited,
mystically anticipated', the *Capita theologica et economica*, from a
later period, speak no longer of the Church ecclesiastically but
only eschatologically. In Riou's words:

> They recall the paschal crossing which has founded the
> Church in its catholicity and, at the same time, the
> eschatological passing over of the Church, which is none
> other than exodus from this world, in God, by the Passover
> of Christ.[99]

Chapter 51 to 70 of those *Opuscula*, in particular, remind the
reader of the realism of the Triduum, and of the need to have
communion with that realism. The Resurrection of Christ is
the eighth day which shows forth to the creation the *tropos* of
the new creation, itself 'above nature and beyond time'.[100] The
following chapters evoke the character of this new creation
which is not a prolongation of nature but its radical innovation.
Its foundation, the life-giving *kenôsis* of the Word, reveals
simultaneously, however, not only the final goal, but also the
original meaning of the creation.

> Whoever knows the mystery of the Cross and the Tomb
> knows the *logoi* of creatures. And whoever is initiated into
> the unspeakable power of the Resurrection knows the
> purpose for which God in the beginning gave subsistence
> to all things.[101]

The passage of the creation to this vocation promised from the
beginning requires its own 'Easter' in the Pasch of the Word.

---

[99]A. Riou, *Le monde et l'Eglise selon Maxime le Confesseur*, op. cit., p. 173.

[100]*Capita theologica et economica* I. 51 (PG 91, 1101C).

[101]*Capita theologica et economica* I. 66 (PG 91, 1108AB).

All visible things need a 'cross', all intelligible things a 'burial'; through such dying of the world to itself:

> The Word who alone exists through himself, as the One rising from among the dead, is manifested anew, circumscribing all that comes from him, though nothing at all has kinship with him by relationship of nature. For it is by grace, not by nature, that he is the salvation of the saved.[102]

It is by his *kenôsis* that Christ gave the Church her foundation, and, in Maximus' telling phrase, 'accomplished the future in advance', becoming, as head of his Church-body, the precursor of humankind before the Father. As the *Capita theologica et economica* put it:

> If for our sake, in his Economy, the Word of God went down into the lower parts of the earth and re-ascended above all the heavens, he who by nature is wholly immobile, and who, in himself, as man, by Economy, accomplished the future in advance, then let anyone who cherishes the love of knowledge consider, mystically rejoicing, how great is the end promised to those who love the Lord. If God the Word, the Son of God the Father, has become son of man, a human being so to make men gods, son of God, we believe that we shall be the same there where, by virtue of being in our condition, Christ is now himself, as Head of the whole Body, having become for us the pioneer with the Father.[103]

In other words, by the Cross and the Descent into Hell, the Son has opened for the world entry into the Father's presence. Or, as Riou would have it:

> The God who did not refuse to die has, by his Cross, planted in the world his own life which is stronger than

---

[102]Ibid., I. 67 (PG 91, 1108B).
[103]Ibid., II. 24-25 (PG 91, 1136BC).

any death; he has made the kenosis more powerful than all the metaphysical absolutes and cosmic idealisms, and has dragged them behind him in his triumph procession.[104]

We can note in conclusion that all of this has a clear *ethical* aspect — and one, moreover, that is not just a matter of 'separated morals' (moral theology has all too often found itself shunted off into a siding of its own in theological history) but which Maximus presents as intimately bound up with the appropriation of salvation. Christ, by the Holy Spirit, frees believers from the passions, and disciplines them in the virtues — an action which both prepares and manifests the Parousia to come. As the *Capita theologica et economica*, again, have it:

In the same way that, before the visible Parousia according to the flesh, the Word of God dwelt noetically among the patriarchs and prophets, prefiguring the mysteries of his Parousia, so also, after that sojourn, he comes to the aid not only of those who are still children — nourishing them with the Spirit and leading them to the age of the perfection that is according to God, but also of the perfect — inscribing in them, as in images, in advance and in a hidden fashion, the character of his coming Parousia. And in the same way that the words of the Law and the Prophets, being precursors of the Parousia of the Word according to the flesh, taught souls in view of Christ's coming, so also the Incarnate Word of God, himself glorified, teaches souls by his own words with a view to the welcome to be given him in his visible divine Parousia. That Parousia he gives actuality to always, transforming from a fleshly state to a spiritual, by the virtues, those who are worthy, and he will actualise it too at the end of the age, when then he reveals visibly what until then has been hidden from all.[105]

---

[104]A. Riou, *Le monde et l'Eglise selon Maxime le Confesseur*, op. cit., p. 177, with an allusion to Colossians 2, 15.

[105]*Capita theologica et economica* II. 28-29 (PG 91, 1137BD).

By what Riou calls the 'kenosis of the passions', the flesh refinds its original dignity and, more than that, becomes the privileged locus of the accomplishment of the divine plan.[106] In the words of the *Commentary on the Pater*:

> The flesh has become both a poison strong enough to make [Satan] vomit out all those whom he had swallowed by confining them in death's dominion, and also life for the human race, which causes the whole of nature to rise like a loaf for a resurrection of life.[107]

Maximus' anthropology, and his soteriology will be, in fact, our last doctrinal topics.

---

[106]A. Riou, *Le monde et l'Eglise selon Maxime le Confesseur*, op. cit., p. 192.
[107]*Orationis dominicae expositio* (PG 90, 880BC).

6

Lars Thunberg on Maximus' Doctrine of Man

The theological anthropology of the Greek Fathers is a combination of Scripture and philosophical Hellenism, and much of its interest lies in seeing who shall be master. Will the (theoretical) reflections of writers in the ancient world on the structure of the human being, and their (practical) investigations of the virtues that lead him or her to their proper flourishing eviscerate the Scriptural revelation, depriving it of its own meaning or truth? Or, conversely, will the revelation given in Scripture and Tradition, the Church's book and the Church's life, find in ancient philosophy and ethics conceptual elements and insights serviceable for the deployment of its proper content? A third possibility also suggests itself, by way of a via media: can natural philosophy and ethics serve as a complement to the understanding of man and the human project which revelation brings within our ken?

General Anthropology

The relation of the human body to the human soul, and both to the being of the human person, is the central topic of anthropology at large. In his study of Maximus' doctrine of man, Lars Thunberg places first and foremost his account of the 'co-existence in principle of body and soul' — a position taken up, evidently, in conscious contrast to that of Origenism, where the postulate of the soul's pre-existence is frequently encountered — in Nemesius of Emesa and Evagrius, as well as

158

in Origen himself.[1] Origen had related the notion to the ampler idea of a double creation — first of souls, and then, thanks to sin, of bodies, the latter a stratagem of God's providential judgment.[2] In Evagrius what is at issue is, strictly, a matter of pure intellects, rather than souls, yet he preserves the wider outlines of Origen's scheme.[3] Maximus was probably aware of an earlier sortie against this position, that of Gregory of Nyssa in his *De hominis opificio*.[4] There Gregory had argued, in Thunberg's pithy summary

> that a fall into the material world would not imply purification, but rather successive falls leading to a complete destruction of the soul, and that if this were not the case, it would, on the contrary, imply a superiority of sensual life over against spiritual life, since the latter would be the cause of the fall and the former of salvation.[5]

Maximus' account is very different. Concerned to safeguard the divine sovereignty, and God's positive purpose for the present created order in its complex integrity, he stresses — in a series of comments in *Ambigua* 42, and, more sketchily, *Ambigua* 7 — that it is impossible for the visible world, which reveals God, to have its cause in evil. Everything that exists has been created according to the divine foreknowledge, and the *logoi* of all things pre-exist in him.[6] And moreover body and soul are always bound by relationship, *schêsis*: they cannot exist in absolute separation.[7] Man has a *phusis sunthetos*, a 'composite nature'.[8]

---

[1]L. Thunberg, *Microcosm and Mediator. The Theological Anthropology of Maximus the Confessor* (Lund 1965), p. 100.

[2]H. Crouzel, *Théologie de l'image de Dieu chez Origène* (Paris 1956), pp. 148ff.

[3]A. Guillaumont, *Les 'Kephalaia gnostica' d'Evagre le Pontique et l'histoire de l'Origénisme chez les Grecs et chez les Syriens* (Paris 1962), pp. 103-113.

[4]Gregory of Nyssa, *De hominis opificio* 218 (PG 44, 229C-233C). See for a comparison of Gregory's doctrine with that of Maximus, E. Stéphanou, 'La coexistence initiale du corps et de l'âme d'après saint Grégoire de Nysse et saint Maxime l'Homologète', *Echos d'Orient* 31 (1932), pp. 304-315.

[5]L. Thunberg, *Microcosm and Mediator*, op. cit., p. 102.

[6]*Ambigua* 42 (PG 91, 1328A-1329D).

[7]*Ambigua* 7 (PG 1101C).

[8]*Letter* 12 (PG 91, 488D).

Whereas the more rigorous Chalcedonian and Neo-Chalcedonian divines had restricted themselves to talk of a composite *hypostasis* in Christ, as a way of speaking of the unity of divine and human in the God-man, their Monophysite rivals had not hesitated to affirm a composite *nature* in Christ.[9] In this Maximus does not follow them, but, by taking that idea into his *anthropology*, he underlines both the reciprocal independence of body and soul and their unbreakable union. Though the *logos* and *tropos* of body and soul differ, the creative will of the Maker makes them one through the principle of a common, composite nature: itself pre-existent, following the usual Maximian theological ontology, in its own *logos* in God. Here Maximus appears to part company from some of his predecessors among the Greek Christian philosophers, insisting as he does that the unity of body and soul is not only hypostatic (a question of rooting in the single personhood), as conceded by, say, Leontius of Byzantium, but also fully natural. Maximus is concerned *both* to stress the *distinction* between body and soul, so as to protect the immortality and predominance of the soul, *and* to emphasise the natural *unity* of body and soul with a view to affirming the body's resurrection and abiding share in humanity.[10] And by an ironic twist of linguistic history, Maximus speaks of soul and body as ceaselessly 'transmigrating' into each other (*metensômatousthai, metempsychousthai*), thus using a favoured turn of phrase of Origen's in the service of a very different anthropology, related at this point to how Maximus understands *perichôrêsis* in the Incarnate Word.[11]

However, this is not the whole story. The individual human being, the *person*, cannot be seen aright unless it is recognised that human nature has a hypostasis of its own, related to the Logos of God. Consequently, for Maximus, personal

[9]J. Lebon, 'La christologie du monophysisme sévérien', in A. Grillmeier and H. Bacht (eds.), *Das Konzil von Chalkedon. Geschichte und Gegenwart* (Würzburg 1951-1954), I. p. 488. C. Moeller, 'Le chalcédonisme et le néo-chalcédonisme', ibid., pp. 680, 692.

[10]For a discussion, and attempted resolution, of the problem that Maximus, like Leontius, also compares the union of body and soul in man to that of the two natures in Christ, see L. Thunberg, *Microcosm and Mediator*, op. cit., pp. 106-110.

[11]Ibid., p. 109.

relationship with God is included in the definition of human nature, and is indeed identical with fully realised human existence.[12] Though man is free, his liberty cannot be wholly actualised until it finds its goal in God. And so, as Thunberg points out, the question of the hypostatic character of the unitary human being cannot be answered without addressing the further question of the spirituality of the human subject, and its situation.[13] And here we confront, in the first place, a trichotomy (and not merely a dichotomy) in Maximus' treatment of man: not only soul and body but mind, *nous,* also. Verbally, this triad comes from the philosophical tradition of Poseidonius and Plotinus.[14] But a cognate trio — soul, body and spirit, *pneuma* — is found in Paul and Irenaeus. Maximus probably followed Evagrius of Pontus in preferring the term *nous* to *pneuma,* but, where the substantive content of his teaching is concerned he is really closer to Gregory of Nyssa, who had himself stressed, in his occasional use of *nous,* its spiritual (not ontological) meaning: it is the *spiritual aspect of soul.* Like Evagrius, Maximus sees *nous* as the contemplative instrument of man's relation with God, the seat of prayer as of hope and love for God.[15] Yet unlike Evagrius Maximus underlines the relationship between *nous* and the other human capacities, and also the unitary created character of man in his difference from God and reliance on the grace of God for the achievement of his end.

> *Nous* is, thus, to Maximus both more or less identified with the soul, as representing the whole of man, and — in its relationship to God — called to be above human nature and above itself in a mystical sense.[16]

And Thunberg suggests, following a hint dropped by Vladimir Lossky, that, within the human totality, the rôle of *nous* corresponds most closely to that of *person* — something the

[12]H. U. von Balthasar, *Kosmische Liturgie* (Einsiedeln 1961²), p. 245.

[13]L. Thunberg, *Microcosm and Mediator,* op. cit., p. 112.

[14]L. Reypens, 'Ame', *Dictionnaire de Spiritualité* I (Paris 1937), col. 435.

[15]*Centuriae de caritate* III. 61; ibid., I. 3.

[16]L. Thunberg, *Microcosm and Mediator,* op. cit., p. 118.

Maximian scholar ascribes to the influence of Christology on Maximus' doctrine of man.[17]

This theme of the spirituality of the human subject cannot be abandoned, however, without glancing at how Maximus deals with that commonplace yet vital motif in patristic theology: man as made in God's image, and to God's likeness. In the tradition of Origen, and above all in Evagrius, man's image character is restricted to *nous*— above all, for the latter writer, because only mind is able to receive God, having itself once shared the divine Unity. The likeness will be given in the end to mind alone. Here we have an extreme case of the spiritualising tendency common to the Alexandrian school, in part, no doubt, for reasons connected with the danger of anthropomorphism. But while Maximus follows the Alexandrians in relating the image to the rational soul, *noera psuchê*, treating *to noeron*, the intelligible aspect of soul, as the mirror of the divine glory, and seeing the new man, risen in Christ, as typified by a knowledge he has acquired by way of *nous*, Maximus also shows a definite tendency to treat the theme of the divine image in close association with that of freedom: the self-determination of the understanding human subject, not simply its divine affinity.[18] The resolute connecting of the image of God in man with freedom is one of Maximus' numerous points of contact with St Thomas Aquinas.[19]

The note had already been sounded by Gregory of Nyssa.[20] Origen may not have been an Origenist, but, faced with Origenism, Nyssa stressed that the goal of human living is not simply a return to an original communion with God but a self-fulfilment in the divine Good thanks to man's deliberate (and thus *free*) decision.[21] In Maximus, freedom takes up the centre

[17]Ibid., p. 119, with reference to V. Lossky, *The Mystical Theology of the Eastern Church* (Et London 1957), p. 201.

[18]*Ambigua* 7 (PG 91, 1096A); ibid., 10 (PG 91, 1204 A); *Letter* 32 (PG 91, 625).

[19]*Summa Theologiae*, Ia. IIae., prologue. The importance of this connexion to any genuinely theocentric account of ethics is highlighted in S. T. Pinckaers, O.P., *Les Sources de la morale chrétienne. Sa méthode, son contenu, son histoire* (Fribourg 1985), pp. 327-399.

[20]J. Gaïth, *La conception de la liberté chez Grégoire de Nysse* (Paris 1953).

[21]*Homilia in Cantica Canticorum* 2 (Jaeger 6, p. 55); *Oratio catechetica* 5 (PG 45, 24C).

of the stage. In his kindness, God has created man self-moved, *autokinêtos*, in his own image, and in such a way that the good of human nature is only achieved through a free act manifesting the divine likeness in man.[22] In the *Disputatio cum Pyrrho*, not surprisingly, then, human self-determination becomes a 'primary expression of man's image character'.[23]

In distinguishing sharply between the image and the *likeness* in this context, Maximus appears to revert to an earlier stage of the Alexandrian tradition — in contrast to his general tendency. Though in Philo the two terms are more or less interchangeable, in Clement and, above all, in Origen (though also, from a very different ecclesial milieu, in Irenaeus) the distinction between them is marked, carrying indeed much of the weight borne later by the difference between 'natural' and 'supernatural' in the developed theology of grace. Thunberg does not hesitate to call Origen's the 'classical form of the idea' and sums up its chief features in this way: while man has received the dignity of image from the beginning, the likeness belongs to the end — both as eschatological gift and as moral achievement. Image is actualised in likeness, by way of a lengthy spiritual process. Man comes to imitate the virtues of God, though what is formed thereby in us is divine sonship, Christ in the soul of the believer. The main lines of this account recur in Maximus — but not in many other orthodox writers such as Athanasius, Nazianzen, Nyssa (probably), Didymus, Cyril and the Western tradition at large, for all of whom the distinction between image and likeness is by no means self-evident.[24] Though Origen's distinction is found again in a spiritual theologian like Diadochus of Photikê, Maximus' acceptance thereof is likely to be not so much a bowing before the authority of tradition as a piece of conscious theologising of his own.[25]

---

[22] *Capita 200 theologica et oeconomica* I. 11 (PG 90, 1088A; ibid., I. 13 (PG 90, 1088BC).

[23] L. Thunberg, *Microcosm and Mediator*, op. cit., p. 126, with reference to the *Disputation* at PG 91, 304C.

[24] L. Thunberg, *Microcosm and Mediator*, op. cit., pp. 128-133.

[25] A clear guide on these matters (in the first five centuries) is G.A. Maloney, S.J., *Man the Divine Icon. The Patristic Doctrine of Man Made in the Image of God* (Pecos, New Mexico, 1973).

In the *Ambigua* we read that man's image character develops as the human being moves closer towards God by contemplation, and *pari passu* God becomes 'incarnate' in man through those human virtues which mirror the divine attributes.[26] How this relates to the distinction between image and likeness becomes clear in the *Centuries on Charity*. Of the four attributes which, according to Maximus, God bestows on his rational creatures, two — being and 'ever-being', given to the creature's substance — pertain to the image, and two — goodness and wisdom, given to the creaturely will and judgment, belong to the likeness. We receive the first pair by nature, the second by the second gift, by grace.[27] The connexion of the likeness with being good and wise accounts for its intimate linkage with *praxis entolôn*, the living out of the divine commands: the man who, in his freedom, uses aright the threefold movement of the soul (mind, reason, sense) adds to the good of nature the 'voluntary good', *to gnômikon agathon*, of likeness. Thereby, Christ is formed in the Christian, who makes his own the presence in the world of the Incarnate Logos, thanks to those virtues which draw with them the activities not only of the mind but of the body too. (Here we rejoin, from an anthropological direction, the theme of Christ's 'incarnation' in the virtues already encountered in the soteriological treatment of Riou.) At the same time, Maximus' writings also hint at the notion of an *imago Trinitatis* in the human soul — comparable to the analogies offered by Augustine in his *De Trinitate* or Gregory Nazianzen in his *Orations*,[28] as well as the anonymous treatise *Quid sit ad imaginem*, printed by Migne among the works of Gregory of Nyssa.[29] But these faint adumbrations are never filled out, a failure which Thunberg ascribes to Maximus' feeling for apophasis: the mystery of the Holy Trinity is humanly inexpressible.[30]

[26]*Ambigua* 10 (PG 91, 113B).

[27]*Centuriae de caritate* III. 25.

[28]*Orationes* 23, 11 (PG 35, 1161C-1164A).

[29]PG 44, 1336AB. I take this phrase from Father Edward Yarnold, S.J.,'s study of grace: *The Second Gift* (Slough 1974).

[30]L. Thunberg, *Microcosm and Mediator*, op. cit., p. 139.

The most interesting aspect of Maximus' theological anthropology in the eyes of Thunberg is that which gives his great study its title: man as microcosm, and, in dependence on this, as cosmic mediator. The theme of the 'little' and 'great' cosmos, man and the world, is endemic both in Oriental religion and Greek philosophy. For the former, man is formed after the pattern of the world, rather than the other way round, though in the latter, and above all in Plato, the world, contrarily, can be described in human terms. In the Christian perspective the difference is crucial: man is more in the image of God than he is of the material creation, and so possesses a supramundane destiny, while at the same time, in their ideal relationship to the Word of God, man and world are equal — since both are made through the Word and for the Father's glory. Maximus' resolution of these tensions is a creative variant on that already found in that rather original Christian Platonist Nemesius of Emesa. For Nemesius, man can be a microcosm, reflecting the outside world, and also created in the divine image, because on the basis of the latter his function is to unify the former. Man is called upon to *act* as mediator, after God's likeness.[31]

In Maximus, the right ordering of man as a microcosmic totality — related through his senses to matter and through his mind to God — is a presupposition for his work as mediator. In *Ambigua* 10 man is said to be the last made of all creatures because he was to be their natural link, *sundesmos*, summoned to bring into one unity, in relation to God, that which was by nature differentiated. But man preferred rather to direct his natural movement towards the created world, and was salvaged only by Christ who, as God Incarnate, fulfilled man's unifying and mediating rôle, being, as he was, the one man in true relationship with God.[32] Or, as Thunberg puts it:

It is made clear from the very beginning that this work of reconciliation and unification is a task, originally set before man, but now fulfilled — because of man's fall —

[31]Ibid., pp. 140-145.
[32]*Ambigua* 10 (PG 91, 1193C-1196B).

by Christ on his behalf, in such a way that he has to live in accordance with this fulfilment and participate actively in it.[33]

But what are the opposed elements which need to be reconciled by man's mediatorial activity? In *Ambigua* 41, Maximus lists five relevant 'divisions': between man and woman, overcome by the establishing of a 'passionless' relationship between them; between paradise and the humanly inhabited world, overcome by holy living, which makes of both one earth; between heaven and earth, overcome by man's imitation of the Angels; between the intelligible and sensuous realms, overcome by a knowledge equal to the Angels', in which knowing and not-knowing are non-diverse; and between created nature and the Uncreated, when by grace man lives in intimate communion with God.[34]

These points, and the citation from Thunberg oblige us to confront Maximus' views on the Fall of man. Adam's destiny was deification, perfect likeness to God, yet this was set before him as a purpose which he must make his own in freedom. In this he failed, making his wrong decision immediately.[35] This does not prevent Maximus from painting a highly coloured picture of Adam's original blessings — in order, so Thunberg suggests, to underline the 'unlimited possibilities which lie ahead, when man has been restored in Christ to his image character ...'.[36] So the pre-lapsarian Adam enjoys spiritual freedom;[37] he has a capacity for spiritual pleasure;[38] he is without sin,[39] and subject to the law of becoming yet physically incorruptible: only after the Fall did man practise sexual intercourse, a means for the preservation of the race, and know death, the supreme sign of human corruptibility;[40] wise, Adam

---

[33]L. Thunberg, *Microcosm and Mediator*, op. cit., p. 147.

[34]*Ambigua* 41 (PG 1304D-1313B); L. Thunberg, *Microcosm and Mediator*, op. cit., pp. 151-152.

[35]*Quaestiones ad Thalassium* 61 (PG 90, 628A).

[36]L. Thunberg, *Microcosm and Mediator*, op. cit., p. 155.

[37]*Ambigua* 42 (PG 91, 1316D).

[38]*Quaestiones ad Thalassium* 61 (PG 90, 628A).

[39]*Ambigua* 42 (PG 91, 1317A).

[40]Ibid.

enjoyed knowledge, *gnôsis*, beyond the reach of any merely natural contemplation.[41] Thunberg is inclined to dismiss the idea that Maximus regarded the changes supervening on human nature after the Fall as a second creation — along the lines of Gregory of Nyssa, and behind him of Origen and Philo. The passions, pain, the law of death, the principle of procreation through conception: these do not constitute a second creation but are providentially introduced consequences of the human misuse of Adamic capacities.[42]

In Maximus' account of the Fall, the Devil seduced man through a stratagem, feigning benevolence while appealing to man's self-love, *philautia*.[43] Yet it was man who in his freedom allowed himself to be swayed by the pleasure, *hêdonê*, which the Devil insinuated, and man, accordingly, who turned his natural capacity for spiritual pleasure towards the sensuous world, and away from God.[44] And so evil entered the human condition, or rather (for Maximus accepts the privative view of evil's ontic status taught by the pseudo-Denys), man failed to direct his natural energies towards his true end.[45] Man's self-love is now turned towards sensual gratification, but God in his Providence introduces into the life of fallen man a counter-principle, at once penalty and purgation: *odunê*, 'pain'.[46] It is indeed as a dialectic of pleasure and pain that Maximus presents the Fall's consequence, following as these do on man's decisive preferring of sense pleasure to its spiritual counterpart. Man's nature is now turned toward passion, corruptibility and death: this is his curse.[47]

More specifically, Maximus maintains that fallen man is ensnared in three basic evils, whence issue the entire array of vices and passions. And these are: *agnoia*, 'ignorance', whereby

---

[41]Ibid. 45, (PG 91, 1353CD).

[42]L. Thunberg, *Microcosm and Mediator*, op. cit., pp. 161-163.

[43]*Epistle* 2 (PG 91, 396D).

[44]Ibid.

[45]*Quaestiones ad Thalassium*, prologue (PG 90, 253B). Cf. the Scholia to the Pseudo-Denys at PG 4, 304D, and the comments of H. U. von Balthasar, *Kosmische Liturgie*, op. cit., p. 143.

[46]*Quaestiones ad Thalassium*, prologue (PG 90, 256A).

[47]Ibid. 45 (PG 90, 408C).

he fails to realise what is truly good, seeking rather for satisfaction in the corruptible realm; *philautia*, 'self-love', the root of all vitiated dispositions which arise at the behest of a multiplicity of impulses mediated from the sensuous realm by the will; and *turannis*, 'tyranny', both of the passions in the individual soul and of some human beings over against others. Love for God perverted into constant self-love at once excludes love for the neighbour.[48] And so, in Thunberg's concluding words on Maximus' general anthropology:

> Maximus thus develops the consequences of fallen man's dependence upon the dialectic of pleasure and pain in a personal way, though he is in general agreement with the ascetic Christian tradition before him.[49]

Psychology

Maximus' psychology is basically trichotomist: that is, he understands the soul as having, basically, three main aspects. Before investigating these, however, it may be well to remind ourselves of the wider context. Though man's microcosmic character consists in his simultaneous relationship to, on the one hand, God and the intelligible world, and, on the other, the world of senses, Maximus treats this distinction in a positive manner. He stresses that the human unity integrates mind and body into a common whole, of which mind is the spiritual subject. As Thunberg points out, there is for Maximus a certain analogy between man's place in the cosmos and that of the soul within the human totality. Just as man is called to mediate a divine vocation to the world as a whole — a world which can only *be* a whole by virtue of man's unifying activity, so also the soul is called to mediate man's spiritual vocation to the body, while the different aspects of the soul bear investigating *both* in relation to what is common to the soul in its entirety *and* in relation to its special position, and function, within the richer

---

[48]*Epistle* 2, especially at PG 91, 397A.
[49]L. Thunberg, *Microcosm and Mediator*, op. cit., p. 171.

totality which is the human being as a whole.[50] And so the basic dichotomy between the intelligible world and the world of sense, taken for granted by the Greek Fathers but frequently excoriated in the modern period as a source of a theologically damaging metaphysical dualism, is in Maximus the presupposition, rather, for a series of what he terms 'natural movements' which mediate between the noetic and the material orders and so, in a way, overcome their difference. While the motion of sense is synthetic, receiving from visible things, in the form of symbols, some insight into their *logoi* which sense refers on to reason; the motion of reason analytic, distinguishing according to causality; and the motion of the mind simple and direct, yet Maximus presents one fundamental natural movement as travelling upwards through all of these, with what is grasped by one motion so functioning in the next as to serve the final outcome of the whole process in God — and thus, as Thunberg comments, with reference to *Ambigua* 10, 'the final transcendence even of the basic dichotomy'.[51]

Maximus' trichotomist doctrine of soul can take various forms—for example, apart from the trio of natural movements which we have just encountered, he can also work with the triad *rational soul* (reasonable, intellectual, imperishable, immortal), *non-rational soul* (appetitive, sensible), *non-sensible soul* (vegetative, nutritive) whereby man unites in himself the characteristic animating principles of, respectively, rational beings, animals and plants. But the predominant threesome in Maximus is that of the soul's *rational, irascible* and *concupiscible* elements, a trinity found almost universally in the philosophical writing of the ancient Greeks and taken over, lock, stock and barrel by their Christian successors, the Fathers. What is distinctive in Maximus is not this tripartite picture of the soul as such, but what he does with it: his insistence that each of the soul's elements has a positive function, restored in Christ, and, furthermore, that all of these elements are *equally* distorted in fallen man, even if it was through the senses that man received that influence on him which would prove so malign.

[50]Ibid., p. 180.
[51]Ibid., p. 182; cf. *Ambigua* 10 (PG 91, 116A).

Against a complex background in Platonic, Aristotelean, Stoic and patristic thought, Maximus singled out those features of a precedent tradition which most attracted him. In his biblical interpretation, largely 'Alexandrian' as this is, the trichotomy of *to logistikon* (rational), *to thumoeides* (irascible), and *to epithumêtikon* (concupiscible) is set to use in ways both negative — underlining man's internal disintegration, and positive or at least neutral — as an expression of unity in differentiation. In *Questiones ad Thalassium* 27, for instance, Maximus treats the animals, reptiles and birds on the great sheet in Peter's vision in the Acts of the Apostles as symbolising the variety of human passions.[52] The creeping animals stand for those whose concupiscible element is attached to worldly things; the wild beasts those whose irascible element is stirred up to the danger of other people; and the birds those whose rational element is puffed up in pride.[53] Yet Maximus at once goes on to make clear that these faculties are not evil in themselves; whether they work for good or for evil turns altogether on their use. Through Peter's sacrifice they are transformed, so that desire-filled souls now long for what is heavenly; anger-filled souls become benevolent towards their fellow-men, and proud souls finish up meek and lovers of God.[54]

Replying to Thalassius on another occasion, Maximus gives an example of the positive significance of the triad. In the Second Book of Chronicles we read how, during the campaign against Judah of Sennacherib, king of Assyria, Hezekiah planned 'with his officers and his mighty men' to staunch the flow of the water-springs outside the city.[55] Maximus interprets this by way of anthropological allegory: Hezekiah, ruling in Jerusalem, is the mind ruling in the soul, and the officers and mighty men the soul's three faculties, spoken of in these terms because they are the soul's premier powers and provide the starting-point for all its movements. A right use of them will extend to faith

---

[52]Acts 10, 12ff.
[53]*Quaestiones ad Thalassium* 27 (PG 90, 356C).
[54]Ibid. at PG 90, 356CD.
[55]II Chronicles 32, 2-3.

(for the rational element), charity (for the concupiscible element), and peace (for the irascible element).[56]

The more neutral evaluation of the irascible and concupiscible elements is illustrated in Maximus' exegesis of Nehemiah 7, 67, where the Jewish historian describes the men-servants and maid-servants of those returned from exile in Babylon. These Maximus interprets as anger and concupiscence, for which the mind ought to take care, so that anger becomes a ceaseless activity of desire and concupiscence likewise desire for divine things: by grace these servants may thus become full members of the community.[57] For Maximus, the reason why Scripture allows for this kind of allegorical interpretation is that God has made it so: an understanding of the human situation is one of the reasons why God has set the Bible before us. Man needs to know the truth about how the different elements in his differentiated unity can both damage him but also help him by serving as the building-blocks of a positive relationship to his divine goal.[58]

Thunberg proceeds to illustrate this in terms of each basic facet of the soul. The concupiscible element concerns desire, *epithumia*, which, according to Maximus played the chief part in the Fall. In post-lapsarian man, *to epithumêtikon* is frequently in a disturbed condition, which is why the Letter to the Ephesians can describe the old nature as 'corrupt through deceitful lusts'.[59] Yet there is also such a thing as a true desire, activating the concupiscible element in a praiseworthy way, turning it, in fact, into joy, symbolised for Maximus by David's dancing before the ark, and John the Baptist's moving in the womb of his mother.[60] When the concupiscible faculty is properly used, it becomes the vehicle of the love of God whereby the man who desires God ardently stays indissolubly linked to what he desires.[61]

---

[56] *Quaestione ad Thalassium* 49 (PG 90, 449BC).
[57] Ibid., 55 (PG 90, 549AB).
[58] L. Thunberg, *Microcosm and Mediator*, op. cit., pp. 210-211.
[59] Ephesians 4, 22; cf. *Epistle* 32 (PG 91, 625D).
[60] *Ambigua* 6 (PG 91, 1068A).
[61] *Quaestiones ad Thalassium* 49 (PG 90, 449B).

The irascible element, while sometimes simply inwardly diseased is more often treated by Maximus in the context of social relationships. When *to thumoeides*, the power of aggression, is placed in the service of *philautia*, self-love, it produces tyranny, not just of one passion over the entire soul but also of oneself over against other people.[62] But by a good use of the irascible element, the soul clings to the peace of God, strengthening that movement of desire for God which ought to animate (as already noted) the concupiscible element. In Letter 2, the power of anger, thus transformed, is said to produce a fighting spirit for the attainment of our divine end.[63]

So far as the rational element in the soul is concerned, while *to logistikon* depends for any vicious exercise on the impulses it receives from the other two elements, Maximus speaks of its own chief misuse in negative terms: and this is *agnoia*, ignorance of its own divine Cause and Goal, which prepares it to fall victim to these imaginations from without. Though ignorance, along with folly and price, are, for Maximus, characteristic *results* of the misuse of the rational faculty, governed ultimately by egoism — the supreme vice of the concupiscible element, and the mother of all vices no matter where found, in another sense he can speak of ignorance, seated in *to logistikon*, as the *source* of all viciousness. For when, by an act of his own freedom, man turns his attention from God to the world of the senses, he empties himself of that natural relationship to God which is furnished by the connexion between the uncreated Logos and the created *logos* of his own human nature. So ignorance is both cause and effect of moral evil, in different aspects. The special importance of a good use of *to logistikon* is that it establishes direct relation with God. By conversion, faith is born in it, filling that faculty with knowledge and prudence. Enlightened and transformed it seeks God by intellectual enquiry, assisted by the virtues proper to legitimate use of its sister faculties.[64]

---

[62]E.g. *Epistle* 2 (PG 91, 397A).

[63]Ibid. at PG 91, 397B.

[64]L. Thunberg, *Microcosm and Mediator*, op. cit., p. 216, with reference to *Centuriae de Caritate* III. 3; and *Quaestiones ad Thalassium* 39 (PG 90, 392B); *Orationis dominicae expositio* at PG 90, 896C) and *Epistle* 2 (PG 91, 397B).

Just as the misuse of any one of these elements tends to involve the degradation of all the rest, and thereby of the mind itself as the spiritual subject of the whole person, so the mind as man's spiritual subject should use all the faculties for the unification and re-integration of man through Christ. As Thunberg puts it:

> The mind should tend towards God, strengthened as it were by its irascible element and aflame with love through the extreme desire of the concupiscible ... The reintegration of man and the fulfilment of his purpose through Christ is a matter not only of the intellect but also of will, emotion and temper — in order that he may arrive at a true relationship to God as man's Cause and End, a relationship carried by the will and manifested not only in 'reasonable' communion, though this is primary, but also in virtues, which engage the whole of man.[65]

But what then of the place of *will*, mentioned here *en passant*, in Maximus' doctrine of man? As some of the main terms, and concepts used in Maximus' account of human volition have already been described, with Piret's help, in the context of Christology, we can concentrate on some new elements.[66]

Although Maximus did not make perfectly clear his understanding of the inter-relation of mind and will,[67] the general direction of his thought is fairly plain. Both mind, *nous*, and will, *thelêsis*, are transcendent faculties in respect to the three 'parts' of the soul discussed under the heading of Maximian psychology so far. Just as man's volitional life cannot be identified, simply, with the functions of the concupiscible and irascible parts, so his intellectual life is not purely the work of the rational part alone.[68] As we have already noted in the

---

[65]L. Thunberg, *Microcosm and Mediator*, op. cit., pp. 219-220.

[66]See above, pp. 102-104.

[67]Polycarp Sherwood speaks of his 'weakness' in this respect, in idem., *The Earlier Ambigua of St Maximus the Confessor* (Rome 1955), p. 154.

[68]L. Thunberg, *Microcosm and Mediator*, op. cit., p. 222.

discussion of Maximus' christological doctrine, will is a rational appetency, belonging to man in virtue of his (intelligible) nature. Though *nous* carries the image of God, willing or self-determination is its heart.[69] The mind is active in relation to the goals to which it is directed, whether this be by *thelêma phusikon*, 'natural will', the rational faculty of self-determination inherent in man, or *thelêma gnômikon*, 'gnomic will', that more ambiguous 'habit' of desire which individuals acquire through use of their capacity for self-determination. The ambivalence of the latter (and so Maximus' eventual decision to exclude it from his account of the make-up of Christ's humanity)[70] derives from the fact that whereas, in Thunberg's words:

> the relationship between the mind and 'natural will' is one which is coherent with the rational character of both as signs of the divine image in man, ... the relationship between the mind and 'gnomic will' may lead either to an irrational disintegration of man (fallen and individualised) or to a restoration of man as directed in accordance with the rational principle of human nature (its *logos phuseôs*).[71]

The Maximian comparison and contrast of *gnômê* with natural will plays much the same rôle in Maximus' thinking as does the couplet free will and freedom (*liberum arbitrium* — *libertas*) in that of Augustine. Free will, however important in the concrete circumstances of human existence, must eventually give way, in its radical indeterminacy, to that permanency of orientation which characterises the saints. Though the human power of self-determination has to be exerted in a personal, 'existential' fashion, it serves, ultimately a higher end. In *Ambigua 7*,

---

[69]Ibid., p. 223.

[70]Ibid., pp. 225-226. Thunberg notes that, in the early *Commentary on the Pater*, though allowing Christ a gnomic will, Maximus speaks of it as without any revolt in relation to human nature from the very outset. In this sense, it effectively coincides with 'natural will', and hence, when the term *gnômê* is used by way of contrast to *thelêma physikon* it is, in the later works, denied of Christ, on the grounds of its uncertainty and ambivalence: ibid., p. 228, with particular reference to the *Disputatio cum Pyrrho* at PG 91, 308D-309A.

[71]L. Thunberg, *Microcosm and Mediator*, op. cit., p. 225-226.

Maximus proposes that true abiding in the good is finally achieved only through a voluntary transcending of human self-determination, which is, however, at the same moment, its 'perfect fulfilment according to the capacity of its nature'.[72]

The building-blocks of Maximus' doctrine of will, his basic terms and concepts, are helpfully arranged by Thunberg in the form of a narrative: the story of action, its genesis, development and final enactment. Actually willing begins in *boulêsis*, wishing, which Maximus defines as an 'imaginative appetency', *orexis phantastikê*.[73] It involves setting a goal, *telos*, which the acting person thus intends. Next comes *zêtêsis*, search, where the rational faculty, conscious of its goal, makes an effort to reach it,[74] both by *skepsis*, a general survey of relevant means,[75] and *boulê*, deliberating about particular means within that survey.[76] This leads to judgment, *krisis*,[77] which can be mistaken owing to wrong disposition, *gnômê*. Good judgment is *diakrisis*, 'discernment'.[78] Judgment eventuates in choice or decision, *prohairesis*, which is the summation of our efforts of personal willing.[79] That expresses itself in *ormê*, impulse, an outgoing activity which takes as its goal the action to be performed itself.[80] And *ormê*, finally, issues in practical action, termed by Maximus *krêsis*, 'use'.[81]

Through the Fall man's capacity for self-determination via this process is perverted in such a way that he is now predisposed to its misuse. The Fall forms in man a sinful disposition of gnomic will, which also affects natural will, the volitional aspect of nature itself. Accepting for himself the misuse of *gnômê*, the

---

[72]*Ambigua* 7 (PG 91, 1076B), cited in ibid., p. 231.

[73]*Opuscula theologica et polemica* 1 (PG 91, 13B).

[74]E.g. Epistle 2 (PG 91, 397AB).

[75]E.g. *Opuscula theologica et polemica* 1 (PG 91, 24A).

[76]Ibid., at 16B.

[77]Ibid. at 13A; 16B; 20A; 24A.

[78]*Centuriae de Caritate* II. 26.

[79]*Opuscula theologica et polemica* 1 (PG 91, 16BC).

[80]Ibid. at 20A; 24A.

[81]R. A. Gauthier, 'S. Maxime le Confesseur et la psychologie de l'acte humain', *Recherches de Théologie Ancienne et Médiévale* 21 (1954), pp. 74-76.

individual person deviates from the natural course of relations with God and neighbour. As Thunberg memorably puts it:

> The fallen *gnômê* as it were *cuts the common human nature into pieces*, since it divides men from each other because of their different opinions and imaginations, which again instigate contrary actions. And this split is, at the same time, a revolt through *gnômê* within nature itself, since there is *no consistency* in its appearance.[82]

Disintegration through the Passions

For Maximus, just as charity sums up and unifies all virtues, so its inverted image, self-love, crowns, grotesquely, all vices. *Philautia* is not only the apex of the hierarchy of vices, it is also the general attitude which finds expression in them all. And so, in the *Centuriae de Caritate*, Maximus calls self-love the 'mother' of both the passions and the vices, as well as the passions' fount and origin.[83] A person filled with self-love has, for this text, all the passions in embryo.[84] Both here and in the prologue to the *Quaestiones ad Thalassium*, Maximus elaborates a grand scheme of vices, for which *philautia* forms the organising centre. Essentially, Maximus has developed hints thrown out by a number of his Christian, Jewish and pagan predecessors, all of whom had regarded love of self as potentially disastrous for the soul's progress: notable here, as Irénée Hausherr has shown, were, among non-Christian writers Plato and Philo Judaeus, and, within the theological tradition, Clement of Alexandria, Evagrius, the Cappadocians, Ephrem Syrus, the Pusedo-Denys, Dorotheus of Gaza and Maximus' friend Thalassius himself — quite a *catena*.[85] One intriguing additional possibility is an influence on Maximus from Augustine, in the course of the

---

[82]L. Thunberg, *Microcosm and Mediator*, op. cit., p. 241 (emphasis original), with reference to *Epistle* 2 (PG 91, 396D) and *Orationis dominicae expositio* at PG 90, 893B.

[83]*Centuriae de Caritate* II. 8; II. 59; III. 57.

[84]Ibid., III. 8.

[85]I. Hausherr, S. J., *Philautie. De la tendresse pour soi à la charité selon saint Maxime le Confesseur* (Rome 1952), pp. 11-42.

former's North Africa sojourn — for Augustine stresses that self-love must, crucially, have a right direction if it is not to become perversely deformed into its own opposite, an evil self-love which expresses the very essence of sinfulness itself.[86]

In both East and West, sinful self-love is at once a matter of sensuality and of pride — though the Eastern tradition, nowhere clearer than in Evagrius, is to place sensuality first; the Western, exemplified classically in Augustine, to give priority to pride. Here Maximus is typically Oriental. Self-love shows itself first and foremost in an inner affection of an irrational and thus disordered kind for bodily sensations and the sensuous world: this in turn generates all the other vices, the culmination of which is pride.[87] However, it must be carefully noted here — so as to save Maximus from any charge of Manichaean distaste for the bodily realm — that self-love can be thus defined not because the body is itself evil, but because 'attachment to the body prevents man's entire attachment to his divine end'.[88] The point about good (*noera*, 'spiritual') self-love is that, by contrast with its vicious counterpart, it orders the whole of man towards a transcendent end, enabling the ordered microcosm to act as universal mediator.

What are, then, for Maximus the vices that branch out from the common root of distorted self-love? In the *Centuries on Charity*, Maximus speaks first of the eight vices identified by Evagrius of Pontus, and then adds four more to the list. Though indebted to the classification of human action made by Evagrius, who was the single most important source for his ascetic doctrine, Maximus lived at a time when, in the Eastern church, the monastic tradition was still adding — and very occasionally subtracting — itemised vices to — or from — the catalogue inherited from Evagrius. Just as in the West, Gregory the Great established a system of seven deadly sins, by

[86]R. Holte, *Béatitude et sagesse. Saint Augustin et le problème de la fin de l'homme dans la philosophie ancienne* (Paris 1962), pp. 238ff. For the possible debt of Maximus to Augustine, see L. Thunberg, *Microcosm and Mediator*, op. cit., pp. 250-252, and G. C. Berthold, 'Did Maximus the Confessor Know Augustine?', *Studia Patristica* XVII, 1 (Oxford 1982), pp. 14-17.

[87]L. Thunberg, *Microcosm and Mediator*, op. cit., pp. 257-261.

[88]Ibid., p. 262.

reconstructing, in a restrictive way, Evagrius' hierarchy of eight vices, so John Climacus in his treatise *The Ladder of Paradise* also opted for seven, whereas it was more usual in the Byzantine context to expand the list — a consequence, according to Thunberg, of the monastic character of the system of vices there, open as this was, then, to fresh influence from practical ascetic experience.[89] Maximus arranges his own list of twelve vices, as his enumeration of the passions, in terms of his tripartite doctrine of the soul — the three basic elements, concupiscible, irascible, rational,[90] even though other principles of distinguishing between vicious impulses may also sometimes be at work in his writing, in a subordinate way.[91] According to Thunberg, the vices Maximus adds over and above the Evagrian eight — namely, rapacity (*pleonexia*), resentfulness (*mnêsikakia*), envy (*phthonos*) and slander (*katalalia*) — are only intended by him as elaborations of the original octet, on which, in fact, he concentrates. This licenses Thunberg's curtailment of his exposition of 'disintegration through the vices' to those shared by Maximus with Evagrius.

The most basic and most bodily of the Evagrian vices is *gastrimargia* — gluttony, a vice of the concupiscible element yet one with multiple consequences for the intellectual aspect of the soul, as Maximus stresses. In the *Quaestiones ad Thalassium*, Michal, the daughter of Saul, is, rather ungraciously, interpreted allegorically as gluttony, on the grounds that she brought up five sons for Adriel — in other words, a five-fold misuse of the senses by the mind.[92] Falling likewise within the ambit of *to epithumêtikon* is *porneia*, fornication, which Maximus, like

---

[89]Ibid., p. 273.

[90]See *Centuriae de Caritate* I. 64-667; III. 3; III.20.

[91]Thunberg mentions in this connexion such subsidiary means of classification as: vices corresponding to the four cardinal virtues of Plato's *Republic*; vices of body, and of soul (or those in the soul, those in the body, and those concerned with the body); vices issuing from the senses, the body's condition and the memory; the Stoic scheme of a dialectic between pleasure and grief, present conditions and future expectations; vices manifesting irrational love, or irrational hate; the notion of a sevenfold fall of human nature: idem., *Microcosm and Mediator*, op. cit., pp. 275-276.

[92]*Quaestiones ad Thalassium* 65 (PG 90, 768B).

Evagrius, links with gluttony as well as carelessness in physical contact.[93] Avarice, *philarguria*, Maximus describes as the passion of a man who receives with joy but gives away with grief.[94] Though belonging mainly to the concupiscible faculty it characteristically expands to affect the whole person. Next come grief and wrath, *lupê* and *orgê*, which together make up the bridge that leads from *to epithumêtikon* to the irascible part, *to thumoeides*. Grief for Maximus is a lack of pleasure closely related to both resentment and envy, while anger is self-explanatory.[95] Accidie or listlessness, *akêdia*, often thought of as the classic monastic vice, Maximus links to grief.[96] While located basically in the irascible faculty, Maximus emphasises that accidie takes hold of all aspects of the soul, and for this reason is harder to bear than any other passion.[97] With vain-glory, *xenodoxia*, we encounter a vice seated chiefly in the rational faculty. For Maximus, vanity is a negation of true knowledge, binding the rational element in the soul and destroying already established virtues.[98] Finally, the vice of pride, *huperêphania*, inhering in the rational faculty, consummates a wrong relationship both to God and to one's neighbour. For Maximus, pride denies the divine Cause both of virtue and nature, refusing to glorify God and to admit human frailty. It is overcome by humility, which rules out a misplaced boldness in relation to God and others, and by knowledge of one's own weakness and God's strength.[99] For Maximus, the peculiar menace of pride is that, rooted as it is in *to logistikon*, it can threaten man even in the state of *theôria*, the contemplative knowledge of God.[100]

In their sum, the vices cause division, not only in the individual person by destroying the unity of the human

---

[93] *Centuriae de Caritate* II. 19.

[94] Ibid., III. 76.

[95] L. Thunberg, *Microcosm and Mediator*, op. cit., p. 288.

[96] *Centuriae de Caritate* I. 52.

[97] Ibid., I. 67.

[98] Ibid., 46; *Quaestiones et dubia* 23 (PG 90, 804A).

[99] *Quaestiones ad Thalassium* 64 (PG 90, 916B); ibid., 54 (PG 90, 513B); *Centuriae de Caritate* III. 87.

[100] *Quaestiones et dubia* 35 (PG 90, 813D-816A).

composite, created as this is with its fundamental principle and
purpose set towards God. In addition, they have the effect of
dividing human beings from each other, since all men are
called by God's providence to be united around this common
human principle and purpose'.[101] The passions and vices can
be distinguished, in fact, in terms of whether they adversely
affect relations with God or with neighbour, while in the *Liber
asceticus* Maximus describes how Christ, who is free from all
philautia, was first obedient to the commandment of love for
God, overcoming in the desert the temptations of the
concupiscible element, and then, in his Passion, showed also
his obedience to the commandment of love of neighbour, by
defeating the temptations of the irascible faculty.[102] As Thunberg
sums up Maximus' account of the vices and anticipates that of
the virtues:

> Now we see that … (the) microcosmic character of man
> on the one hand leads to vicious destruction, when self-
> love rules in him, for self-love invites all the passions to
> perform their disintegrating function in accordance with
> the differentiated nature of man himself; but on the other
> that man's truly microcosmic character is fully established,
> when love in both its aspects rules in man, for love invites
> all the virtues to perform their task of transformation of
> the different human faculties, through their victory over
> the vices and their good use of these faculties.[103]

Reintegration through the Virtues

Until quite recently, an account of the good life in terms of
virtues — dispositions constitutive of human flourishing as
construed in the popular, as well as literary and, ultimately,
theological tradition of the human city — would have been
regarded as impossibly old hat by moral philosophers. Today,
however, thanks notably to the salvage work of the Northern

---

[101]L. Thunberg, *Microcosm and Mediator*, op. cit., p. 197.

[102]*Liber asceticus* 10-15 (PG 90, 920A-924C).

[103]L. Thunberg, *Microcosm and Mediator*, op. cit., p. 301.

Irish philosopher Alasdair McIntyre, himself a recent convert to Catholicism, an ethics of the virtues is taken seriously once more.[104] A disprized, if not despised, aspect of the work of Plato, Aristotle, Augustine, Thomas Aquinas and Dante, has been re-evaluated and found, by some, invaluable. The process of *ressourcement* should extend to the Greek-speaking Fathers and ecclesiastical writers of the early centuries — and not least to St Maximus.

Maximus' hierarchy of virtues is even more closely modelled on that of Evagrius than are the spreading branches of his tree of vices. In Maximus' list, at the opening of the *Centuries on Charity*, we find faith, the fear of God, self-mastery, patience and long-suffering, hope in God, detachment and love.[105] Differences from Evagrius are minimal with one vital exception. Love is the absolute terminus of Maximus' list, though he adds straight afterward a chapter on contemplative knowledge. In Evagrius, on the other hand, love simply concludes the practical life, and leads on to the higher virtue of *gnôsis*. We shall return to this, but must note first the existence of other, if less emphasised, catalogues of the virtues of Maximus — which add to the total: humility, *tapeinôsis*; meekness, *praotês*; gentleness, *praüpatheia*; mercy, *eleos*; poverty, *aktêmosunê*, as well as the Platonic tetrad of courage, temperance and justice, and other virtues defined by the simple negation (using the 'alpha privative') of various vices, such as lack of resentfulness, lack of wrath, lack of envy, of vainglory, of avarice. Compared with Evagrius, Maximus is not especially concerned with showing the correspondence between particular vices and virtues, possibly for the reason which Thunberg adduces with reference to the two aspects of the love-command, love of God and love of neighbour.

> Since the different vices can be understood as belonging to these two types of self-love, performing its disintegrating function in man, the corresponding virtues, as positive

---

[104]A. McIntyre, *After Virtue: A Study in Moral Theology* (London 1981). See also, idem., *Whose Justice? Whose Rationality?* (London 1988).

[105] *Centuriae de Caritate* I. 4.

expressions of the two aspects of integrating love, must be more than mere counterparts to their vices. They must be seen as manifold expressions of one and the same love, in its double character.[106]

It was mentioned that Maximus places love, *agapê*, not merely at the summit of the virtues of the practical life, as in Evagrius, but at the apex of the virtues *tout court*. In the wider sense in which Maximus uses that key term of Christian ethics and spirituality, love already involves a preference for the knowledge of God above all other things, and in any case it has the power to transport the human being,[107] not least in his or her intellectual capacity, into a state of full communion with God. In comparison with Evagrius, Maximus' understanding of the rôle of detachment, *apatheia*, in growth in holiness, is not so much negative — a matter of escape from the tyranny of the passions (though this aspect is certainly affirmed), as positive — a matter of using all one's faculties with a view to the divine goal, in the service of love.[108] Compared with Evagrius, then, Maximus is less interested in establishing an equilibrium between the virtues and vices, and more concerned with underlining the positive functions of the soul's different faculties, as developed in a multi-faceted living out of the virtues. Or, in Thunberg's words, Maximus is not, like Evagrius, interested in

a departure from the lower elements in man, but in a restoration and re-integration of man as a whole.[109]

[106]L. Thunberg, *Microcosm and Mediator*, op. cit., pp. 315-316.

[107]*Centuriae de Caritate* I. 1.

[108]*Quaestiones ad Thalassium* 54 (PG 90, 512A), where the habitus of detachment is also a state in which the 'face' of the soul, lifted up towards God in praise, is said to be 'formed by many and varying virtues'.

[109]L. Thunberg, *Microcosm and Mediator*, op. cit., p. 327. For Evagrius, with his sharply dualistic anthropology, the virtues conquer the vices and so establish in the soul an equilibrium which enables the mind to devote all its intellectual attention in love to God.

It is because this re-integration can only happen through *agapê* that love is for Maximus the integrating keystone in the house of the virtues.

In fact, Maximus' presentation of *agapê* lends itself to investigation from three angles: charity in relation to other virtues; charity as love of God and love of neighbour, in relation to the faculties of the soul; charity in its relationship to knowledge and to deification.[110]

First: for Maximus, charity unifies the other virtues. In *Letter* 2 he claims for her that she possesses or includes all the other virtues, in such a way that no 'form' of good can be found outside of her.[111] Not that charity is some kind of perfect substitute for the other virtues; rather, charity unifies them in a higher synthesis, supporting the human being by their strength.[112] The virtues, after all, as the good use of man's natural powers are never superfluous as expressions of human nature. In the old conundrum, *erôs* or *agapê* ?, Maximus' position is clear: human charity is the marriage of natural desire and aspiration, *erôs*, with divine gift, *agapê*,[113] the two of which, becoming one, form in man an integrated love, fulfilling the virtues, and enabling man as microcosm to perform his function of mediation.[114]

In the second place, Maximus, in the context of the virtues, both differentiates love of God and love of neighbour and unites them, regarding love of neighbour as included in the love of God. As he puts it in the first of the *Centuries on Charity*:

> The one who loves God cannot help but love also every man as himself even though he is displeased by the passions of those who are not yet purified. Thus when he

[110]Ibid.

[111]*Epistle* 2 (PG 91, 393C-396B).

[112]As noted by J. Pegon in *Maxime le Confesseur, Centuries sur la Charité* (Paris-Lyons 1945), p. 54.

[113]Cf. P. Sherwood, O.S.B., *St Maximus the Confessor, The Ascetic Life, and The Four Centuries on Charity* (London 1955), p. 83.

[114]L. Thunberg, *Microcosm and Mediator*, op. cit., p. 330.

sees their conversion and amendment, he rejoices with an unbounded and unspeakable joy.[115]

Negatively, love of God excludes hatred for one's neighbour;[116] positively, love for God causes love of neighbour.[117] Indeed, the person who is detached and now lives by charity loves all with an equal love, a condition which Maximus formulates in the paradox that 'he who loves nothing human, loves all men'.[118] As Thunberg glosses this last claim of the *Centuries on Charity:*

> He who devotes his loving desire entirely to God is not affected by any partial attachment to the world, and is thus able to love all men equally in limitation of God's love for all.[119]

Moreover, not only are the virtues for Maximus forms of love in both of these aspects, Godward and 'neighbourward', they are also virtues of one or another of the elements of the soul — thus showing that, while love integrates it does not thereby occlude the differentiated character of the human microcosm. For example, in *Letter* 2, Maximus speaks of the concupiscible faculty as itself transformed by charity into a holy desire for God, moving man towards his goal.[120] Again, charity to one's neighbour produces in the irascible faculty the virtues of long-suffering and patience;[121] such neighbourly love, according to Maximus, comes to qualify *to thumoeides* itself.[122] And where *to logistikon*, the rational faculty is concerned, the fear of God, presupposing the knowledge of God in faith, leads to a form of humility, namely reverence, which is a virtue of that element.[123] Likewise the intellectual activity of what Maximus terms 'pure

[115] *Centuries on Charity* I. 13.

[116] Ibid., II. 15-16.

[117] Ibid., II. 9.

[118] Ibid., III. 37.

[119] L. Thunberg, *Microcosm and Mediator*, op. cit., p. 333.

[120] *Epistle* 2 (PG 91, 397B).

[121] *Centuriae de caritate* I. 40; IV. 55.

[122] Ibid., IV. 15.

[123] Ibid., I. 81-82.

prayer' is an expression of the love for God.[124] The *Centuries on Charity* IV. 15 gives lapidary expression to Maximus' ideal of our logical worship:

> The soul is moved reasonably when its concupiscible element is qualified by self-mastery, its irascible element cleaves to love and turns away from hate, and the rational element lives with God through prayer and spiritual contemplation.

Lastly, Maximus' doctrine of charity can be expounded in terms of love's contribution to man's deification. Charity alone, for Maximus, brings man into a condition of mystical union with God, but it does not do so without some positive relationship to the other supernatural theological virtues; faith and hope. Though Maximus has a clear teaching on faith, which he regards as a baptismal gift, at once power and calling,[125] and also a true knowledge of things that are above mind and reason, albeit one that flows from undemonstrable principles,[126] he has much less to say about hope.[127] In Letter 2, however, he speaks of it as pointing to the object of both faith and charity by asserting the substantiveness of the divine realities.[128] Effectively, Maximus regards faith, hope and charity as inter-related on the model of one of his favourite triads — *archê* — *mesotês* — *telos*, beginning, middle, end — a trio characteristic, in his thought about created beings. As Thunberg, at any rate, interprets the enigmatic *Centuries on Charity* III. 100 on this point:

> Virtually, ... faith is attached to the beginning — it lays the foundation of Christian life — while hope performs a task of mediation, since it indicates that which is believed and

---

[124]Ibid., II. 7.

[125]*Mystagogia* 1; 24 (PG 91, 668A; 705B).

[126]*Capitula theologica et economica* I. 9 (PG 90, 1085D).

[127]J. Heintjes, 'Een onbekende leeraar van ascese en mystiek: Sint Maximus Confessor', *Studia Catholica* 11 (1935), pp. 189ff.

[128]*Epistle* 2 (PG 91, 393D-395B).

makes real that which is the object of love. And charity is above all related, to the end, the consummation of all.[129]

For charity alone grants man full enjoyment, *apolausis*, of what is believed on and hoped for:[130] that is, in the term hallowed for this subject since Gregory of Nyssa, mystical communion with God, what Maximus elsewhere calls 'participation in supernatural divine things'.[131] Whereas such communing-love is conditioned by believing-knowledge, and in turn conditions that knowledge, were we to hand the palm to one of them, it is for Maximus love that is the higher gift. As Thunberg understands *Centuries on Charity* I. 100:

> According to Maximus, even the illuminated mind seeks, in its desirous love, for something in God which it is not allowed to find, but in this very desire and love it is, nevertheless, allowed to be united with him.[132]

In all this, little if anything has been said explicitly about Jesus Christ. In fact for Maximus, the work of integration whereby man serves God by a unified effort of all his faculties is also a continuing incarnation of the Logos in mankind. Or, as Thunberg puts it, there is, in Maximus:

> a clear correspondence between the integrating function of love as a unified movement towards God as man's true end and Christ's own act of differentiation, through which he as the Logos allows himself to be incarnate in the manifold human virtues themselves.[133]

In itself, the idea of an incarnation of Christ in the virtues is not original to Maximus. Talk of the birth and formation of Christ the Word of God in the hearts of the believers was shared by a

---

[129]. Thunberg, *Microcosm and Mediator*, op. cit., p. 338.

[130]*Epistle* 2 (PG 91, 393D-396C).

[131]*Quaestiones ad Thalassium* 59 (PG 90, 608D).

[132]L. Thunberg, *Microcosm and Mediator*, op. cit., p. 341.

[133]Ibid.

number of the early Fathers.[134] For Origen, who tried to think speculatively about this process, while man has virtues, Christ is personally identical with them, so that the Christian imitation of Jesus Christ entails some kind of participation in Christ's very being.[135] Gregory of Nyssa, accordingly, regards the virtues as the 'colours' of the divine image in man,[136] while Evagrius treats them as media of communication with Christ insofar as by means of them man reaches *apatheia* — his distinctive emphasis.[137] Maximus builds on the work of these predecessors by affirming a divine incarnation in the virtuous living of man. More specifically, it is faith, as the source of virtues, which for Maximus is the mother of the presence of the Logos in believers.[138] Those who keep the commandments, as Thunberg explains:

> communicate morally with the Logos, by developing virtues which are natural, since they imply a right relationship of these Christians to their own principle of nature.[139]

True, Maximus also stresses that, beyond the ethical striving of the 'practical life', the believer will also be raised up into a quality of contemplative insight higher than all commandments, a perception of the one God who is the source of principles and rules in their multiplicity: Maximus' version of the *Shema*, 'The Lord our God is one Lord'.[140] But the divinity known in mystical contemplation is precisely the God of the

[134]K. Rahner, 'Die Gottesgeburt. Die Lehre der Kirchenväter von der Geburt Christi im Herzen des Gläubigen', *Zeitschrift für katholische Theologie* 59 (1935), pp. 339-383.

[135]H. Crouzel, *Théologie de l'image de Dieu chez Origène* (Paris 1956), pp. 228-229; cf. also M. Harl, *Origène et la fonction révélatrice du Verbe incarné* (Paris 1958), pp. 291ff.

[136]J. Daniélou, *Platonisme et théologie mystique. Essai sur la doctrine spirituelle de Grégoire de Nysse* (Paris 1954²), p. 101.

[137]H. Gressmann, *Nonnenspiegel und Mönchsspiegel des Evagrios Pontikos* (Leipzig 1913), p. 163.

[138]*Quaestiones ad Thalassium* 40 (PG 90, 1068A).

[139]L. Thunberg, *Microcosm and Mediator*, op. cit., pp. 347-348.

[140]*Quaestiones et Dubia* 61 (PG 90, 833BC); cf. Deuteronomy 6, 4.

commandments, so moral perfection, in Maximus, constitutes an abiding aspect of man's deification, not a stage which has to be reached and then transcended.[141] The flowering of our natural capacities as a moral expression of the divine attributes is also our unification with God through desiring charity. Indeed, in his second *Letter*, Maximus even allows that deifying love, uniting both God with the man and individual human beings among themselves, justifies a communication of idioms — what he calls in this context a 'relational exchange', *antidosis schetikê* — comparable to that which takes place through the hypostatic union between the divinity and humanity of the Word incarnate. In his great love God allows himself to be differentiated in terms of the amount of practical virtue found in each person, so that human virtue in all its variations can find its true significance in him.[142]

Asceticism and Ecstasy

It remains to consider Maximus' view of the growth of the spiritual life in relation to that human being whom we have so far considered in terms of both general anthropology and psychology, as well as of his or her disintegration through the passions, and reintegration by way of the virtues. Maximus generally distinguishes three aspects of the Christian life which Thunberg, for the sake of convenience, labels: *vita practica; vita contemplativa* and *vita mystica.*[143] Seen as three stages — what will later be termed purification, contemplation and union, this distinction goes back to Origen who in the prologue to his commentary on the Song of Songs saw it as the best way to make sense of the inter-relation between three Old Testament books: Proverbs, Ecclesiastes, and the Song of Solomon itself.[144] Evagrius, developing Origen's thinking on this point, finds that Christian existence unfolds by way of: first, *praktikê,* exercise in virtuous living according to the commandments, something

---

[141]L. Thunberg, *Microcosm and Mediator*, op. cit., p. 348.
[142]*Epistle* 2 (PG 91, 401B).
[143]L. Thunberg, *Microcosm and Mediator*, op. cit., p. 352.
[144]*Commentarium in Canticorum cantica*, prologue.

which, for him, is symbolised by the flesh of Christ; secondly, *phusikê*, the contemplation and understanding of the nature of created things, symbolised by the blood of Christ; and lastly, *theologikê*, a higher contemplation implying the knowledge of God himself and symbolised by the heart of Christ.[145] Fundamentally, Maximus follows Evagrius here; but he also adds important refinements which change the inflexion of Evagrius' system.

Most especially: even though, like Evagrius, Maximus distinguishes between the 'practical' and 'theoretical' aspects of Christian living, he also maintains that there is an interplay between them. Just as God's truth cannot be separated from his goodness, so too in man contemplation and practice, wisdom and prudence, knowledge and virtue go hand in hand, not least because while the image of God in man, linked with *nous*, is related to God as truth, the divine likeness in him is connected by Maximus to the freedom of man's reasonable nature, and relates to God as goodness.[146] Maximus, accordingly, gives a higher value to the practical life than does Evagrius, and while treating it as a stage does not see it as a merely preparatory stage.[147] In the *Quaestiones ad Thalassium* 3, Masimus sets out to interpret in this sense the passage in Luke 22 where the Lord sends on Peter and John to prepare for the Last Supper, with the information that they will meet a water-carrier, and should follow him into a house where they must ask the steward for a suitable room to prepare the Passover.[148] Peter signifies the practical life, John contemplation. The water-carrier represents those who carry the grace of God by practical philosophy in the arms of the virtues. The house is the true piety, where the practical mind comes with its virtues; the steward, who possesses these virtues as his second nature, is the theoretical mind, illumined by the light of mystical understanding. Lastly, the passover lamb which is to be brought inside, to nourish those

---

[145] *Centuriae gnostica* I. 10.
[146] *Opuscula theologica et polemica* 1 (PG 91, 12A).
[147] L. Thunberg, *Microcosm and Mediator*, op. cit., p. 360.
[148] Luke 22, 8-12.

gathered there, is the Logos himself.[149] The presence of the Logos, to be appropriated by human beings, is bestowed only on a house prepared by both the natural virtues and the divine light. Maximus can even suggest that the water-carrier and the stewart, as *praktikos* and *gnôstikos* respectively, are from one point of view separate persons, yet in view of their common nature, they are one and the same.[150] And summing up a number of texts of this kind, gathered together by Père Irénée-Henri Dalmais,[151] Thunberg concludes:

> This connection not only implies that they are both important, and that one cannot be isolated from the other, or substituted for the other. It also implies that they support each other in their own functions, and thus condition the perfection of each other — though this perfection — as in the Alexandrian tradition — is considered to start on the basis of faith with the *vita practica*, and to continue through contemplation which is related to the wisdom of God and which leads us into a union with him which is beyond all knowledge and all merely human effort.[152]

It coheres with this that Maximus' favourite names for the practical life is the laudatory one of *praktikê philosophia*: this is not something to concern only dumb groundlings.

And if, at Maximus' hands, Evagrius' teaching on the 'practical life' emerges looking rather different, the same is true of the next stage or aspect in their shared scheme, 'natural contemplation'. Maximus accepts Evagrius' scheme of the five *theoriai* or kinds of contemplative knowledge: of these, two, related to divine providence and divine judgment, are really more a matter of world history than of the nature of things, while one, contemplation of the Holy Trinity, goes beyond the

---

[149] *Quaestiones ad Thalassium* 3 (PG 90, 273BC; 276A).

[150] Ibid., at PG 90, 273C.

[151] I.-H. Dalmais, 'La doctrine ascétique de s. Maxime le Confesseur d'après le *Liber asceticus*', *Irénikon* 26 (1953), pp. 24ff.

[152] Thunberg, *Microcosm and Mediator*, op cit, p.

category of natural contemplation altogether. So far as *physikê theôria*, strictly speaking, is concerned, we are left, then, with two kinds, which Evagrius distinguished in terms of whether they involved visible and corporeal beings, or beings invisible, incorporeal.[153] Comparison between Maximus' *Centuries on Love* and the *Gnostic Centuries* of Evagrius suggests that Maximus wanted to separate the five sorts of contemplative knowledge (called by him the five 'teachings', *dogmata*) from the Origenistic scheme in which Evagrius had embedded them. Moreover, in the second *Letter* and the *Liber asceticus* Maximus envisages an entry upon deification and union with God by-passing natural contemplation altogether, possibly because for those not contemplatively gifted communion with the Logos through the moral life was, to his mind, enough. Again, while certainly approving of 'natural contemplation', provided that its place in the Christian life is not exaggerated, Maximus connected it with the interpretation of Scripture, which throws light, evidently, on the divine purpose of the world, and thus saves the practitioner of natural *gnôsis* from absorption in any mere cosmic mysticism.[154] Anticipating the statement of the symbolist poet Stéphane Mallarmé 'La nature est une forêt de symboles', Maximus considered that not only nature but history too is 'a forest of symbols', if read in the perspective of Scripture. As Thunberg points out:

> It is the task of 'natural contemplation', not only to see the *logoi* of created beings both in their differentiation according to natures — as indications of the purpose of God for each nature — and in their relationship to their common Cause the Logos, who keeps them together, but also to see them in their symbolic relationship, a hierarchical relationship of a prophetic character which points in the direction of the attributes of God and is closely linked with his providence and judgment.[155]

---

[153]For Maximus' debt to Evagrius here, see R. M. Viller, 'Aux sources de la spiritualité de saint Maxime', *Revue d'Ascètique et de Mystique* 11 (1930), pp. 243ff.

[154]L. Thunberg, *Microcosm and Mediator*, op. cit., pp. 368-371.

[155]Ibid., p. 372.

One last point relevant to natural contemplation concerns Maximus' paschal interpretation of spiritual experience. Like Evagrius, Maximus sees the purgative process of the *vita practica* as involving a death with Christ, and spiritual ascent through contemplation as a resurrection with Christ.[156] Unlike Evagrius, he also regards contemplative experience as not only a miniature Easter, but also a continuing Good Friday. The Christian gnostic does not transcend crucifixion, the sacrifice of Christ which is the pivot of the world, but shares in it in his own way.[157] There is spiritual crucifixion in the practical life, through a dying to the temptations of the sensuous world. For Maximus, this imitates the crucifying of the flesh of Christ. There is also spiritual crucifixion, secondly, in the life of natural contemplation, by way of abandonment of the mind's symbolic contemplation of natural realities, and its entry on a simple, unified path into the mystery of God. For Maximus, this imitates the crucifying of the soul of Christ. Lastly, there is a crucifixion in the stage — even — of *theologia*, divine contemplation itself, thanks to the mind's ultimate obligation to deny, apophatically, the divine qualities, so as to move closer to God as he is in himself, in his own simplicity. Though Maximus does not explicitly say that this is an imitation of the crucifying of the mind of Christ, Thunberg believes that such a statement would faithfully reflect his meaning.[158]

And so we come to the third great stage of man's spiritual journey, as charted by both Evagrius and Maximus — after the life of the virtues, and natural contemplation, there is *theologia*, the knowledge of God. Whereas for Evagrius, with his Origenistic intellectualism, the third stage develops naturally from the second with which it is closely linked, for Maximus, the last stage is supremely the gracious gift of divine love, and so is related to the other two in a manner more discontinuous than continuous.[159] One way in which this is brought out lies in Maximus' corrective appeal, vis-à-vis Evagrius, to the

---

[156]E.g. *Capita theologica et economica* II. 95 (PG 90, 1169CD).

[157]*Ambigua* 47 (PG 91, 1360CD).

[158]L. Thunberg, *Microcosm and Mediator*, op. cit., p. 375.

[159]Ibid., p. 377.

apophaticism of Denys: *theologia* is a relationship, beyond all knowledge, with the God who is himself above knowledge.[160] Again, for Maximus, pure prayer is not simply purified prayer — that is, prayer purged of those thoughts suggested by the passions. Much more is it a prayer formed by God alone, who by his grace reveals himself to the lover of God, and, through ecstasy draws the latter toward his inmost mystery.[161] In pure prayer, the mind of man passes beyond all created things, 'emigrating' towards God. And if Evagrius could say as much, Maximus emphasises that such rapture takes place in love, notably through the latter's aspect of desire, *erôs tês agapês*, and that, in this 'emigration', the mind finds a divine treasure which leaves it unaware now even of itself.[162] Maximus also modified the Pseudo-Denys' notion of ecstasy as *pati divina*, 'to suffer the divine'. In the context of the Monoenergist and Monothelite disputes, there was quite a possibility that such a formula could have been invoked to exclude human activity in deification: perhaps, indeed, that was Denys' intention. So Maximus' reinterprets the *pati divina* as a matter of our suffering ourselves to be moved by God thanks to our active love for him: for the one who loves something surely suffers ecstasy towards that thing as loved.[163] In Maximus' spiritual doctrine, then:

> Suffering is transferred to the realm of movement and will, and excites an activity instead of eliminating it.[164]

And, above all, what is thus 'suffered' is divine grace: the very idea of ecstatic passivity signifies for Maximus the sovereignty of God's grace in our deification. Without diminishing the supreme rôle of grace, Maximus carefully avoids the Monothelite implications of Denys' formulae, and teaches an

---

[160]As in *Centuriae de Caritate* III. 99.

[161]L. Thunberg, *Microcosm and Mediator*, op. cit., pp. 386-391.

[162]See *Centuriae de Caritate* I. 12; and for Maximus' doctrine of ecstasy at large, P. Sherwood, O.S.B., *The Earlier Ambigua of St Maximus the Confessor* (Rome 1955), pp. 124-154.

[163]*Ambigua* 7 (PG 91, 1073BC).

[164]L. Thunberg, *Microcosm and Mediator*, op. cit., p. 450

inseparable oneness of God and man as united in mystical union, while maintaining with all possible rigour the conviction that a gulf nonetheless sunders the created from the Uncreated.[165] In other words, he offers a fully *Chalcedonian* version of what, in Christendom, the mystical marriage of God and humanity might mean. Athanasius' dictum, 'The Logos became man in order that we should become gods',[166] finds its own explication in terms of a theological doctrine of man itself founded on the orthodox doctrine of Christ. The foundation for deification is not nature but grace, and more specifically the hypostatic union of divinity and humanity in the Incarnation. Yet the deifying effect of the Incarnation is by no means contrary to nature, for God meant the creation for this from the beginning — to become in man participation in the divine life. So far, this concerns Jesus Christ: but in Baptism, the Son, with the Holy Spirit which is his, liberates sinful man so as to choose freely what is good for him. And so another incarnation takes place in the believer — an incarnation in his virtues, realised as a revelatory movement of God towards man.

> Man exerts his virtuous activity and receives by grace reflections of the divine attributes in himself ... Man has deified himself through the gift of charity, while at the same time God's divine attributes are made effective in him.[167]

Just as, the two natures, operations, wills compenetrate, but without mixture or confusion, in the person of the Redeemer, so in the persons of believers, the two streams of human willing and divine grace interact by a similar *perichôrêsis* based ultimately on the divine Son's condescension itself. All in all, Maximus' teaching, as set forth by Thunberg, fully warrants the judgment made on the Fathers' contribution to moral theology by the Flemish Dominican historian of ethics Servais Pinckaers.

---

[165]Ibid., pp. 450-451.
[166]*De incarnatione Verbi* 54 (PG 25, 192B).
[167]L. Thunberg, *Microcosm and Mediator*, op. cit., p. 458.

If ... the moral thinking of the Fathers was nourished directly on Scripture in all its amplitude; if it knew how to harvest, and judiciously exploit, the riches contained in Greek and Latin culture; if, lastly, it presented as the crowning of morals, such potent and effective spiritualities as those of martyrdom, monasticism and virginity for Christ, then we certainly cannot speak of that epoch as poorly favoured in the realm of moral thought and theology, nor compare it to an infancy. On the contrary: as for theology at large, the age of the Fathers was a golden age when the foundations of Christian moral teaching and living were laid. Those foundations would form the great Tradition, and, thanks to repeated renewals, resist the flux of centuries.[168]

---

[168]S. T. Pinckaers, *Les Sources de la morale chrétienne*, op. cit., p. 212.

7

Juan-Miguel Garrigues on Maximian Soteriology

It remains to draw together the threads of these various themes by looking, in conclusion, at Maximus' vision of Christian salvation. It has long been customary to contrast 'physical' with 'moral' theories of redemption in the soteriology of the Fathers. But while a didactic notion of redemption as, essentially, enlightenment can be found early enough among the Apostolic Fathers, and receives at the hands of the Apologists of the later second and third centuries the benefit of a rational foundation in the doctrine of Christ as the Logos, the Fathers at large customarily associate such liberation from intellectual and moral ignorance and error with a more comprehensive divine action aimed at the healing and transformation of human nature as a whole. As J. N. D. Kelly has pointed out in his classic treatment of this subject, the various theological elucidations of the climactic redemptive act of Good Friday and Easter — Christ's death as a sacrifice, or as a superabundant payment for the devil's 'rights', all presuppose the truth of this more comprehensive account of which the 'physical' theory of salvation is itself an elaboration. And this soteriological thread running through the work of all the Fathers, of whatever school, is the theme, first Pauline and then Irenaean, of *recapitulation*.

> Just as all men were somehow present in Adam, so they are, or can be, present in the second Adam, the man from heaven. Just as they were involved in the former's sin, with all its appalling consequences, so they can participate in

the latter's death and ultimate triumph over sin, the forces of evil and death itself. Because, very God as he is, he has identified himself with the human race, Christ has been able to act on its behalf and in its stead; and the victory he has obtained is the victory of all who belong to him.[1]

It is just such a renovation of human being, transcending the categories of 'physical' and 'moral' and founded on a new, gracious solidarity with God in Christ, which Maximus' soteriology holds out as hope for the world. It is from this eschatological perspective, indeed, that Maximus' doctrine of salvation is best unfolded.

Human Nature's Fulfilment in God

Père Juan-Miguel Garrigues, in his study of Maximus' soteriology, underlines the eschatological novelty of the Christian life, as Maximus conceives it.[2] Garrigues points out that the early Christian author of the Epistle to Diognetus had affirmed the eschatological unity of faith and morals, theory and practice, in the phrase *thaumastê kai paradoxos politeia*, 'a wonderful and paradoxical citizenship' or 'way of living'.[3] Maximus takes up the crucial term *politeia* in his own attempt to express the goal of the appearance on earth of the divine Son. That goal is: 'to teach the ways of life, and a heavenly manner of living'.[4] This Maximus understands in a thoroughly realistic way, however, as a refusal to turn away from those who persecute us, and a loving of those who hate us.[5] And with a reference to the Johannine writings, Garrigues comments that:

---

[1] J. N. D. Kelly, *Early Christian Doctrines* (London 1977[5]), p. 377.
[2] J. M. Garrigues, *Maxime le Confesseur. La Charité, avenir divin de l'homme* (Paris 1976), pp. 79-80.
[3] *Letter to Diognetus* V. 4.
[4] *Liber Asceticus*, PG 90, col. 920D.
[5] Ibid., 917C.

The eschatological character of extremest charity, prior
to any dialectic of thought and action, is what articulates
the being of the Christian.[6]

For Maximus, the whole 'matter' of existence, whether thought
or action, is not just renewed but 'innovated' — recreated from
the roots up — by entrance upon the life of the children of
God. As Creator, the Logos furnishes man with these 'materials',
but as Word Incarnate, he communicates to him the new life
which 'innovates' nature in his person.

> Life becomes the person of the Logos, the Logos the
> nature of life, thus sketching out the man who is truly new,
> according to Christ: he who carries, by means of faithful
> imitation, the image and likeness.[7]

Garrigues' account of the 'metamorphoses of divinisation'
unfolds in terms of the three principal stages of Maximus' life.
He discusses Maximus' earliest 'monastic' writings under the
heading 'divinisation as the fulfilment of human nature in
God'. In the period which opens with his flight to Africa come
reflections on the theme of 'divinisation as personal adoption
in the Son'. Finally, from the years of persecution which were
heralded by the imperial *Ecthesis* of 639, the story is rounded off
by consideration of the divinisation motif as 'event of the
Trinitarian love'. Although one might reasonably consider
that a trifle too schematic, its value can only really be tested by
considering the light it throws as it unfolds.

Though no work of the very first monastic years of Maximus
has come down to us, Garrigues believes that the dedicatory
letter of *Ambigua* II to his former superior, John of Cyzicus,
provides give-away phrases for his understanding of the monastic
life as an 'eminent fulfilment in man of the mystery of salvation'.[8]

> All the world praises, and doubtless justly, on the grounds
> of their appetite for knowledge, those who desire good

[6]J. M. Garrigues, *Maxime le Confesseur*, op. cit., p. 79.
[7]PG 91, col. 12A.
[8]J. M. Garrigues, *Maxime le Confesseur*, op. cit., p. 83.

things with greater ardour, who apply themselves thereto with more urgency so as to have knowledge of them, who go to the best masters and to those who teach the best subjects, for — acquiring by asking the gnosis and knowledge of what they did not know, they are freed from ignorance and inexperience, and from the opprobrium which flows therefrom ... But you, you are the pastor of the spiritual sheep, you know how to lead them to the fold which is above by the sounds of a spiritual flute, and you have received a singular habit for the mystical gnosis which is not accessible to others, by reason of which, considered as a governor of the Church of Christ, you direct it knowingly, as a ship freighted with faith and worthily rigged out with the life which is according to God, to the shore of the divine will, without suffering any damage from the buffetings of the floods of life.[9]

Read in the light of the spiritual currents of the monasticism of the day, the passage is revealing. Garrigues finds in it two lines of thought. The first is an intellectual mysticism, a mysticism of the mind, which betrays the influence of Evagrius, and, behind Evagrius, of Origen.[10] But the text speaks in a second voice: it points to a link between the desire for mystical knowledge and the liberation which such understanding brings about. And here it announces the presence of a more existential spirituality, not unconnected with a concept of spirit as, precisely, freedom. This suggests another lead — to the spiritual theology of Gregory of Nyssa, though, in the work of that Cappadocian Father, we have, from one viewpoint, simply the development of yet another aspect of Origen's teaching. This time what is at stake is the notion of the liberty of the human spirit as facing the constant risk that it may, by 'satiety', *koros*, turn away from God,

---

[9]*Ambigua*, PG 91, 1061A-1064A.

[10]Cf. I.-H. Dalmais, O.P., 'L'héritage évagrien dans la synthèse de Maxime le Confesseur', *Studia Patristica* VIII (Berlin 1966), pp. 356-363.

directing its impatience towards deceptive goods which make it their thrall.[11]

Garrigues finds here, however, not simply the (unintegrated) co-presence of these two fundamental spiritualities, but a happy attempt to marry them with each other, and so to achieve a balance which either lacks by itself. Maximus yields neither to the intellectualism of Origen, for the soul's ship in Maximus is equipped with faith and a godly life, nor to the 'dramatic existentialism' of Nyssa, for Maximus avoids the idea of an infinite *epektasis* of desire, understood in terms of the instability of free will, replacing that key-notion with his own prospect of a sure and serene ascent to the fullness of repose of the heavenly harbour. Sketched out in advance, we encounter here the mature mystical theology of Maximus with its balance between:

> the free and personal decision in which man wagers ('joue') his salvation, and the silent aspiration of his nature towards God, for whom it has been made. This natural dynamism, once freed and transposed by grace into a personal liberty, gives to nature the stability and energy necessary for it to be attached to its final Good.[12]

This notion of a journey towards God sustained at once by the 'ascensional dynamism' of natural aspiration, and by the 'theurgic mediation' of a higher authority (the spiritual leader of the Letter to John of Cyzicus), is reminiscent of the mysticism, simultaneously ontological and ecclesial, of the Pseudo-Denys. At the same time, Maximus', accents are more personalist than those of Denys: though nature is oriented in man towards the good of communion with God, divinisation happens only by way of a personal turning, *tropos*, within human freedom.

---

[11]See on this P. Sherwood, O.S.B., 'Maximus and Origenism', in *Berichte zum XI Internationalen Byzantinischen Kongress* (Munich 1958); idem., The *Earlier 'Ambigua' of St Maximus the Confessor* (Rome 1955), pp. 181-204; M. Harl, 'Recherches sur l'origénisme d'Origène: la "satiété" (*koros*) de la contemplation comme motif de la chute des âmes', *Studia Patristica* VIII (Berlin 1966), pp. 373-405.

[12]J. M. Garrigues, *Maxime le Confesseur*, op. cit., p. 85.

However, if we may follow Garrigues' imaginative reconstruction, a theology of divinisation as, essentially, the fulfilment of man's nature in God, fits better with Maximus' monastic experience than with the turbulent events, both political and ecclesial, of his later years. For this way of seeing the mystery is centred chiefly on the initiation of the mind and heart into the Christian mysteries in a homogeneous, ruptureless, unfaltering progress, based on the natural desire for God. By contrast, the Persian invasion introduced a note of eschatological disruption into Maximus' life: it made of the monk moving from perfection to perfection a wanderer, seeking in the disintegration of his historical world the anticipatory signs of He-who-Comes. On Garrigues' reading, Maximus now begins to see that human nature cannot receive its divine fulfilment without undergoing a paschal 'innovation': 'a Christic resurrection, and no longer just a theurgic completion in a pre-established cosmic order'.[13] Exile, by opening Maximus' life to an 'eschatological wandering', inaugurated a new stage of his confession, and led him to a transformed view of the Christian mystery, and the divinisation which it accomplishes.

Where the basic soteriological scheme of Maximus' early period is concerned, Garrigues would identify two fundamental themes. And these are: first, that of the 'ecstatic finality of nature', turned as nature is, by the very fact of its existing, towards the absolute Good; secondly, the innovation or transformative renewal of nature in and by its mode of existing. From what we have seen of Maximus' thought in the preceding pages, it will not surprise us to find that Garrigues considers Maximus' first main soteriological theme in connexion with his debt to Evagrius, Gregory of Nyssa, and Denys; and the second main motif in terms of his Christology.

Though learning soteriologically from all three of Evagrius, Nyssen and Denys, Maximus also found, eventually, much to correct in all. While Evagrius' ascetic doctrine, with its advocacy of detachment from the world of matter, intended no condemnation of the materiality of creation *as such*, it failed to

[13]Ibid., p. 87.

distinguish between what Garrigues terms the moral 'passionality' of the human person, due to sin, his tendency to be overwhelmed by the passions, and that 'passibility' of the human being which is natural to his spirit.[14] Such an anthropology would draw with it nefarious consequences: if personal peccability is ultimately indistinguishable from natural passibility, then Christ, who possesses moral immutability in his personal free will, would have to be absolutely impassible by nature. Such a radical docetism could only empty the Christian doctrine of salvation of its very substance. On the threshold of the Evagrian trap, Maximus did not, however, walk into it: passibility for him is not sin; it is sin's consequence — and that is something very different.[15]

Maximus corrected Evagrian asceticism, founded as that was on an intellectualistic concept of salvation, by a soteriology centred on freedom, and inspired by Gregory of Nyssa.[16] In the latter's existentialist anthropology, the passion of the will, at the root of sin, is *désir de soi*, a 'desire in its own right, for desire' which progresses by 'vampirising' everything that falls within its grasp as 'materials of desire'.[17] Relatedly, in the words of Maximus' second 'century' on charity, evil is 'the passion which affects our representation'.[18] The passion for self, *philautia*, turns the spirit, in its innermost functioning, into a serf.

Yet, for Garrigues, just as Maximus corrects the Platonic dualism of Evagrius, so too does he moderate Gregory's radical existentialism.

> For Maximus, man is not only liberty: if his person be irreducible to his nature, his being is not just purely and simply convertible into freedom.[19]

---

[14]Ibid., p. 89.

[15]Compare *Questiones ad Thalassium* 1 (PG 90, 268D-269A) with the same work at no. 42 (PG 90, 405C).

[16]Cf. here A. Siclari, *Volontà e scelta in Massimo il Confessore e in Gregorio di Nissa* (Parma 1984).

[17]J.-M. Garrigues, *Maxime le Confesseur*, op. cit., p. 90.

[18]*Centuries on Charity*, II. 15.

[19]J.-M. Garrigues, *Maxime le Confesseur*, op. cit., p. 91.

The adventure of human liberty belongs for Maximus with man as called to live in God's likeness, with the freedom of his person exercised in imitating God's good wisdom. But more primordial still is the gift by God to man as in-his-image of a natural existence, tensed between its origin and its goal in God — being, and ever-being.

And it was here, for Garrigues, that Maximus found the Pseudo-Denys of such high utility. What did this entail? The chance to integrate the drama of freedom within an ontology of the world as structured, and rendered dynamic, by participation.

> Maximus attempted the grandiose task of combining, in a manner at once original and free of concordism, the two greatest Christian *Weltanschauungen* of the patristic epoch: the cosmic economy of Origen and the cosmic ontology of Denys.[20]

And though he needed to refer, behind Denys, to Aristotle, so as to disengage from out of Denys' excessively emanationist view of creation the idea of a creaturely nature, in all its finite consistency, Denys *tout seul* was able to provide him with the basic doctrine that he needed at this juncture: that of God as the primary Cause, bearing in that primary causality on a world at once ordered and multiple.[21] Whereas Origenism had identified as the origin of the saving Economy that sinful movement of freedom which provoked in its turn the material, manifold world, Maximus made the movement of the created issue from the creative Act itself.[22] The natural dynamism of the creature is thus withdrawn from the uncertainties of sheer personal liberty and re-situated within the ontological finality whereby everything that is tends towards its perfect good. Nevertheless, what is given potentially in the creative causality of being must, for man, be converted into terms of free choice, if he is to find rest in his own fulfilment in God. As *Ambigua* 65 has it:

[20]Ibid., p. 92.
[21]*Ambigua* 7 (PG 91, 1077C).
[22]Ibid., 23 (PG 91, 1257D).

Notice that the principle of the origin of existing things comprises being, well-being and ever-being. The first is given to existent things by essence; the second is given by free choice to those who have liberty of movement; and the third is bestowed by grace. One can say that the first covers the power; the second the act; and the third the repose.[23]

Convincing as this synthetic scheme of Maximus' is, and remarkable for its anticipation of the structure of Thomas Aquinas' theological vision, Garrigues finds himself obliged at this point to enter a *caveat*. Does not personal freedom enter in here simply so as to join together two moments in natural causality: nature's origin and nature's goal? To go to God, all the person has to do, it would seem, is to make his or her own the natural aspiration towards the Good. As Garrigues puts it, with particular reference to *Ambigua* 7, a classic statement of the doctrine of divinisation by ecstasy:

In his anxiety to correct the Origenist personalism which maintains free will even in the blessed condition of the saints, ... Maximus managed to fall into a natural mysticism of desire, in which freedom appears only as a stage, quickly passed, in the assent to the contingent being's irresistible need for plenitude.[24]

In trying to describe how freedom is stabilised by the divine energy which overcomes it, Maximus was betrayed into presenting human action as a mere passivity. Such 'Monoenergism' in the realm of ascetical and mystical doctrine could only prepare the way for a christological Monoenergism — on which, of course, Denys' notorious phrase, 'the new theandric energy' could bestow the official motto.[25] Garrigues

---

[23]Ibid., 65 (PG 91, 1392A).

[24]J.-M. Garrigues, *Maxime le Confesseur*, op. cit., p. 97, with reference to *Ambigua* 7 (PG 91, 1073C-1076A).

[25]J. M. Garrigues, *Maxime le Confesseur*, op. cit., p. 98, with reference to *Ambigua* 7 at PG 91, 1076 BC.

notes, moreover, that such an option has the further, unintended, effect of de-valuing the eschatological dimension of specifically Christian existence in the here-and-now. The flowering of the 'glorious freedom of the sons of God', re-vivified as these are by Baptism, now appears as simply a transition to a post-mortem divinisation. In Garrigues' words:

> It is understandable that, in the absence of that eschatological dimension opened up by a spirituality based on Baptism, the mystical life in the Holy Spirit is conceived first and foremost as a negative asceticism, intended to strip the human being of any *personal* motion, which would be suspect from the start as placing possible obstacles in the way of the divinising finality of the only motion that is truly 'natural': namely, the divine activity.[26]

The Lord of providence and history was, however, about to shake Maximus' confidence in such an eschatology, and to bid him confess more boldly the mystery of redemption by death and resurrection with Christ.

It is here that Garrigues turns, then, to the christological inspiration of the sea-change which Maximus' doctrine of nature's fulfilment in God underwent at the start of his period of exile. The effect of the Persian invasion, and Maximus' consequent flight from his monastic home was (so Garrigues maintains, in what must be considered, however, a somewhat audacious proposal of speculative biography) to make Maximus more acutely aware of the proper standing of personhood, which latter is in fact as thoroughly original — constitutive of the human being in his or her source — as is that of nature. Hurled into the unpredictable, Maximus could no longer regard personal freedom as simply acquiescence in ontological finality. He realised that the personal order is, rather, a 'creative imagining' which constitutes a constant 'innovation' of the order of nature.[27]

---

[26]J.-M. Garrigues, *Maxime le Confesseur*, op. cit., pp. 98-99.
[27]Ibid., p. 100.

By happy coincidence, this disruption of the rhythm of life took place at more or less the same time as the christological crisis provoked by the policies of Heraclius and Sergius, and so was followed at once by Maximus' call to become the witness of Jesus Christ in his authentic divine and human mystery. In Garrigues' perhaps over-tidy presentation, just as he was led by the harsh facticity of events to discover the irreducibility of person to nature, so Maximus was also stimulated by christological reflection to confess the co-originality, or simultaneously constitutive character, of nature and hypostasis in the Word Incarnate.[28] And Garrigues finds abundant evidence for this confession in the later *Ambigua*, above all, in the *Book of Ambiguities* 42. In the twofold distinction of *genesis*, the creation of nature, and *gennesis*, the birth of the person, on the one hand, and on the other, of *logos*, nature in its permanent intelligible structure, and *tropos*, the changeable mode of existence of such a nature (distinctions we have already studied in this work),[29] Maximus found the instruments he needed to articulate his new discoveries. Just as in the order of salvation the hypostasis of the Son of God must be granted a certain priority over his divine nature, so in that same order as it affects ourselves, how salvation transforms us now is by touching us in our personal freedom, expressed in the New Testament by the theme of our new (personal) birth.[30] At first, in the second set of the *Ambigua*, Maximus stresses the negative aspect of this discovery: the *tropos* of personal innovation, newness of life, which salvation brings, is understood as liberation from an iron law of pleasure-seeking, of individualism and corruption which rules over the birth of human persons since the Fall. But signs soon begin to appear of a more positive way of seeing this new way of being personal, introduced by Christ. The new *tropos* is, in Garrigues' words,

---

[28]Ibid., pp. 102-103.

[29]See above, pp. 63, 90-91, 93, 98-100, 109, 131-133, 136, 160.

[30]Cf. *Ambigua* 42 (PG 91, 1316D-1317B; also ibid., 31 (PG 91, 1280AC) for the *genesis-gennesis* distinction; *Ambigua* 42 (PG 91, 1341D and 1344D) and ibid., 31 (PG 91, 1280A) for the *logos-tropos* distinction.

a filial freedom which man has corrupted by his free-will, and which only a hypostatic order, innovating nature, can bring about.[31]

Faced with the mystery of the Incarnate Word, Maximus at last grasped that man is not divinised by a simple prolongation of his natural dynamism, but by a change which fulfils his natural aspiration only through transposing it into a new key, in that realm of being and action proper only to persons. Henceforth, where salvation is concerned, divinisation and Christology will form one single mystery.[32]

Man's Personal Adoption in the Son

At the moment, then, when circumstances obliged Maximus to take up the defence, on the level of doctrine, of the human energy of the Son, he also, according to Garrigues, in his own personal experience discovered how, by human action, we may ourselves 'put on' Christ. In Maximus' own words:

The Word was born once for all according to the flesh, but, because of his philanthropy, he desires to be born ceaselessly, according to the Spirit, in those who desire him. He makes himself a little child and is formed in them at the same time as the virtues are. He manifests himself in the measure that he knows the one who receives him is able. In acting thus, it is not by jealousy that he attenuates the radiance of his own grandeur, but because he judges and measures the capacity of those who desire to see him. And so the Word of God ever reveals himself to us in the manner which befits us and yet remains invisible, because of the immensity of his mystery.[33]

Maximus now goes on, therefore, to situate his discovery of the two 'co-original' orders — the genesis and *logos* of nature, the

---

[31]J.-M. Garrigues, *Maxime le Confesseur*, op. cit., p. 110.
[32]Ibid., p. 112.
[33]PG 90, 1181A.

birth and mode of existing of persons — in terms of the mission of the Son, and of the Spirit. The Word, Image of the invisible God, presides over the creation of human nature in God's image; the Holy Spirit gives new birth to man as person, free for a life of likeness to God. But as Adam had betrayed the vocation whereby he was called to a free communion with God in personal resemblance, only the Son of God could give back to man that filial adoption which he lost when he preferred the carnal birth of sin to birth in the Holy Spirit. To re-create us in a Godly mode of existence, Christ, who assumed our nature in the Incarnation, accepted Baptism in the Holy Spirit at Jordan, so that the Father might once again recognise man as his son.[34] Such a linkage of Christology and Pneumatology by way of exegesis of the narratives of Jesus' Baptism, and the accompanying notion that the Baptism sealed the filial adoption of our humanity as assumed in the Incarnation, had been a commonplace of Greek patristic theology since Irenaeus. Maximus now goes back behind Evagrius and Denys so as to root his doctrine of salvation-divinisation-in what Garrigues terms 'the profoundest intuitions of ante-Nicene theology'.[35] The filial *tropos* is a pneumatic vocation to personal freedom, a liberty in which God and man co-operate. As the *Liber asceticus* has it

> The Lord has given us the *tropos* of salvation and the eternal power to become sons of God; henceforth, our salvation is in our power.[36]

Yet there is here no Pelagianism, or even Semi-Pelagianism: because, in Garrigues' words:

> The hypostatic mode of freedom 'innovates' the natural will by giving it re-birth according to an unheard of manner of existing which, however, fully respects that same natural will in its own order of essence and energy.[37]

[34] J.-M. Garrigues, *Maxime le Confesseur*, op. cit., p. 117, with reference to *Ambigua* 42 (PG 91, 1348AB).

[35] J.-M. Garrigues, *Maxime le Confesseur*, op. cit., p. 118.

[36] *Liber asceticus*, at PG 90, 953B.

[37] J.-M. Garrigues, *Maxime le Confesseur*, op. cit., p. 119.

Hypostatic adoption as sons and daughters of God is not so much a dignity conferred once and for all, as a communion with the Father mobilising all man's natural energies for a life of divine likeness.[38] In this conception of salvation as rooted in the baptismal mystery, which regenerates human nature in holiness, Maximus was influenced, so Garrigues believes, by the *Homilies* of the Pseudo-Macarius where, of all the texts come down to us from the ancient Eastern church, this motif is most clearly indicated. Though ascribed to the celebrated fourth century Egyptian anchorite Macarius the Great, those homilies were probably written in the Syro-Palestinian milieu, perhaps in circles affected by Messalianism, a 'charismatic' movement concerned, as all such movements are, with the felt experience of grace. They may well come from the pen of Symeon of Mesopotamia, himself a pupil of the Cappadocian Fathers and the head of a monastic community. Whether via Maximus' Palestinian friend and mentor Sophronius of Jerusalem, or via the fifth century ascetic author Diadochus of Photikê, who made use of them, or directly, these *Homilies* have left a trace here, it would seem, on Maximus' own doctrine of salvation.[39] The divine form which inaugurated the Reign of God in man, and gives a new quality and direction to his action, will be for Maximus, from this time onwards, that 'Christic' form imprinted in the human heart by the Holy Spirit at Baptism: 'christening'. Eschatology is no longer postponed till after death: it begins now.

This is not to say, however, that the End becomes available to human beings in some way wholly independent of a dying. There can be no new birth without initiation into the mystery of Easter; of Christ's passing, through the gate of the death, into the risen world. As Garrigues has it:

> The paschal Christ is not continuously born in man according to nature. The Christ whom the Holy Spirit makes to be born in human beings is Christ in his eschatological futuring —

[38]Cf. *Orationis dominicae expositio* at PG 90, 884.

[39]J.-M. Garrigues, *Maxime le Confesseur*, op. cit., pp. 121-123, with reference to, especially, *Quaestiones ad Thalassium* 6 (PG 90, 280CD-381B).

an English neologism which may be allowed to stand for Garrigues' French pun: 'le Christ en à-venir eschatologique'.[40] Man, restored as image by the Economy of Christ in the flesh, is made new by a paschal birth in the Spirit which leads him to manifest in his personality the still invisible traits of the Christ who is coming. In *Letter* 43, Maximus remarked:

> The day when we realise that it is our friendship with the Devil which has brought us to perdition, we will welcome the pacific Advent of Christ, that gentle king of peace, which is being produced invisibly in us.[41]

In this way, hypostatic likeness, itself eschatological in character, transposes the teleological dynamism spontaneously native to human nature as created in God's image, and, in transposing it, confirms it. Hence the intimate relevance of the christological debates over Monoergism and Monothelitism to the doctrine of salvation: it is not by an ontological necessity of a superior causality weighing upon human nature and activity that Christ has saved us, as even such moderate Monophysites believed. The new reality which Christ has brought about in human acting comes solely from the new mode of hypostatic existence he has given us: itself the 'imprint', *hypotypôsis*, of his own eternal personhood as the Son of God.[42] To cite Garrigues again:

> In order to save man, Christ had to assume his will in its natural being, and his instinct of self-preservation, but to fulfil these in an unheard of hypostatic mode, namely, that of filial obedience to the Father unto death.[43]

It is that hypostatic mode's imprint, found in us as filial adoption, which assures the unconfused communion of our will with that of God.

[40]J.-M. Garrigues, *Maxime le Confesseur*, op. cit., p. 128.

[41]*Epistle* 43 (PG 91, 640AC).

[42]*Opuscula theologica et polemica* 20 (PG 91, 241A); cf. J.-M. Garrigues, *Maxime le Confesseur*, op. cit., pp. 134-135.

[43]Ibid., p. 147.

And here we can take a further, and final, step in the exposition of Maximus' soteriology. The *hypotypôsis* or profile of existence, that was sketched out by Christ in the moment of his extremest humiliation in obedience to death on Calvary, and thanks to the Spirit breathed out by him on the Cross in his expiring, and imprinted in us as the hypostatic mode of filial freedom, has a name, and that name is *charity*.[44]

The Advent in Humanity of the Trinitarian Love

Garrigues introduces the subject in this way. The only thing that can bind men with the divine Son in filial adoption is the hypostatic connexion, just described, which the Holy Trinity in its philanthropy offers to the world. But the hypostatic mode of this philanthropic stooping down, *kenôsis*, of God involves a twofold 'innovation' vis-à-vis the order of the natures concerned. First, the Son of God appears among us as the hypostatic subject of an historical and passible human existence since, by condescension, he was able to attach himself to the lot of sinful man — even to the death of the Cross. But secondly, man appears in Christ as 'innovated' or transformatively renewed, not only inasmuch as he is delivered from his sin, but also insofar as he is drawn beyond the limits of his nature in the grace of filial adoption. For Garrigues, this twofold modality of hypostatic communion between God and his adopted creature — at once the human *kenôsis* of the incarnate Son and the filial 'innovation' of divinised mankind, is deployed from within the only mystery which can properly be called 'theandric', and that is: love.[45] As God stoops down in the person of his Son by philanthropy, loving-kindness towards men, so man rises to him in divinisation as the son of God by charity.[46]

In God, what the divine Goodness is for the divine nature, that charity is for the divine Persons in their hypostatic communion. The Trinitarian 'counsel' of those Persons is, in turn, at the source of a plan of love whereby the hypostatic

[44]Ibid., p. 151.
[45]Ibid., p. 155.
[46]Cf. II *Ambigua* 60 (PG 91, 1385BC).

communion itself is personally engaged. The Son, that is, has to accomplish it by coming to exist in a human nature, and finally in that nature to die. As Maximus expresses that in *Letter* 44:

> God as the Good One having in times past by the Law and the Prophets instituted in manifold ways the law of charity for men, as Friend of Man become man at the end of time, has accomplished that law himself. He has not only loved us as himself, but above himself, as is clearly taught by the power of the mystery to those who have piously received the confession of faith in him. Indeed, if he has deliberately delivered himself up to the Passion and the Death, willing to take responsibility in our place , we who *should* have suffered as responsible, it is clear that he has loved us more than himself, we for whose sake he gave himself to death, and — though the expression be bold — it is clear likewise that, as More than Good, he elected to suffer those outrages which were willed at that moment in the Economy of our salvation, preferring them to his own natural glory, as more worthy of him. Going beyond the dignity of God, and transcending the glory of God, he made of the return to him of those who were removed far away a more insistent expression and manifestation of his own glory. Nothing is more fitting to the principle of his glory than man's salvation. For that is every word and every mystery, and what is henceforth the most mysterious of all mysteries: that God himself really became man by charity, assuming flesh endowed with intellectual soul, and welcoming into himself without change the passions of human nature so as to save man and to give himself to us as the imprint of virtue, and having the image of charity and benevolence towards him and our neighbour, to mobilise all our powers so that we might correspond as we ought with our salvation.[47]

---

[47]*Epistle* 44 (PG 91, 641D-644B).

The personal *kenôsis* of the Word manifests that intimate life of the Trinity, charity, which is at once the hypostatic transposition of the essential attributes of the *ens perfectissimum*, and the explanation of how One of the Trinity was able, without alteration of God's intrinsic immutability, to come in person, as the Lover of Mankind, impressing his charity in the human heart not from without — by the power of a higher causality, but from within — by the transformation worked through love.[48]

By interpreting the mystery of salvation as filial adoption in charity, Maximus was able, accordingly, to safeguard the specificity of the distinct natures in the communion of God with man in Christ. Though the cosmic dimension of salvation is not rejected — far from it!, it is transmuted, transposed eschatologically into that hypostatic union of God with man which transcends all notions of natural participation. And here Garrigues stresses that the hypostasis of the Son does not enter into competition with individuated human existence but transmutes it at its source into the personal *tropos* of the Son of God, who transformatively renews it without altering its being.[49] Maximus' doctrine of salvation was enormously helped by his incorporation of Chalcedonian Christology into the trinitarian theology inherited from the Cappadocians. In no way does the hypostatic mode of the Son's being and its subsequent 'history' in the Incarnation threaten the simplicity of the divine consubstantiality, since it is *not a natural property*. In this impossibility of deducing the trinitarian hypostatic modalities from the starting-point of the divine *ousia* lies true Christian apophaticism — which has, then, little if anything to do with the Neo-platonic *via negativa* of approach to 'the One'.[50]

But how is the charity of the Son made man to be salvifically appropriated by ourselves? For Maximus, charity was from the beginning that manner of life which should have characterised

---

[48]Cf. *Opuscula theologica et polemica* 15 (PG 91, 156C).

[49]J.-M. Garrigues, *Maxime le Confesseur*, op. cit., p. 169, with reference to *Opuscula theologica et polemica* 16 (PG 91, 205AC).

[50]J.-M. Garrigues, 'Monarchie et théologie', *Istina* (1970), pp. 435-465.

the human person. Only charity could fulfil in a *personal* way our natural desire; namely, in the self-gift of ourselves to God, and in communion with other persons. But man chose instead the way of *philautia*, and understanding his individual existence as independent vis-à-vis God, took up a position which was contrary to his freedom, and no longer at its source, as well as the rival of other individual humans in what Garrigues terms the 'megolamania of desire'.[51] In comparison with that passion for self whereby the natural man daily seeks survival, charity is now an eschatological manner of life. Only such charity can transform the free-will which encloses us in the egoism of individual existence and awake us to our true hypostatic — that is, personal — vocation. Playing on the counter-position of individual and person, familiar in French Catholic philosophy since Jacques Maritain and echoed in the modern Orthodox dogmatics of Lossky, Garrigues writes:

> The hypostasis, as life of charity, implies intimate communion with our co-natural fellows, in the likeness of the consubstantiality of the trinitarian Persons. Charity thus 'innovates' our free will into that glorious freedom which can 'enhypostatise', by intention, the self-same human nature into a personal communion, thus fulfilling, in a way that is beyond itself, the aspiration of our nature which free will claimed to satisfy in the absolutisation of its 'I'.[52]

Such charity is, for Maximus, found concretely in the *ecclesial* life, called pregnantly by Ignatius of Antioch, in the preface of his *Letter to the Romans*, 'The Charity'. Unlike free will, which is enclosed within individual existence, it is characteristic of hypostatic life that it can be affected by others — in the likeness of the Son of God who attached himself to us even to the point of appropriating our sinful state. Rediscovering in Christ's Church-body their filial adoption, human beings are drawn

---

[51]Idem., *Maxime le Confesseur*, op. cit., p. 177.
[52]Ibid., pp. 180-181; cf. *Epistle* 2 (PG 91, 396CD).

into that same kenotic movement which marks out the philanthropy of the divine Son.[53] Charity as the hypostatic seal of filial adoption, can thus divinise man, rendering him in God's likeness, not suppressing distinctively human activity but adapting the latter to God in a free personal *sunergia*, 'co-acting'.[54] It opens the way for a kenotic spirituality, of the maximalist kind preached by Dostoevsky's character Father Zosima in *The Brothers Karamazov*.[55] More specifically, however, and not in fictional space and time but that of geography and history, such a kenotic vocation was lived out to the end in Maximus' own martyrdom, his confession.

> By being born of God in charity, Maximus advanced ever further in the trinitarian eschatology of his hypostatic vocation. This he brought to its consummation in the martyrdom which configured him in a definitive way to the likeness of the Son of God in *his* hypostatic kenosis. But in this kenosis, he enhypostatised eschatologically the destiny of the Church of his time, and from his bloody confession in humble love there came forth a converting power stronger than that power which had thought to extinguish his voice for ever.[56]

[53]J.-M. Garrigues, *Maxime le Confesseur*, op. cit., p. 184; cf. *Epistle* 12 (PG 91, 504D-505B).

[54]Ibid. 2 at PG 91, 401C.

[55]J.-M. Garrigues, *Maxime le Confesseur*, op. cit., pp. 189-190. Rich materials on this theme lie in J. Saward, *Perfect Fools. Folly for Christ's sake in Catholic and Orthodox Spirituality* (Oxford 1980).

[56]Ibid., p. 199. With this we can compare Dom Basil Studer's cognate comment: 'not only was it ever his heart's desire to anchor the entire Christian life in the Incarnation of the eternal Word and to seek the ground of all unity in the Logos become man, but also he had to experience in his own body what it means to step out in the footsteps of the God who was crucified for us.'
'Zur Soteriologie des Maximus Confessor', in F. Heinzer — C. Schönborn (eds.), *Maximus Confessor. Actes du Symposium sur Maxime le Confesseur, Fribourg, 2-5 September 1980* (Fribourg 1982), p. 241.

8

Conclusion

The Bavarian Byzantinist Hans-Georg Beck, in his monumental study *Kirche und theologische Literatur im byzantinischen Reich*, concluded that Maximus the Confessor was:

> the most universal spirit of the seventh century, and perhaps the last independent thinker of the Byzantine church.[1]

There is a certain disparity between Maximus' achievement and the comparative paucity of his later influence.

In the West, Maximus was known, after the ninth century, as the interpreter of the Pseudo-Denys — though much of the relevant materials, the *Scholia* on the *Corpus Areopagiticum*, may be in fact the work of John of Scythopolis. Alongside the *Scholia*, translated by pope Nicholas I's Greek librarian, Anastasius, could also be consulted, however, the *Ambigua* and the *Questiones ad Thalassium*, put somewhat freely into Latin, from a Greek not always understood, by John Scotus Eriugena. Quite why the emperor Charles the Bald, rightly dissatisfied with the highly defective version of Denys' writings done under the direction of abbot Hilduin of St Denis, at the request of Charles' predecessor Louis the Pious for the glory of the royal abbey which bore Denys' name, should subsequently have taken it into his head to ask Eriugena not only to prepare a new

---

[1]H.-G. Beck, *Kirche und theologische Literatur im byzantinischen Reich* (Munich 1959), p. 436.

translation of Denys but to add the *Ambigua* of Maximus as well, is not known. We possess, however, the preface written by Eriugena, and addressed to his imperial patron, in which the Irish scholar expresses his high regard for Maximus' name.

> It is [Eriugena wrote] a very difficult task that you have confided to me to translate this work of Maximus from Greek into Latin ... and you requested me to do it in a hurry ... I have sought to achieve it as quickly as possible, and thanks be to God have finished. I would not have faced such darkness except for the fact that it is a most excellent apologia, and that I have noted that the blessed Maximus frequently in his work affirms and clarifies the very obscure ideas of Denys the Areopagite, whom in the past I was also commissioned to translate.[2]

Despite occasional mistakes, Eriugena's work was a tour de force. Anastasius the Librarian considered it, indeed, a miracle that such learning should belong to a barbarian whose home was *in finibus mundi*: 'at the ends of the earth'.[3] In his own theology, Eriugena took from Maximus, according to D. J. Geanakoplos, his teaching on God's transcendence and simplicity, as well as his doctrine of the Spirit's procession from Father through Son, and, more characteristically Maximian in tenor, the notion that the divine attributes 'descend' into the human virtues, as man rises towards God by charity.[4] It was as the combined translating work of Eriugena and Anastasius, that the associated texts of Denys and Maximus were handed down in the West: the *Corpus Anastasianum*. Anastasius also produced a Latin summary of the *Mystagogia*, under the title

---

[2] *Versio Maximi* (PL 122, 1195a). See on this M. Cappuyns, *Jean Scot Erigène. Sa vie, son oeuvre, sa pensée* (Paris-Louvain 1933), p. 162; idem., 'La *Versio Ambiguorum Maximi* de Jean Scot Erigène', *Recherches de théologie ancienne et médiévale* 30 (1963), pp. 324-329.

[3] PL 122, 1027-1028.

[4] D. J. Geanakoplos, 'Some Aspects of the Influence of the Byzantine Maximos the Confessor on the Theology of East and West', *Church History* 38 (1969), pp. 150-163. For a fuller account, see E. Jeauneau, 'Jean Scot Erigène et le Grec', *Archivium Latinitatis Medii Aevi* 41 (1979), pp. 5-50.

Historia mystica Ecclesiae catholicae Maximi,[5] and a series of
extracts from the writings connected with the Lateran Council
of 649, entitled *Collectanea ad controversiam et historiam
Monothelitarum spectantia.*[6] Later, the *Centuriae de Caritate* were
translated in twelfth century Hungary by the Venetian monk
Cerbanus, though little, apparently, disseminated.[7] That work
would be re-translated, in the later fifteenth century, by Petrus
Balbus, bishop of Tropea, who added for good measure the
Liber asceticus and Maximus' *Letter to John the Chamberlain.*[8]

But whatever profit Western Christians may have found in
Maximus' ascetical and mystical writings, it was as a student,
and corrector, of Denys that they were most influenced by him.
They found it, however, extremely difficult to disentangle the
contributions of Denys, Maximus and John of Scythopolis: at
any rate, it was the combined work of the latter two which
stabilised for the Latin theological tradition the Catholic
interpretation of Denys. In this sense, a chain of influence
winds through Bernard and Hugh of Saint Victor, Albert and
Thomas, Grosseteste, Eckhart and the Rhineland mystics to, in
the later Middle Ages or early Renaissance, Nicholas of Cusa
and his friend and secretary Petrus Balbus.

In the East, by contrast, Maximus was read more
independently of Denys, whose fame stood higher in the West
which, when alive, he had never known. Geanakoplos warns,
though, that much remains to be excavated from the literary
remains if we are to judge the effect of Maximus' influence on
specific scholars and theologians in the middle and later
Byzantine period. Investigation of one such figure, John
Cyparissiotes, from the fourteenth century, a Greek who,
under the influence of Dominican theologians residing in the

---

[5]S. Pétridès, 'Traités liturgiques de saint Maxime et de saint Germain traduits par Anastase le bibliothécaire', in *Revue de l'Orient chrétien* 10 (1905), pp. 289-313; 350-364.

[6]E. Dekkers, 'Maxime le Confesseur dans la traditione latine', in C. Lagan, J. A. Munitiz and L. van Rompay (eds.), *After Chalcedon. Studies in Theology and Church History Offered to Professor A. van Roey for his Seventieth Birthday* (Leuven 1985), pp. 11-21.

[7]A. B. Terebessy (ed.), *Translatio latina sancti Maximi Confessoris, De caritate ad Elpidium, libri I-IV, saeculo XII. in Hungaria confecta* (Budapest 1944).

[8]E. Dekkers, 'Maxime le Confesseur dans la tradition latine', art. cit.

East and the Thomistic circle of Kydones at the Byzantine court, became a Latinophile, moving eventually to the West and working, indeed, for pope Gregory IX both at Avignon and at Rome, shows Maximus to have been a leading source for a writer who, though 'Latin' in the presentation of his theology, where he utilised numerous Scholastic devices, was entirely Greek in the literary content of his work.[9]

Geanakoplos' surmise that, in Byzantium where, after the 'Triumph of Orthodoxy', emphasis was laid above all on the preservation of the theological pronouncements of the ecumenical Councils and the teachings of the Greek Fathers, Maximus' example was invoked, not to bring about innovation in theological thought, despite his own creativity of mind, but to strengthen what was already accepted, is, broadly speaking, confirmed by Jaroslav Pelikan in his essay 'The Place of Maximus Confessor in the History of Christian Thought'.[10] For Pelikan, Maximus' chief use to the Byzantine church lay in his re-thinking of Denys' philosophical theology in terms of the trinitarian and christological doctrine bequeathed by the Cappadocian Fathers. Pointing out that, for the latter, apophatic theology was essentially a foil to the radiance of a cataphatic account of the God who, in his Word, had made to a degree available to human understanding what, by essence, was utterly unknowable to man, Pelikan wrote:

> Hence, with due allowance for the spectrum from Gregory of Nyssa to Basil the Great to Gregory the Theologian, we may say that the corollary to Cappadocian apophaticism was a theological method that was Christocentric and Scriptural, in a way that the system of the pseudo-Dionysius was neither Christocentric nor Scriptural. One of the most important ways to identify the place of Maximus

[9]D. J. Geanakoplos, 'Some Aspects of the Influence of the Byzantine Maximos the Confessor on the Theology of East and West', art. cit., which makes use of the full study of John by B. Dentakis, published at Athens in 1965 as *Ioannês Kyparissiotês, ho sophos kai philosophos.*

[10]J. Pelikan, 'The Place of Maximus Confessor in the History of Christian Thought', in F. Heinzer — C. Schönborn (eds.), *Maximus Confessor. Actes du Symposium sur Maxime le Confesseur* (Fribourg 1982), pp. 387-402.

Confessor in the history of Christian thought is to see him in his rôle of an interpreter of Denys the Areopagite, as the one who turned apophatic theology around, from the speculative nihilism that was its potential outcome back to a concentration on the person of Jesus Christ.[11]

Maximus' was, in the full sense of the word, a Byzantine *Gospel*.

Though until the nineteenth century Maximus' greatness was largely lost to view, and he became, as in the cover-illustration of this book, just one more tiny Byzantine saint on the jewelled surface of a manuscript, his reputation today has never stood higher since his own lifetime. The explanation must be sought in the richness of his message. The themes of his Gospel, as expressed in the main monographs studied in this book, explain his attractiveness to (especially) Orthodox and Catholic theologians today. For here we have not only a profoundly trinitarian reading of the Gospel story, corresponding to the desire of the best twentieth century dogmatics that theology be triune reflection through and through. We find also a cosmology which presents man as the priest of nature, unifying, through the Word Incarnate, its myriad forms and powers. That all of this finds its issue in the liturgical cultus of the Church, seen as anticipatory participation in the unity of the Age to Come, only adds to its attractiveness: for the Great Church can neglect neither the order of creation, highlighted today as ecological awareness, nor creation's more wonderful re-making in the sacramental mysteries of the God-Man and their final outcome in glory. If Hans Urs von Balthasar, the pre-eminent Catholic theologian of the twentieth century's second half, could laud Maximus as the transcriber of the 'Cosmic Liturgy', John Zizioulas, the most acute Orthodox theologian of the same period, found inspiration at the same source for his ideas of 'cosmological prophecy' and 'eucharistic cosmology'.[12] Here, once the sense of strangeness at a far-off world is overcome, lies a feast for thinking and devotion, for mind and heart.

[11]Ibid., p. 398.
[12]J. Zizioulas, 'Preserving God's Creation (1)', *Theology in Green* 5 (1993), pp. 15-26.

Appendix

The Rediscovery of Maximus: A Brief History of Maximian Scholarship

Before the second half of the nineteenth century, little was known about Maximus the Confessor by students of the Fathers, even though his writings were in principle available to them. In 1675, as part of the *mouvement de ressourcement* of the French *grand siècle*, the learned Dominican patrologist François Combefis had published the first two volumes of three, which together were intended to offer the Confessor's *opera omnia*. In the French National Archives are conserved Combefis' working papers for the last volume, which would have comprised a major treatise by Maximus (the *Book of Ambiguities*), a minor work on matters calendrical and chronological (the *Computus ecclesiasticus*), and the 'scholia' on the writings of Denys the Areopagite, a commentary now ascribed to John of Scythopolis. With its exhaustive indices, Combefis' work is a marvel of early modern thoroughness and dedication.[1] Though the expanded edition of Cardinal Baronius' *Annales Ecclesiastici* published at Lucca in 1742 contained in its eleventh volume substantial references to Maximus' life, an appendix explained that, while the Vatican library (of which Baronius was librarian) contained

---

[1] *S. Maximi Confessoris graecorum theologi eximiique philosophi Operum tomus primus (secundus) ex probatissimis quaeque mss. codicibus, Regiis, Card. Mazarini, Seguierianis, Vaticanis, Barberinis, Magni Ducis Florentinis, Venetis, etc. eruta, nova versione subacta, notisque illustrata, opera et studio R. P. F. Combefis* (Paris 1675). The survey of Maximian scholarship in this chapter is indebted to M. L. Gatti, *Massimo il Confessore. Saggio di bibliografia generale ragionata e contributi per una reconstruzione scientifica del suo pensiero metafisico e religioso* (Milan 1987), pp. 136-351.

several copies of Maximus' disputation with his Monothelite opponent Pyrrhus of Constantinople, it had been decided to omit this work, lest its prolixity tire the reader. As a comment passed in a book whose title is ninety-nine words long, this was rather rich.[2]

The modern study of Maximus begins with a study by the great conciliar historian Karl Joseph Hefele in the *Theologische Quartalschrift* for 1857.[3] Reversing the judgment of the author of the appendix to volume eleven of Baronius' *Annales ecclesiastici*, Hefele underlines the importance of the *Disputatio cum Pyrrho* as the best defence of the two wills of the Word Incarnate come down to us from the age of the Monothelite debate. In the same year, by chance, F. Oehler produced at Halle the first printed version of Maximus' *Book of Ambiguities*, basing himself, however, on but one fourteenth century manuscript.[4] Two years later, the first attempt at an overall characterisation of Maximus' theological work saw the light of day. With a remarkable comprehensiveness, the pages devoted to Maximus in J. Huber's *Die Philosophie der Kirchenväter* anticipate many of the conclusions of later research.[5] Huber presents Maximus as the most mature theologian of the Greek church. His speculative gifts found expression, so Huber reports, in an ordered variety of ways: in mystical contemplation; in the exposition of doctrine, to whose service he pressed an

[2]*Annales Ecclesiastici, auctore C. Baronio Sorano e Congregatione Oratorii S. R. E. presbytero Cardinali Tit. SS. Nerei et Achillei et Sedis Apostolicae Bibliothecario, una cum critica historico-chronologica P. A. Pagii Doctoris Theologi Ordinis Minorum Convent. S. Francisci, in qua rerum narratio defenditur, illustratur, suppletur, ordo temporum corrigitur et Periodo Graeco-Romano munitur, additur praetera Dissertatio Hypatica eiusdem Pagii; et Epistola consularis H. Card. Norisii, in hac vero editione Fasti Consulares ab A. U. C. 709 ad annum Christi 567 illustrantur, supplentur, et castigantur. Accedunt animadversiones in Pagium, et praecipue circa Chronologiam inferioris aevi ab eo digestam, Tomus undecimus* (Lucca 1742).

[3]K. J. Hefele, 'Sophronius und Maximus über die zwei Willen in Christus', *Theologische Quartalschrift* (1857), pp. 189-223.

[4]*Tou en hagiois Patros hêmôn Maximou tou Homologêtou Peri diaphorôn aporiôn tôn hagiôn Dionysiou kai Grêgoriou pros Thôman ton hêgiasmenon, Sancti Patris nostri Maximi Confessoris De variis difficilibus locis SS. PP. Dionysii et Gregorii ad Thomam v. s. librum ex codice manuscripto Gudiano, descripsit e in latinum sermonem interpretatus post I. Scoti et Th. Galae tentamina nunc primum integrum edicit F. Oehler* (Halle 1857).

[5]J. Huber, *Die Philosophie der Kirchenväter* (Munich 1859), pp. 341-358.

allegorical style of biblical interpretation; and in the construction of a Christian *Weltanschauung* which incorporates whatever is best in the thinking of his theological predecessors. J. P. Migne's *Patrologia Graeca* reached the works of Maximus in 1865,[6] and consisted in an amalgam of the work of Combefis and Oehler. It remained the usually cited text until the new editions produced by the scholarly équipe of *Corpus Christianorum* in the 1980s. In 1867, J. Carnadet's edition of the *Acta Sanctorum* reached the middle days of August, including Maximus' death-day, 13th August. The opportunity was taken to gather together numerous texts relevant to the life of the Confessor.[7]

The remaining nineteenth century contributions to Maximian studies can be dealt with fairly summarily. The Freiburg Catholic encyclopaedia, *Wetzer und Welte's Kirchenlexikon*, did Maximus justice in an ample article by one Knöpfler, which called for more ambitious study of the Confessor's work.[8] In point of fact, the first doctoral thesis on Maximus' work had appeared, in Germany, nearly a quarter of a century previously, but it was many years before its exploration of Maximus' Christology and soteriology — which its author presented as both original and remarkably coherent — was taken further.[9] The more generous study which Knöckler's encyclopaedia entry desiderated appeared, however, with commendable timing, in 1894, the year after the Freiburg Lexikon itself. F. A. Preuss' *Ad Maximi Confessoris de Deo doctrinam*

---

[6] *Patrologiae cursus completus, seu bibliotheca universalis, integra, uniformis, commoda, oeconoma, omnium SS. Patrum, Doctorum Scriptorumque Ecclesiasticorum, sive Latinorum, sive Graecorum, Series Graeca prior* 90 [91] (Tournholt 1865).

[7] *Acta Sanctorum, quotquot toto orbe coluntur, vel a catholicis scriptoribus celebrantur, ex latinis et graecis, aliarumque gentium antiquis monumentis collecta, digesta, illustrata a J. B. Sollerio, J. Plinio, G. Cupero, P. Boschio, editio novissima, curante J. Carnadet, Augusti tomus tertius, quo dies XIII, XIV, XV, XVI, XVII, XVIII, XIX, continentur* (Paris and Rome 1867).

[8] Knöpfler, 'Maximus, der heilige, beigenannt Confessor', *Wetzer und Welte's Kirchenlexikon, oder Enzyklopädie der katholischen Theologie und ihrer Hülfswissenschaften, zweite Auflage, in neuer Bearbeitung, unter Mitwirkung vieler katholischen Gelehrten, begonnen von J. Hergenröther, fortgesetzt von F. Kaulen, Band VIII* (Freiburg 1893), cols. 1096-1103.

[9] H. Wester, 'S. Maximi Confessoris praecepta de Incarnatione Dei et deificatione hominis exponuntur et examinantur' (Halle-Berlin 1869).

adnotationes ranged widely through such themes as Maximus' understanding of apophatic and cataphatic theology, his concept of revelation, of the creation of the cosmos, of Trinity, Incarnation, and Redemption, of charity, deification and salvation.[10] This book was a hopeful augury for twentieth century interest in Maximus' achievement.

Although 1902 saw an essay on Maximus' eschatology, which its author, M. Michaud, considered little divergent from Gregory of Nyssa's doctrine of *apokatastasis*, the final restoration of all things in a world without Hell,[11] the most substantial early twentieth century studies of Maximus concerned his Christology. H. Straubinger's *Die Christologie des heiligen Maximus Confessor* set out to identify Maximus' rôle in the development of christological dogma. After a preliminary survey of the emergence of Monothelitism, Straubinger presented the Confessor's doctrine of Christ's two natures and their activity, following the scheme: operation, will, passions, and considers the significance of the Word's assumption of these for Maximus' account of the Atonement.[12] An article of the following year by the same author, on Maximus' relation to Sophronius of Jerusalem, his friend and ally, inaugurated the habit of comparing Maximus with Thomas Aquinas — by no means a merely formalistic *démarche* of the Thomistic revival, for real parallels exist.[13] Meanwhile in 1903 the Protestant equivalent of the Freiburg *Kirchenkexikon*, the *Realencyklopädie für protestantische Theologie und Kirche*, had offered its own entry on Maximus. While entering a caveat as to just how successful the Confessor had been in integrating, within a harmonious unity, the different elements of Christian thought he had inherited, the two authors concurred in finishing with high praise. Not

---

[10]F. A. Preuss, *Ad Maximi Confessoris de Deo doctrinam adnotationes* (Schneeberg 1894).

[11]M. Michaud, 'S. Maxime le Confesseur et l'apocatastase', *Revue internationale de théologie* 10 (1902), pp. 257-272.

[12]H. Straubinger, *Die Christologie des heiligen Maximus Confessor* (Bonn 1906).

[13]Idem., 'Die Lehre des Patriarchen Sophronius von Jerusalem über die Trinität, die Inkarnation und die Person Christi. Mit besonderer Berücksichtigung in ihren Hauptpunkten zugleich verglichen mit den Sätzen des hl. Thomas', *Der Katholik*, 3rd series. XXXV (1907), pp. 81-109; 175-198; 251-265.

only was Maximus one of the main channels whereby many waters of theological and mystical teaching from the Christian East and antiquity had reached the Western Church and Middle Ages. He was also, in all relevant respects

> one of the ... most estimable, one of the greatest, Christian thinkers of all time, known and valued, except from afar, by few, yet nonetheless in the firmament of the Christian Church a star of the first magnitude.[14]

The first decade of the new century closed with two contributions of the chronology of Maximus' life: one, with that title, was an ambitious overview; the other concentrated on the arrest and trial, with particular reference to Maximus' companions, Anastasius the Monk and his homonym, Anastasius the Apocrisarius.[15] Of those two, Montmasson's chronological study was the first of a number of distinguished essays on Maximus published from Constantinople by the journal of the Pères Assomptionistes, *Echos d'Orient* — now the *Revue des Etudes Byzantines*.

The new decade opened with a severely technical study, J. Dräseke's 'Maximus Confessor und Johannes Scotus Erigena'. While confirming that Maximus' influence on Eriugena — and via him on the development of Western theology — was considerable, Dräseke pointed out that the Irish doctor had not always understood Maximus' Greek. However, the very literalness of Eriugena's translations is a help to the textual critic of Maximus' works—and indeed the *Corpus Christianorum* edition of the *Liber Ambiguum*, published in 1988, would print in parallel columns Eriugena's Latin version.[16] In 1911

---

[14]A. I. Wagenmann – R. Seeberg, 'Maximus Konfessor', *Realencyclopädie für protestantische Theologie and Kirche, begründet von J. J. Herzog, in dritter verbesserten und vermehrter Auflage unter Mitwirkung vieler Theologen und anderer Gelehrten, herausgegeben von A. Hauck, Band XII* (Lepizig 1903), pp. 457-470, and here at p. 470.

[15]E. Montmasson, 'Chronologie de la vie de saint Maxime le Confesseur', *Echos d'Orient* 13 (1910), pp. 149-154; J. Stiglmayer, 'Der heilige Maximus "mit seinen beiden Schüler"', *Der Katholik* 88 (1908), pp. 39-45.

[16]J. Dräseke, 'Maximus Confessor und Johannes Scotus Erigena', *Theologische Studien und Kritiken* 84 (1911), pp. 20-60; 204-229.

Montmasson heralded the post-Great War interest in Maximus as a figure in the history of spirituality by his eassay on the handling by Maximus of the *apatheia* theme.[17] And in the last pre-Great War contribution, the English Benedictine, John Chapman, later abbot of Downside, wrote a careful appraisal for the *Catholic Encyclopaedia* — the first modern account in the English tongue.[18] Here it may be noted that, because of the tendency of Anglican divinity to regard the first four Ecumenical Councils only as authoritative for Christian theology, and of the consequent practice, in the old Anglican Universities, for the syllabus to terminate, where early Christian doctrine was concerned, with Chalcedon in 451, or, at best, with the death of Leo the Great in 461, Maximus is simply too 'late' a Father to have been the object of much concern.

No such inhibitions were felt in Russia. In 1915 S. L. Epifanovich published at Kiev his comprehensive survey *Prepodobnyi Maksim Ispovednik i vizantiiskoe bogoslovie*, whose characteristic mark it is to stress at once Maximus' position as synthesiser of the preceding Greek patristic tradition and also — and this was Epifanovich's own emphasis — his rôle as initiator of a new epoch in Christian thought: Byzantine theology.[19] Epifanovich proposed to follow up this work by a new edition of all the texts of Maximus, including documents relevant to his life and various fragments come to light in patristic *florilegia* and elsewhere. However, the outbreak of the Great War and the two revolutions of 1917 put an end to this hope. Nonetheless, Epifanovich was able, before the curtain of Bolshevism finally descended, to bring out a curtailed version of this latter project: a substantial compendium of 'materials'

---

[17]E. Montmasson, 'La doctrine de l'apatheia d'après saint Maxime', *Echos d'Orient* 14 (1911), pp. 36-41.

[18]J. Chapman, 'Maximus of Constantinople, Saint', *The Catholic Encyclopaedia. An International Work of Reference on the Constitution, Doctrine, Discipline and History of the Catholic Church*, Edited by C. G. Herbermann, E. A. Place, C. B. Pallen, T. J. Shahan, J. J. Wynne, Assisted by Numerous Collaborators, Fifteen Volumes and Index, Volume X (New York 1913), pp. 78-81.

[19]S. L. Epifanovich, *Prepodobnyi Maksim Ispovednik i vizantiiskoe bogoslovie* (Kiev 1915).

for the life of Maximus, and indications of the whereabouts of a number of fragments.[20]

Before the decade was out, two Western scholars added brief contributions: W. M. Peitz on the inter-related rôles of Maximus and pope Martin I in the Monothelite crisis, and A. Saudreau, in the course of a resumé of Maximus' spiritual doctrine, on the relation of the virtues, and the grace of the Holy Spirit, to contemplation.[21]

The 1920s offered examples of four of the main kinds of enquiry we have noted so far. First, there were studies, by V. Grumel and R. Devreesse, devoted to Maximus' biography.[22] Secondly, Grumel also wrote an overview of the encyclopaedia entry sort — this time for the *Dictionnaire de Théologie Catholique*.[23] Thirdly, Maximus' burgeoning reputation as a representative of the Eastern spiritual tradition found expression in a German translation, with introduction, of the *Liber asceticus*.[24] Fourthly, Grumel made yet another appearance — but now as interpreter of Maximus' dogmatic theology. His 'L' union hypostatique et la comparaison de l'âme au corps chez Léonce de Byzance et saint Maxime le Confesseur' broke fresh ground in its effort to locate Maximus' in relation to the Neo-Chalcedonian theologians of the previous century and their attempt to work out a 'metaphysic of the Incarnation'.[25] Grumel pointed out

---

[20]Idem., *Materialy k izucheniiu zhizni i tvorenij prep. Maksima Ispovednika* (Kiev 1917).

[21]W. M. Peitz, 'Martin I, und Maximus Confessor. Beiträge zur Geschichte des Monotheletenstreites in den Jahren 645-668', *Historisches Jahrbuch* 38 (1917), pp. 213-236; 429-458; A. Saudreau, 'Saint Maxime', *La Vie spirituelle* 1 (1919-1920), pp. 255-264.

[22]V. Grumel, 'Notes d'histoire et de chronologie sur la vie de saint Maxime le Confesseur', *Echos d'Orient* 26 (1927), pp. 24-32; R. Devreesse, 'La vie de s. Maxime le Confesseur et ses récensions', *Analecta Bollandiana* 46 (1928), pp. 5-49.

[23]V. Grumel, 'Maxime de Chrysopolis ou Maxime le Confesseur (Saint)', *Dictionnaire de Théologie Catholique, contenant l'exposé des doctrines de la Théologie Catholique, leur preuves et leur histoire, commencé sous la direction de A. Vacant, et E. Mangenot, continue sous selle de E. Amann, tome X, partie 1* (Paris 1928), cols. 448-459.

[24]M. Garbas, *Des heiligen Maximus Confessor Buch vom geistlichen Leben (Liber asceticus) aus dem Griechischen ins Deutsche übertragen und mit einer Einleitung versehen* (Breslau 1925).

[25]V. Grumel, 'L'union hypostatique et la comparaison de l'âme et du corps chez Léonce de Byzance et saint Maxime le Confesseur', *Echos d'Orient* 25 (1926), pp. 393-406.

that, while Maximus took from Leontius of Byzantium a concept of the hypostasis as *einai kath' heauto*, self-subsistence, and the notion of *enhypostaton*, the 'enhypostatised', as well as valuable clarifications of such terms as *phusis, hypostasis, henôsis phusikê, henôsis hypostatikê* — 'nature', 'person', 'physical union', 'hypostatic union', he also recognised that Leontius' defective anthropology, with its tendency to treat body and soul as two complete substances, united hypostatically, led to an equally deficient Christology, with a three-natured Redeemer, body, soul, divinity. There is no natural union in Christ, only a hypostatic one, and Grumel applauded Maximus for stressing that the union of the Incarnation is strictly incomparable with any 'composition' that the created order can propose as comparison.

In the 1930s interest in Maximus was almost entirely confined to his place in the history of Christian spirituality. Writing in *Echos d'Orient*, M. T. Disdier located the 'dogmatic foundations' of Maximus' spirituality in his doctrines of man made to God's image, of original sin, and of the restoration of the image by grace.[26] A much more influential study, however, was M. Viller's investigation of Maximus' debt, as an ascetic writer, to Evagrius of Pontus.[27] Spiritual development, from the 'practical' life of the virtues to the 'gnostic' life of contemplation, follows the same route, with the same stages, in Maximus as in Evagrius. And yet, as Viller was not slow to point out, Maximus also corrected the Evagrian scheme, avoiding those aspects of both Origen and Evagrius which had suffered condemnation in the course of the sixth century, and holding fast to the elements in the teaching both of the Alexandrian doctor and the monk of Scetis, that were of enduring orthodox value. A few years later Irénée Hausherr, comparing the influence on Maximus of Evagrius and Denys, would hand the palm unhesitatingly to the

---

[26]M. T. Disdier, 'Les fondements dogmatiques de la spiritualité de saint Maxime le Confesseur', *Echos d'rient* 29 (1930), pp. 296-311.

[27]M. Viller, 'Aux sources de la spiritualité de S. Maxime. Les oeuvres d'Evagre le Pontique', *Revue d'Ascétique et de Mystique* 11 (1930), pp. 156-184; 239-268; 331-336.

former.[28] Tracing the river of spiritual influence in its *down*stream course, Etienne Gilson, about the same time, identified Maximus as a major figure, mediated by Eriugena, in the background of St Bernard.[29]

In addition, the 1930s saw two translations of the *Mystagogia*, into Italian and French successively.[30] As to the interpretation of Maximus' dogmatic works, those who read Russian could find an excellent overview in G. V. Florovskii's *Vizantiiskie Ottsy V-VIII [vv.]*. Surveying Maximus' life and work, and its outcome in the Sixth Ecumenical Council as well as his theology, Florovskii emphasised the holistic and indeed systematic character of the Confessor's theological vision. He alerted his readers to the wider significance (beyond the Monothelite-Dyothelite clash) of Maximus' stress on volitional factors. The Christian life is founded not only on grace, through the sacraments, but also, via grace, on *podvig* — ascetical effort. Maximus' Gospel is, in a punning Russian phrase, based on *otrechenie, ne mol'ko otblechenie,* 'renunciation, not just distraction', and thus anticipates a major theme of Florovskii's own dogmatics, the synergy of divine grace and human effort or grace-awakened freedom.[31] Readers lacking Russian had to be content with E. Stéphanou's 'La coexistence initials du corps et de l'âme d'après saint Grégoire de Nysse et saint Maxime l'Homologète', which suggested how, while both the Cappadocian Father and the Confessor had set out to combat the notion of the soul's pre-existence, of the two *Maximus'* doctrine was the more refined and rich, owing to the reflection

---

[28]I. Hausherr, 'Ignorance infinie', *Orientalia Christiana Periodica* 2 (1936), pp. 351-362.

[29]E. Gilson, 'Maxime, Erigène, S. Bernard', in *Aus der Geisteswelt des Mittelalters. Studien und Texte M. Grabmann zur Vollendung des 60. Lebensjahres von Freunden und Schülern gewidmet, herausgegeben von A. Lang, J. Lechner, M. Schmaus, Halbband I* (Münster 1935), pp. 188-195.

[30]*S. Massimo Confessore, La Mistagogia ed altri scritti, a cura di R. Cantarella* (Florence 1931); M. Lot-Borodine, 'Mystagogie de Saint Maxime', *Irénikon* 13 (1936), pp. 466-472; 595-597; 717-720 14 (1937), pp. 66-69; 182-195; 282-284; 444-448. 15 (1938), pp. 71-74' 185-186; 276-278; 390-391; 488-492.

[31]G. V. Florovskii, *Vizantiiski Ottsy V-VIII [vv]* (Paris 1933), pp. 195-227; Et. *The Byzantine Fathers of the Sixth to Eighth Century* (Vaduz, Liechtenstein 1987), pp. 208-253.

on his metaphysical and anthropological concerns of his exemplary Christology.[32]

The 1940s were epochal in Maximian studies thanks to, above all, the appearance of two new students of his thought: Hans Urs von Balthasar, later to become the finest Catholic dogmatic theologian of the century, and — at first on a much more modest scale — the French Dominican Irénée-Henri Dalmais, whose many articles on Maximus would prevent the interest of a younger generation from flagging, when the post-conciliar crisis in Catholic theology had cast into oblivion much of the early twentieth century patristic revival. While on the one hand, Balthasar demonstrated that the commentary or *scholia* on the treatises of Denys the Pseudo-Areopagite, and traditionally ascribed to Maximus, were in overwhelmingly large part the work of John of Scythopolis,[33] on the other hand he vindicated the Maximian authorship of another work, whose authenticity had been sometimes denied: the *Capitula theologica et economica* or 'Gnostic Centuries'. Dealing in turn with 'Origenistic motifs', 'Evagrian motifs', and what he termed 'counter motifs', *Gegenmotive*, Balthasar underlined the importance of Origen and Denys (and not simply of Evagrius) for the making of Maximus' thought, as well as the latter's strongly synthetic character.[34] Of greater interest and accessibility to a wider public was Balthasar's attempt to expound the inner riches of that synthesis, *Kosmische Liturgie*, the concluding volume of a trilogy whose other members concerned respectively Origen and Gregory of Nyssa.[35] Though in this work Balthasar considered Maximus more of a compiler than an original mind, he applied to him his own nuanced generalisations about the Fathers at large. The more we know them the smaller they appear (because much in Christian

---

[32]E. Stéphanou, 'La coexistence initiale du corps et de l'âme d'après saint Grégoire de Nysse et saint Maxime l'Homologéte', *Echos d'Orient* 31 (1932), pp. 304-315.

[33]H. U. Von Balthasar, 'Das Scholienwerk des Johannes von Skythopolis', *Scholastik* 15 1940), pp. 16-38.

[34]Idem., *Die 'Gnostischen Centurien' des Maximus Confessor* (Freiburg 1941).

[35]Idem., *Kosmische Liturgie. Maximus der Bekenner. Höhe und Krise des griechischen Weltbilds* (Freiburg 1941).

thought is still embryonic in their work) but also the greater (because, when their writings are penetrated with love, their significance extends towards that further horizon). Similarly, as our understanding grows, so does their distance from us (because their situation was much different from ours) and their closeness (because their struggle is our struggle).

Dalmais' earliest essay on Maximus hails him as 'doctor of charity' and, by way of a detailed examination of Letter 2, speaks of his doctrine as fundamentally Pauline — but developed within a theology nourished philosophically by Platonism and Stoicism.[36]

Meanwhile, further translations were seeing the daylight: the *Liber asceticus* was put into Italian, with an introduction, and, in similar format, the *Centuries on Charity* into French.[37]

Two studies of Maximus' doctrine, one large, one small, round off a portrait of the 1940s. J. Loosen's *Logos und Pneuma im begnadeten Menschen bei Maximus Confessor* traced the roles of Word and Spirit in man's transfiguration by grace in Maximus' thought, while D. J. Unger published in *Franciscan Studies* an essay on Maximus' Christocentrism intended to link him to such Franciscan masters of the Latin Middle Ages as St Bonaventure.[38]

In the 1950s Maximian studies revolved around a small number of highly productive figures. In the first place comes Dalmais who wrote both on Maximus' spirituality, and on his cosmological ideas. Dalmais claimed for Maximus' *Commentary on the Pater* the status of climax of his spiritual writings, its often tortuous meanderings the result of its author's effort to express a thought by now rich to excess.[39] The *Liber asceticus* he

---

[36] I.-H. Dalmais, 'Saint Maxime le Confesseur, Docteur de la Charité', *La Vie spirituelle* 79 (1948), pp. 294-303.

[37] *S. Massimo Confesore, Il libro ascetico, traduzione del greco ed introduzione a cura di M. Dal Pra* (Milan 1944); *Maxime le Confesseur, Centuries sur la Charité, introduction et traduction de J. Pegon* (Paris 1945).

[38] J. Loosen, *Logos und Pneuma im begnadeten Menschen bei Maximus Confessor* (Münster 1941); D. J. Unger, 'Christ Jesus Centre and Final Scope of all Creation according to St Maximus Confessor', *Franciscan Studies* 9 (1949), pp. 50-62.

[39] I.-H. Dalmais, 'L'eouvre spirituelle de saint Maxime le Confesseur. Notes sur son développement et sa signification', *Supplément à la Vie spirituelle* 6 (1952), pp. 216-226.

regarded as Maximus' spiritual testament; compared with more famous monuments of Greek Christian asceticism such as the Basilian rules, its theological density is striking, and is owed especially to Maximus' conviction that both creation and history find their *skopos*, their ultimate point, in the Incarnation of the Word.[40] Returning to Maximus' exposition of the Lord's Prayer, Dalmais treats it as a real *compendium theologiae*, the seven requests of the *Pater* disclosing the seven chief mysteries: the revelation of God; filial adoption by grace; the equality of human beings with the Angels; participation in life eternal; the restoration of human nature from distorted passions; liberation from the law of sin; the destruction of the tyranny of the Evil One. Dalmais particularly stressed the value, in this text, of Maximus' anthropology.[41] In the one primarily cosmological essay among these, Dalmais offers a succinct exposition of the Maximian doctrine of the *logoi*. Like Origen, Maximus presents a threefold embodiment of the Word: in creatures, in Scripture, in the flesh — and sees the Word Incarnate in Jesus as the bond of all.[42]

With Dom Polycarp Sherwood's 'Notes on Maximus the Confessor', published in the opening issue of the *American Benedictine Review*, a new authority made its weight felt.[43] Hoping to fill the lacunae in the biography of the Confessor left by Grumel and Devreesse, Sherwood's modestly entitled essay betrayed a master hand. Two years later, he brought the same skills to bear on the dating of Maximus' writings — this time in the fuller space of a monograph.[44] A work of similar scale on the earlier *Ambigua* and Maximus' case against Origenism soon joined these.[45] Its philosophical-theological centre was again

[40]Idem., 'La doctrine ascétique de S. Maxime le Confesseur d'après le *Liber asceticus*', *Irénikon* 26 (1953), pp. 17-39.

[41]Idem., 'Un traité de théologie contemplative. Le *Commentaire du Pater* de S. Maxime le Confesseur', *Revue d'Ascétique et de Mystique* 29 (1953), pp. 123-159.

[42]Idem., 'La théorie des *logoi* des créatures chez S. Maxime le Confesseur', *Revue des Sciences Philosophiques et Théologiques* 36 (1952), pp. 244-249.

[43]P. Sherwood, 'Notes on Maximus the Confessor', The *American Benedictine Review* 1 (1950), pp. 347-356.

[44]Idem., *An Annotated Date-List of the Works of Maximus the Confessor* (Rome 1952).

[45]Idem., *The Earlier 'Ambigua' of Saint Maximus the Confessor and his Refutation of Origenism* (Rome 1955).

displayed in Sherwood's contribution to the Munich international congress of Byzantinists in 1958.[46] Sherwood stresses that for Maximus the incarnate Christ is the *telos*, goal, of creation, in view of which all things receive their *archê*, beginning. If this essay had reference chiefly to the *Book of Ambiguities*, Sherwood's account of Maximus' biblical exegesis, published in the same year, treating mainly of the *Quaestiones ad Thalassium*, came to the same conclusion: namely, that for Maximus, the mystery of Christ is the hermeneutical centre of all Christian reference.[47] Finally, Sherwood offered his conclusions for a wider readership in the extended introduction to his translations of the *Liber Asceticus* and the *Centuriae de Caritate*.[48]

Irénée Hausherr also expanded his earlier work on the Confessor. In *Philautie* Hausherr analysed Maximus' concept of (evil) self-love, with its identification of the source of vices in a directing of the natural faculties to an end that is not their own. Destructive of unity as it is, *philautia* is cured by the knowledge of God, by *askêsis*, and by charity: hence the latter part of Hausherr's book is devoted to 'signes de libération', both exterior — *philadelphia* — and interior, authentic self-love, turned as this is to ethical perfection.[49] Hausherr went on to write the brief but informative entry on Maximus in the *Enciclopedia Cattolica*.[50]

Among other pieces of the jigsaw of Maximus studies, three more may be singled out for the 1950s. R. A. Gauthier's 'Saint Maxime le Confesseur et la psychologie de l'acte humaine' points out that, via Burgundius of Pisa's translation of John

---

[46]Idem., 'Maximus and Origenism. *Archê kai telos*', *Berichte zum XI. Internationalen Byzantinisten-Kongress, München 1958* (Munich 1958), pp. 1-27.

[47]Idem., 'Exposition and Use of Scripture in St Maximus as Manifest in the *Quaestiones ad Thalassium*', *Orientalia Christiana Periodica* 24 (1958), pp. 202-207.

[48]Idem., *Saint Maximus the Confessor, The Ascetic Life, The Four Centuries on Charity*, Translated and Annotated by P. Sherwood (Westminster and London 1955).

[49]I. Hausherr, *Philautie. De la tendresse pour soi à la charité selon saint Maxime le Confesseur* (Rome 1952).

[50]Idem., 'Massimo il Confessore, santo', *Enciclopedia cattolica* VIII (Rome 1952), cols. 307-308.

Damascene, Maximus' account of the human act reached St Thomas Aquinas — for the *De fide orthodoxa* of Damascene is patently indebted to the Confessor's work. Much of Aquinas' understanding of *imperium, consensus, electio*— crucial terms in the phenomenology of will— derives, therefore, from Maximus' synthesis of Hellenic philosophical elements in the new form provided by his preoccupation with the twofold will of Christ.[51] Endre von Ivánka, the Hungarian theologian and student of 'Plato Christianus', also presented Maximus as transcending his inherited philosophical materials— going beyond Platonic dualism and Aristotelian immanentism to establish a Christian philosophy of the creature, even though certain lines of Platonis thinking remain, within that, of importance.[52] Finally, an unpublished Louvain dissertation of 1957 prepared the work for the new critical editions of the 1980s.[53]

In the 1960s the *elenchus* of Maximian scholars was not greatly expanded. Balthasar brought out a second, much revised, edition of *Kosmische Liturgie*.[54] Balthasar now saw Maximus' work as much more of an internal unity. Impressed by Sherwood's conclusions, he withdrew his earlier comments about an 'Origenist crisis' in Maximus' own intellectual life, accepting that the elements the Confessor had retained from Origen were a positive factor in his work. Compared to the first edition, Balthasar gave greater emphasis to Maximus' dogmatic theology, and his (Neo-Chalcedonian) Christology. Though appealing for further study of Maximus' relation to Denys, to the Cappadocians, and to the Neo-Chalcedonians, as well as to the Byzantine liturgy, to Augustine, to the biblical exegesis of the *catenae* and John of Scythopolis' commentaries on Denys,

[51]R. A. Gauthier, 'Saint Maxime le Confesseur et la psychologie de l'acte humaine', *Recherches de théologie ancienne et médiévale* 21 (1954), pp. 51-100.

[52]E. von Ivánka, 'Der philosophische Ertrag der Auseinandersetzung Maximos des Bekenners mit dem Origenismus', *Jahrbuch der Oesterreichischen Byzantinischen Gesellschaft* 8 (1958), pp. 23-49.

[53]G. Mahieu, 'Travaux préparatoires à une édition critique des oeuvres de S. Maxime le Confesseur' (Thesis, Louvain 1957).

[54]H. U. von Balthasar, *Kosmische Liturgie. Das Weltbild Maximus des Bekenners*, zweite, *völlig veränderte Auflage* (Einsiedeln 1961).

Balthasar felt sufficiently confident that he had at least the measure of Maximus' system to identify its watchword as: *asunchytôs*, 'without mixture', a key term of the Chalcedonian Definition.

> The synthesis of Christ becomes a world-theodicy not only for the world's existing but for all its essential structures; all things are inserted into syntheses of an ever fuller kind, even though these themselves are but provisional in the light of the ultimate, all-justifying synthesis of Christ.[55]

Balthasar included in this work translations of the *Mystagogia* and the *Centuriae de Caritate*, as well as large tracts of his earlier presentations of the *Capitula gnostica* and the *Scholia* of John of Scythopolis.

Dalmais maintained his stream of articles in full spate. In a useful phrase, he now spoke of Maximus' 'spiritual anthropology', intending by that a conception of man as finalised in the fulfilment of his vocation, which is to share in the divine life.[56] Re-born into a better condition than that of nature by the Incarnation, all the cosmic syntheses of which man's being forms part are to be unified by charity and integrated, through the hypostatic union of the two natures, into a final synthesis, embracing Creator and creature alike. This scheme, Dalmais went on to show, enabled Maximus to bring out the value of traditional asceticism and the already classic teaching of his monastic predecessors on contemplation, and so help to resolve the 'crisis of Origenist monasticism'.[57] The significance of Maximus' contrast between Adam, the divided man, and Christ, the reconciled man, seemed to Dalmais of ecumenical importance in the year of opening of

---

[55]Ibid., p. 57.

[56] I.-H. Dalmais, 'L'anthropologie spirituelle de saint Maxime le Confesseur', *Recherches et Débats du Centre Catholique des Intellectuels Français* 36 (1961), pp. 202-211.

[57]Idem., 'Saint Maxime le Confesseur et la crise de l'Origénisme monastique', in *Théologie de la Vie monastique. Etudes sur la Tradition patristique* (Paris 1961), pp. 411-421.

the Second Vatican Council.[58] He also approved, in a paper given at the third of Canon F. L. Cross' Patristic Conferences at Christ Church, Oxford, of Maximus' integration of liturgy and asceticism in the *Mystagogia*.[59] Returning to Christ Church for the fourth of those events, Dalmais took advantage of A. Guillaumont's translation from the Syriac of Evagrius' *Kephalaia gnostica* to suggest that Maximus had deliberately inverted Evagrius' triad *stasis-kinêsis-genesis* (stability-movement-becoming) in order to combat the Origenism condemned at Constantinople II.[60] Then in his offering for Marie-Dominique Chenu's *Festschrift* he described, more prosaically, Maximus' vocabulary for human acts, the key terms of his anthropology.[61]

Ivánka brought out an anthology of texts from the *Ambigua* and the *Quaestiones ad Thalassium*, emphasising Maximus' unified vision of creation and salvation: the Incarnate Word turns to himself, by grace, the 'dynamism of ascent' inscribed in the creature, and unites the created and the Uncreated in himself.[62] His *Plato Christianus*, in its seventh chapter, devoted to Maximus, resumes his 1958 essay on the Maximian critique of Origenism.[63]

Grumel, writing for the thirteenth centenary of Maximus' death, painted a pen portrait of the Confessor, and, lamenting the lack of a liturgical commemoration in the then Latin

[58]Idem., 'La fonction unificatrice du Verbe incarné d'après les oeuvres spirituelles de Saint Maxime le Confesseur', *Sciences ecclésiastiques* 14 (1962), pp. 445-459.

[59]Idem., 'Place de la *Mystagogie* de saint Maxime le Confesseur dans la théologie liturgique byzantine', *Papers Presented to the Third International Conference on Patristic Studies held at Christ Church, Oxford, 1959, Part III, Liturgica, Monastica et Ascetica, Philosophica*, Edited by F. L. Cross (= *Studia Patristica* V, Berlin 1962), pp. 277-283.

[60]Idem., 'L'héritage évagrien dans la synthèse de saint Maxime le Confesseur', *Papers presented to the Fourth International Conference on Patristic Studies held at Christ Church, Oxford, 1963, Part II, Patres Apostolici, Historica, Liturgica, Ascetica et Monastica*, Edited by F. L. Cross (= *Studia Patristica* VII, Berlin 1966), pp. 356-362.

[61]Idem., 'Le vocabulaire des activités intellectuelles, volontaires et spirituelles dans l'anthropologie de S. Maxime le Confesseur', in *Mélanges offer à M. D. Chenu, maître en théologie* (Paris 1967), pp. 189-202.

[62]E. von Ivánka, *Maximos der Bekenner. All-Eins in Christus, Auswahl, Uebertragung, Einleitung* (Einsiedeln 1961).

[63]Idem., *Plato Christianus. Uebernahme und Umgestaltung des Platonismus durch die Väter* (Einsiedeln 1964).

calendar, called for his canonical nomination as a doctor of the Church.[64]

Sherwood produced a 'Survey of Recent Work on St Maximus the Confessor' which, unlike the present catalogue, was a good deal more ambitious than simply telling a story.[65] Sherwood brings out the sharp contrast in approach between himself and Balthasar. While the author of the survey had started reading Maximus under the stimulus of teachers who presented him as the *locus classicus* for Byzantine theology, and had always tried to present him in his own context (if also with reference to the Latin theological tradition), Balthasar's perspective was markedly different. The *ratio formalis* of Balthasar's patristic trilogy was given by de Lubac: the relation of the mystery of Christ to modern man. This explains those features of *Kosmische Liturgie* most offputting to specialists: the desire to incorporate Maximus' bold synthesis within a coherent vision of reality including all the values of a post-Cartesian epoch, such as those of German Idealism and modern science. For Balthasar, Maximus had made the Chalcedonian definition into a key unlocking all reality — hence the otherwise inexplicable references to Hegel. Sherwood found this unhelpful: the centre of Maximus' work is not so much the conciliar Christology as the Pauline uniting of all things in Christ. He also called for a study of the participation theme in Byzantine theology, from Denys to Palamas, which might clarify the finite-Infinite, created-Uncreated relationship.

But as well as old favourites, some new names must also be signalled. Beginning from a background in Dionysian studies,[66]

---

[64]V. Grumel, 'Un Centenario, San Massimo Confessore (662-1962)', *Unitas* 18 (1963), pp. 1-23.

[65]P. Sherwood, 'Survey of Recent Work on St Maximus the Confessor', *Traditio* 20 (1964), pp. 428-437.

[66]W. Völker, 'Der Einfluss des Pseudo-Dionysius Areopagita auf Maximus Confessor', in *Universitas. Dienst an Wahrheit und Leben, Festschrift für Bischof Dr A. Stohr, im Auftrag der Katholisch-theologischen Fakultät der Johannes Gutenberg Universität Mainz, herausgegeben von L. Lenhart, Band I* (Mainz 1960), pp. 243-254; idem., 'Der Einfluss des Pseudo-Dionysius Areopagita auf Maximus Confessor', in *Studien zum Neuen Testament und zur Patristik E. Klostermann zum 90. Geburtstag dargebracht, herausgegeben von der Kommission für spätantike Religionsgeschichte* (Berlin 1961), pp. 331-350.

W. Völker produced a monumental study of Maximus as 'master of the spiritual life'.[67] In his investigations of Maximus' debt to Denys, Völker focussed on the theme of divine transcendence. To the dialectic of God's presence in, *en*, creatures and his being beyond, *huper*, them, there corresponds, both for Denys and for Maximus, the contrast of cataphatic and apophatic theology. Not unrelated to this is their shared concept of *ekstasis*, 'ecstasy', whereby the creature must 'stand out of itself' to be in relation with the Uncreated. But Völker also stressed that many streams fed Maximus' river — and noted especially that he sometimes combined Aristotelean ideas with Dionysian. Somewhat later, Völker would enquire further into Maximus' ontology, maintaining that he profited much from Aristotle, notably on the value of the sensuous world, the nature of the soul, and the idea of movement, but deployed these gains within a Neo-Platonic and Dionysian vision of the relation between the One and the Many.[68] His study of Maximus as a spiritual theologian completed the series on Greek-speaking Christian and Jewish mysticism which he had begun as early as 1931, moving from Origen, via Philo of Alexandria, to the Alexandrian Clement, and so to Gregory of Nyssa and Denys. Drawing attention to the rich and nuanced quality of his spiritual teaching, Völker spoke of Maximus as the point of confluence of many doctrinal currents of the patristic age, as well as the departure-point of Byzantine theology proper.

Entirely worthy to be compared with Völker's work, itself written against a background of 'history-of-religions' research rather than theology, was L. Thunberg's *Microcosm and Mediator. The Theological Anthropology of Maximus the Confessor*, which appeared at Lund, Sweden, in the same year and the first, chronologically, of the monographs studied in this book.[69] Thunberg's work treated Völker's themes; sin, the passions,

---

[67] Idem., *Maximus Confessor als Meister des gestlichen Lebens* (Wiesbaden 1965).

[68] Idem., 'Zur Ontologie des Maximus Confessor', in . . . *und fragten nach Jesus. Beiträge aus Theologie, Kirche und Geschichte. Festschrift für E. Barnikol zum 70. Geburtstag* (Berlin 1964), pp. 57-79.

[69] See above, pp. 120-130, 157-194.

the foundations of the spiritual life, action and contemplation, but replaced them in their christological and cosmic — or, more properly *christocentric* context. The idea of man as microcosm, mirroring in himself the variety of the created world, can be taken, Thunberg explains, in a negative sense — in relation to the 'disintegrating' effect of the multitudinous passions and vices of humanity. But it can also be understood in a positive way — in relation to the integrating, or re-integrating, effect of the ascetic life, where by imitation of Christ the virtues abound in their diversity. Thanks to man's creation in God's image and his redemption by Christ, the microcosm cannot be separated from the mediator.[70]

Other contributions of the 1960s can be more summarily indicated. M. Candal discussed an isolated reference of Maximus' to 'uncreated Grace', and concluded that the Palamite interpretation of his theology was poorly founded.[71] R. Bornert devoted to Maximus and his *Mystagogia* the second chapter of his study *Les commentaires byzantins de la Divine Liturgie*.[72] P. Miquel, in the context of the theological recovery of the notion of Christian experience, characteristic of post-War Catholicism, wrote of *peira*: gracious experience as a unique mode of knowledge, going beyond *logos*, concepts and discourse.[73] C. Vona, writing in the *Bibliotheca Sanctorum*, describes the grave of Maximus as still venerated in the nineteenth century — and sums up the evidence of the Byzantine *synaxaria* on his cultus.[74] D. J. Geanakoplos traced Maximian influence, both in the West — via Eriugena's

---

[70]L. Thunberg, *Microcosm and Mediator. The Theological Anthropology of Maximus the Confessor* (Lund 1965).

[71]M. Candal, 'La gracia increada del *Liber ambiguorum* de san Máximo', *Orientalia Christiana Periodica* 27 (1961), pp. 131-149.

[72]R. Bornert, *Les commentaires byzantins de la Divine Liturgie du VIIe au XVe siécle* (Paris 1966).

[73]P. Miguel, 'Peira. Contribution à l'étude du vocabulaire de l'expérience religieuse dans l' oeuvre de Maxime le Confesseur', in *Papers presented to the Fourth International Conference on Patristic Studies held at Christ Church, Oxford, 1963, Part I, Editiones, Critica, Philologica, Biblica*, edited by F. L. Cross (= *Studia Patristica* VI, Berlin 1966), pp. 355-361.

[74]C. Vona, 'Massimo il Confessore, santo', *Bibliotheca Sanctorum* IX (Rome 1967), cols. 41-47.

paraphrases as improved by Anastasius the Librarian, and this *corpus Anastasianum*, Geanakoplos believed, affected Bernard, Hugh of St Victor, Albert the Great, Thomas, and Grosseteste, and possibly also Eckhart, Nicholas of Cusa and Peter Balbus, and also in the East — notably through the fifteenth century John Cyparissiotes, who, though a Byzantine, lived for a while also at Avignon and at Rome.[75]

Finally, new translations also appeared. Hugo Rahner presented some of the documents of Maximus' trial.[76] Père Adalbert Hamman attempted a new translation of the *Mystagogia* into French.[77] A. Argyriou did the same for a number of the *Quaestiones ad Thalassium*.[78] In 1964 P. Canart published, with a translation, the missing second letter of Maximus to Thomas, mentioned by Photius, discovered by Thomas Gale of Trinity College, Cambridge, in 1681 but subsequently lost to view.[79] Lastly, the *Centuriae de Caritate* were done into Italian by A. Ceresa-Gastaldo, in a version which included his own exhaustive investigation of the manuscript tradition of this, perhaps the most readily accessible, to the general reader, of Maximus' works.[80]

In the 1970s the pattern, inevitable for a transient *homo studiens*, of old names gradually supplanted by new is again visible. Dalmais returned to the topic of the *Mystagogia*, which he described as at once one of Maximus' best-planned yet enigmatic works — enigmatic because it does not, in fact, treat of Christian initiation, but, by and large develops the

---

[75]D. J. Geanakoplos, 'Some Aspects of the Influence of the Byzantine Maximos the Confessor on the Theology of East and West', *Church History* 38 (1969), pp. 150-163. See above, pp. 218-219.

[76]H. Rahner, *Kirche und Staat im frühen Christentum. Dokumente aus acht Jahrhundert und ihre Deutung* (Munich 1961).

[77]A. Hammann, *L'Initiation chrétienne. Textes receuillis et présentés, introduction de J. Danièlou* (Paris 1963), pp. 211-246.

[78]A. Argyriou, *Saint Maxime le Confesseur, Le Mystère du Salut, textes traduits et présentés avec une introduction de I. H. Dalmais* (Namur 1964).

[79]P. Canart, 'La deuxième lettre à Thomas de S. Maxime le Confesseur', *Byzantion* 34 (1964), pp. 415-445.

[80]*Massimo Confessore, Capitoli sulla carità, editi criticamente con introduzione, versione e note da A. Ceresa-Gastaldo* (Rome 1963).

characteristic themes of monastic anthropology.[81] A little later, Dalmais proposed that the *Mystagogia* was written for a monastic community, perhaps that of Cyzicus.[82] Dalmais summarised present knowledge of Maximus' life thought and influence in a minor *tour de force* for the encyclopaedia *Catholicisme* in 1979.[83]

Other familiar figures had less to say. Sherwood, in collaboration with F. X. Murphy, brought out a study of the Fifth and Sixth Ecumenical Councils which had perforce to deal with Monothelitism, and so with Maximus.[84] Ceresa-Gastaldo spoke at the Augustinianum, the Roman Patristic Institute, on Maximus' exemplary handling of the nature-supernature relationship, and renewed Grumel's call that he should be declared *doctor Ecclesiae*.[85] Bornert, returning, like Dalmais, to the *Mystagogia*, described Maximus' view of mystagogy as *thêôria* — contemplation: like the biblical words, the Church's cultus will be abolished in the liturgy of eternity.[86]

The lion's share of 70's publications falls, though, to the newcomers. The most productive was J.-M. Garrigues. He found Maximian inspiration in the Sixth Ecumenical Council's presentation of the divine nature as 'energetic' but not as

[81]I.-H. Dalmais, 'Mystère liturgique et divinisation dans la *Mystagogie* de Saint Maxime le Confesseur', in *Epektasis. Mélanges Patristiques offerts au cardinal J. Daniélou, publiés par J. Fontaine et C. Kannengiesser* (Paris 1972), pp. 55-62.

[82]Idem., 'Théologie de l'Eglise et mystère liturgique dans la *Mystagogie* de S. Maxime le Confesseur', in *Papers presented to the Sixth International Conference on Patristic Studies held in Oxford, 1971, Part II, Classica et Hellenica, Liturgica, Ascetica*, edited by E. A. Livingstone (= *Studia Patristica* XIII, Berlin 1975), pp. 145-153.

[83]Idem., 'Maxime le Confesseur' (Saint), in *Catholicisme hier aujourd'hui demain, encyclopédie publiée sous la direction du Centre Interdisciplinaire facultés catholiques de Lille, tome VIII* (Paris 1979), cols. 995-1003.

[84]F. X. Murphy – P. Sherwood, *Constantinople II et Constantinople III*, in *Histoire des Conciles Oecuméniques, 3, publiée sous la direction de G. Dumeige* (Paris 1974).

[85]A. Ceresa-Gastaldo, 'Dimensione humana e prospettiva escatologica in Massimo Confessore', *Renovatio* 12 (1977), pp. 324-329; idem., 'Per la proclammazione di S. Massimo a Dottore della Chiesa', ibid., pp. 135-137.

[86]R. Bornert, 'Explication de la Liturgie et interprétation de l'Ecriture chez Maxime le Confesseur', in *Papers presented to the Fifth International Conference on Patristic Studies held at Oxford, 1967, Part I, Editiones, Critica, Philologica, Biblica, Historica, Liturgica et Ascetica*, Edited by F. L. Cross (= *Studia Patristica* X, Berlin 1970), pp. 323-327.

formally distinct from the divine 'energies' — as Palamism would
have it — and presented Maximus' doctrine of grace more
generally for good measure.[87] Turning to Maximus' Christology,
the same author expounded the rationale of his belief in the
'composed hypostasis' of Christ, over against the Severan
'composed nature'.[88] Garrigues also unravelled the complicated
evidence for Maximus' trial,[89] and investigated his forthright
doctrine of the Roman primacy.[90] Garrigues' full length study of
Maximus, *Maxime le Confesseur. La Charité, avenir divin de l'homme*,
studied above[91] after a detailed account of the saint's life and
writings, considers divinisation from a variety of angles: as the
fulfilment of human nature in God, as personal adoption by the
Son, and as communion of human willing and divine in the Word
Incarnate.[92] If, in the words of Garrigues' title, charity is the divine
future of man, then, by the same token, *philanthropia*, loving
kindness towards man is the human 'future' of God.

Others made substantial offerings, whether as books or
articles. A. Riou's *Le monde et l'Eglise selon Maxime le Confesseur*
was as we have seen dedicated to cosmology and its
transformation by the missions of the Son and the Holy Spirit.[93]
Another work whose conclusions are presented in this book, V.
Croce's *Tradizione e ricerca* took as its subject Maximus'
theological method, treating, after a general overview, Maximus'
biblical exegesis, his appeal to apostolic and patristic Tradition,
and his conception of the rôle of philosophy vis-à-vis revelation.[94]
J. J. Prado's *Voluntad y naturaleza. La antropología filosófica de*

[87]J.-M. Garrigues, 'L'énergie divine et la grâce chez Maxime le Confesseur',
Istina 19 (1974), pp. 272-296.

[88]Idem., 'La Personne composée du Christ d'après saint Maxime le Confesseur',
Revue Thomiste 74 (1974), pp. 181-204.

[89]Idem., 'Le martyre de saint Maxime le Confesseur', ibid., 26 (1976), pp. 410-452.

[90]Idem., 'Le sense de la primauté romaine chez saint Maxime le Confesseur',
Istina 21 (1976), pp. 6-24.

[91]See above, pp. 195-234.

[92]Idem., *Maxime le Confesseur. La Charité, avenir divin de l'homme* (Paris 1976).

[93]A. Riou, *Le monde et l'Eglise selon Maxime le Confesseur* (Paris 1973). See above,
pp. 130-157

[94]V. Croce, *Tradizione e ricerca. Il metodo teologico di San Massimo il Confessore*
(Milan 1974). See above, pp. 24-63.

Máximo el Confessor concentrates, in a presumed context of crisis of the traditional categories of Western humanism, on Maximus' notion of natural will.[95] For Prado, 'movement' and 'difference' are, in Maximus' scheme, the foundational terms for an understanding of created being. Movement is ontologically constitutive of every created nature, and the final unity to which all things tend is a dynamic one, where differences are recuperated, not negated. Consequently, to deny to human nature its natural will — which is its active power of spiritual movement — would be to mutilate it in its specific *logos*. Lastly, among such full-scale studies, comes F.-M. Léthel's *Théologie de l'agonie du Christ*, whose sub-title explains its topic: 'The human freedom of the Son of God and its soteriological importance, as illuminated by St Maximus the Confessor': an account of the crucial mystery, for Maximus' debate with Monothelitism, of the prayer of Christ in the Garden of Gethsemane.[96]

Among articles: in 1973 Sebastian Brock published an anonymous Syriac life of the Confessor: its early sections are, perhaps, imaginative, not least because, emanating as it does from a Monothelite milieu, its author is not always preoccupied with showing Maximus in the best light.[97] A more gracious tribute from a modern source was the essay 'Les deux volontés du Christ selon saint Maxime le Confessur' by the French philosopher Jean-Luc Marion.[98] The Lutheran polymath Jaroslav Pelikan devoted to Maximus' concept of theological authority his contribution to the *Festschrift* in honour of George Florovskii, regarding his fusion of orthodox dogma with 'faith seeking understanding' as masterly.[99] Two articles studied the

[95] J. J. Prado, *Voluntad y naturaleza. La antropología filósofica de Máximo el Confesor* (Rio Cuarto 1974).

[96] F.-M. Léthel, *Théologie de l'agonie du Christ. La liberté humaine du Fils de Dieu et son importance sotériologique mises en lumière par Saint Maxime le confesseur* (Paris 1979).

[97] S. Brock, 'An Early Syriac Life of Maximus the Confessor', in *Analecta Bollandiana* 91 (1973), pp. 299-346.

[98] J.-L. Marion, 'Les deux volontés du Christ selon saint Maxime le Confesseur', *Résurrection* 41 (1973), pp. 18-66.

[99] J. Pelikan, 'Council or Father or Scripture. The Concept of Authority in the Theology of Maximus Confessor', in *The Heritage of the Early Church. Essays in Honour of G. V. Florovskii on the Occasion of his Eightieth Birthday*, edited by D. Neiman and M. Schatkin (Rome 1973), pp. 277-288.

studiers: one, by L. Negri, descriptively, the other, by M. Doucet, more critically — and with a note of warning against undue inflation of Maximus' reputation.[100]

Translations continued to trickle forth: The *Commentary on the Pater* and the first century of the *Capita theologica et economica* into French,[101] the *Liber ambiguum* into modern Greek,in the series *Epi tas pêgas*, 'Back to the Sources', founded by Panagiotis Nellas as a modest companion to *Sources Chrétiennes*.[102] And as to the texts themselves, while G. G. Sotiropoulos brought out his critical edition of the *Mystagogia*,[103] the editors of *Corpus Christianorum* prepared the ground for their work by the relevant section of their exhaustive guide to the texts, *Clavis Patrum Graecorum*.[104] The *Disputatio Maximi et Pyrrhi* was, however, held over until 1980, where it would be discussed under the heading of 'Councils and Catenae'.[105]

Pride of place in the 1980s must go to the new editions: in 1980 itself C. Laga and C. Steel brought out their critical text of the first fifty-five *Quaestiones ad Thalassium*, along with the relevant sections of Eriugena's Latin translation itself earlier than our earliest manuscripts of the *Quaestiones*, which are tenth century. Taking this set of exegetical questions and replies to be, along with the *Book of Ambiguities*, Maximus' most important speculative work, the editors date both to the first years of his African sojourn, between 630 and 634.[106] The

---

[100]L. Negri, 'Elementi cristologici ed antropologici nel pensiero di S. Massimo il Confessore. Nota critica sulla bibliografia dell'argomento', *La Scuola Cattolica* 101 (1973), pp. 331-361; M. Doucet, 'Vues récentes sur les "Métamorphoses" de la pensée de saint Maxime le Confesseur', *Science et Esprit* 31 (1979), pp. 269-302.

[101]A. Riou, *Le monde et l'Eglise selon Maxime le Confesseur*, op. cit., appendix 3.

[102]D. Staniloae, *Philosophika kai theologika herôtêmata* ('Peri diaphorôn aporiôn tôn hagiôn Dionysiou kai Grêgoriou') *tou Hagiou Maximou tou Homologêtou. Eisagôgê-scholia, Metaphrasê* I. Sakales, tomos A. (Athens 1978).

[103]C. G. Sotiropoulos, *Hê Mystagôgia tou hagiou Maximou tou Homologêtou: eisagôge – keimenon – kritikon hypomnêma* (Athens 1978).

[104]*Clavis Patrum Graecorum, volumen III, A Cyrillo Alexandrino ad Ioannem Damascenum, cura et studio M. Geerard* (Turnhout 1979).

[105]*Clavis Patrum Graecorum, volumen IV, Concilia, catenae, cura et studio M. Geerard* (Turnhour 1980).

[106]*Maximi Confessoris Quaestiones ad Thalassium, I, Quaestiones I-LV, una cum latina interpretatione Joannis Scotti Eriugenae iuxta posita, ediderunt C. laga – C. Steel* (= *Corpus Christianorum, Series Graeca*, 7, Turnhout 1980).

Questiones ed dubia, edited by J. H. Declerk, followed in 1982. Remarkably, Declerk's version has two hundred and thirty-nine of these *herôtapokriseis,* whereas in the Combefis text of 1675 no more than seventy-nine are given. The explanation lies in the patient work of specialists on the Byzantine florilegia and exegetical *catenae,* who have managed to augment Combefis' total by such a factor.[107] In 1988 E. Jeaneau contributed to *Corpus Christianorum* his edition of the *Ambigua* as found in Eriugena's Latin translation or 'interpretation', as Jeaneau circumspectly calls it.[108] At the close of the decade, Laga and Steel would take the *Quaestiones ad Thalassium* up to *Quaestio* 65.[109] In a class by itself is Michel van Esbroeck's edition, with introduction and French translation, of the Georgian life of the Virgin ascribed to Maximus and described in chapter four of the present work.[110] To these may be appended two related essays: P. Allen's 'Blueprint for the Edition of *Documenta ad vitam Maximi Confessoris spectantia'*, a look ahead to the *Corpus Christianorum* edition of those documents, not yet in press,[111] and, with reference to the Eriugena paraphrase, E. Dekkers' Maxime le Confesseur dans la tradition latine'.[112] Jeaneau provided the historical background to Eriugena's translation (at once a command of Charles the Bald and a reflection of his personal interest in all things relevant to the Areopagite), as well as an investigation of the themes and

---

[107] *Maximi Confessoris Quaestiones et dubia, edidit J. H. Declerk* (= *Corpus Christianorum, Series Graeca,* 10, Turnhout 1982).

[108] *Maximi Confessoris Ambigua ad Johannem iuxta Johannis Scoti Eriugenae latinam interpretationem Nunc primum edidit Eduardus Jeaneau* (Turnhout 1988).

[109] *Maximi Confessoris Quaestiones ad Thalassium, II, Quaestiones LXI-LXV, una cum latina interpretatione Johannis Scotti Eriugenae iuxta posita, ediderunt Carl Laga et Carlos Steel* (Turnhout 1990).

[110] M. van Esbroeck (ed.), *Maxime le Confesseur, Vie de la Vierge* (Louvain 1986, = *Corpus Scriptorum Christianorum Orientalium* 478, *Scriptores iberici* 21). Idem. (tr.), *Maxime le Confesseur, Vie de la Vierge Louvain 1986,* = *Corpus Scriptorum Christianorum Orientalium* 479, *Scriptores Iberici* 22). See above, pp. 111-119.

[111] P. Allen, 'Blueprint for the Edition of *Documenta* ad *vitam Maximi Confessoris spectantia',* in *After Chalcedon. Studies in Theology and Church History Offered to Professor A. Van Roey for his Seventieth Birthday* (Leuven 1985), pp. 11-21.

[112] E. Dekkers, 'Maxime le Confesseur dans la tradition latine', in ibid., pp. 83-97.

language of the two texts, in his contribution to the 1980 Fribourg symposium on the Confessor's work.[113]

So far as the life of Maximus was concerned, Dalmais announced his conversion, at least in part, to the view that the Syriac *Vita* provides genuine information, otherwise irrecuperable, about Maximus' early years. Rather than rely on the later Greek hagiographical tradition, which placed Maximus' formation in Constantinople, Dalmais gave credence to the Monothelite biographer's claim that Maximus (or prior to his monastic profession, 'Moschion') was a Palestinian who, as a young man, entered the monastery of St Chariton, known in the sixth century as a centre of Origenism — thus explaining Maximus' profound grasp of Origenist thought.[114] A full survey of the biographical sources could be found, after 1980, in R. B. Bracke's *Ad Sancti Maximi Vitam.*[115]

Among attempts at synthesis, Dalmais contributed a very full entry in the *Dictionnaire de Spiritualité.*[116] Ceresa-Gastaldo provided the appropriate, if shorter, equivalent in the *Dizionario Patristico.*[117] Above all, Lars Thunberg, from a distance of two decades since his *Microcosm and Mediator*, wrote an introduction to Maximus for the general reader, comprising, in turn, an account of the Confessor's life; the trinitarian dimension of his theology; its soteriological aspect; Maximus' 'theandrism'; his understanding of nature and society; and his view of the

---

[113]E. Jeaneau, 'Jean l'Erigène et les *Ambigua ad Johannem* de Maxime le Confesseur', in *Maximus Confessor. Actes du Symposium sur Maxime le Confesseur, Fribourg, 2-5 September 1980, édités par F. Heinzer et C. Schönborn* (Fribourg 1982), pp. 343-364.

[114]I.-H. Dalmais 'La vie de saint Maxime le confesseur reconsidérée?' *Studia Patristicam* Volume XVII, in Three Parts, edited by E. A. Livingstone, Part One (Oxford 1982), pp. 26-30. Cf. our remarks above, pp. 15-16.

[115]R. B. Bracke, *Ad Sancti Maximi vitam. Studie van de biographische documenten en de levensberijvingen betreffende Maximus Confessor, ca. 580-662* (Louvain 1980).

[116]I.-H. Dalmais, 'Maxime le Confesseur, moine et théologien byzantin', in *Dictionnaire de Spiritualité, Ascétique et Mystique, Doctrine et Histoire, fondé par M. Viller, F. Cavallera, J. de Guibert, continué par A. Rayez, A. Derville et A. Solignac, avec le concours d'un grand nombre de collaborateurs*, tome X (Paris 1980), cols. 836-847.

[117]A. Ceresa-Gastaldo, 'Massimo il Confessore', in *Dizionario Patristico e di Antichità Cristiane, diretto da A. di Berardino*, II (Casale Monferrato 1984), cols. 2169-2172.

Liturgy and sacraments. In a closing chapter Thunberg provided some final reflexions on such themes as the relation between Maximus' notion of the *archai* of creation and modern science, between his doctrine and that of Palamism, and between eschatology and mystical union.[118] It was helpful that, meanwhile, more translations into modern languages had appeared: the *Capita theologica et oecumenica* and a number of the *Opuscula theologica et polemica* into Italian,[119] and the *Mystagogia* into English — twice, once by Dom Julian Stead,[120] and then by Father George Berthold as part of the latter's substantial anthology of Maximus' 'selected writings, which also includes his translations of the (first) trial of Maximus; the *Chapters on Charity*; the *Commentary on the Our Father*, and the *Gnostic Centuries*.[121] This collection is introduced by an historical sketch of Maximus' life and work by Pelikan.

Two major dogmatic studies of Maximus came out in the 1980s. F. Heinzer's *Gottes Sohn als Mensch* concentrates on the high importance, for Maximus' Christology, of the distinction between *logos*, or the unchanging pattern of a nature, and *tropos*, its mode of existing and acting.[122] P. Piret's *Le Christ et la Trinité selon Maxime le Confesseur*, the main lines of whose difficult but rewarding discussion are set forth above, sees Maximus' Christology and his trinitarian theology in strict relation, joined not only by an inherited vocabulary of *ousia* and *hypostasis*, but also by Maximus' more personal language of 'identity' and 'difference' — in whose dialectic Piret places in

[118]L. Thunberg, *Man and the Cosmos. The Vision of St Maximus the Confessor*, with a Foreword by A. M. Allchin (New York 1983).

[119]*Massimo Confessore, Il Dio-Uomo. Duecento pensieri sulla conoscenza di Dio e sull'incarnazione di Cristo, introduzione, traduzione e note di A. Ceresa-Gastaldo* (Milan 1980); *Massimo il Confessore, Meditazioni sull' agonia di Gesù, traduzione, introduzione et note a cura* di A. Ceresa-Gastaldo (Rome 1985).

[120]J. Stead, *The Church, the Liturgy and the Soul of Man, The 'Mystagogia' of St Maximus the Confessor*, translated, with historical note and commentaries (Still River, Massachusetts 1982).

[121]*Maximus Confessor. Selected Writings*, translation and notes by George C. Berthold (New York 1985).

[122]F. Heinzer, *Gottes Sohn als Mensch. Die Struktur des Menschseins Christi bei Maximus Confessor* (Fribourg 1980).

turn Maximus' account of God as one and three, and of the Redeemer's two natures, two wills and two operations.[123]

Most shorter essays on Maximus in the 1980s are to be found collected in the extremely rich Fribourg symposium proceedings, entitled simply *Maximus Confessor*. Apart from the contribution of Jeaneau, already noted above, we find: E. Bellini on Maximus as interpreter of the Pseudo-Denys, considers that Maximus did not 'correct' Denys' Christology but simply developed it in a sympathetic manner, for Denys' appearance of quasi-Monophysitism is an illusion created by the fact that, addressing himself to Platonists, he did not delay on the clarification of terms;[124] George Berthold excavated 'The Cappadocian Roots of Maximus the Confessor', arguing that the spirit of Maximus' theology is essentially Cappadocian — he emulated Nazianzen in theology and Christology, Nyssen in anthropology;[125] R. B. Bracie proposed that the *Book of Ambiguities* may not be a unity — the amalgamation of the *Ambigua ad Joannem* and the *Ambigua ad Thomam* (*Ambigua* I and *Ambigua* II in Sherwood's terminology) may have been a tenth century affair;[126] Ceresa-Gastaldo stressed that Maximus innovated linguistically only by enriching ancient terms and turns of phrase;[127] P. Christou read Maximus' anthropology in a Palamite perspective;[128] Croce and B. Valente collaborated to set out Maximus' sensitive doctrine of Providence — God in Christ saving the world in its creaturely autonomy, to which difference and movement are vital;[129] B. E. Daley argued that Maximus was, despite the opinions of some critics, extremely

[123]P. Piret, *Le Christ et la Trinité selon Maxime le Confesseur* (Paris 1983). See above, pp. 64-110.

[124]E. Bellini, 'Maxime interprète de Pseudo-Denys l'Aréopagite. Analyse de l'*Ambiguum ad Thomam* 5, *Maximus Confessor*, op. cit., pp. 37-49.

[125]G. C. Berthold, 'The Cappadocian Roots of Maximus the Confessor', ibid., pp. 51-59.

[126]R. B. Bracke, 'Some Aspects of the Manuscript Tradition of the *Ambigua* of Maximus the Confessor', ibid., pp. 97-109.

[127]A. Ceresa-Gastaldo, 'Tradition et innovation linguistique chez Maxime le confesseur', ibid., pp. 123-137.

[128]P. Christou, 'Maximos Confessor on the Infinity of Man', ibid., pp. 261-271.

reserved about the notion of a final restoration of all things, found in Origen and Gregory of Nyssa, and took as a real possibility the self-destruction of the creature by its free refusal of grace;[130] Dalmais, in the inaugural speech of the conference, presented the divine Word, in Maximus, as creator, legislator and redeemer, and so as source of the three-fold law of beings — the law of nature, the biblical law and the spiritual;[131] J. H. Declerk explained the manuscript tradition which lay behind his edition of the *Quaestiones et dubia*, then in preparation;[132] E. des Places looked at Maximus' probable knowledge of the Greek ascetic Father Diadochus of Photikê;[133] J.-M. Garrigues presented Maximus' *logos-tropos* distinction as the solution to the Western debate between Scotists and Thomists over the rationale of the Incarnation; in its *logos* of divinisation divine grace was always intended to raise humankind to share the life of God, while the *tropos* of its concrete modality — the saving Incarnation — turns on the fall of man;[134] Heinzer underlined the bond between the 'Theology' and the 'Economy', as summed up in Maximus' statement that 'the Word Incarnate teaches the Theology' in the *Commentary on the Pater*;[135] Laga spoke of Maximus as a stylist: despite the coals heaped on the latter's head, his language can boast a vast range of expressiveness;[136] for M. J. Le Guillou, Constantinople III is not, in its doctrinal teaching a mere corollary of Chalcedon, but required, to reach its own formulations, the light brought

[129]V. Croce – B. Valente, 'Provvidenza e pedagogia divina nella storia', ibid., pp. 247-259.

[130]E. E. Daley, 'Apokatastasis and "Honourable Silence" in the Eschatology of Maximus the Confessor', ibid., pp. 309-339.

[131]I.-H. Dalmais, 'La manifestation du Logos dans l'homme et dans l'Eglise. Typologie anthropologique et typologie ecclésiale d'après *Qu. Thal.* 60 et la *Mystagogie*', ibid., pp. 13-25.

[132]J. H. Declerk, 'La tradition des *Quaestiones et dubia* de S. Maxime le Confesseur', ibid., pp. 85-96.

[133]E. des Places, 'Maxime le Confesseur et Diadoque de Photicé', ibid., pp. 29-35.

[134]J.-M. Garrigues, 'Le dessein d'adoption du Créateur dans son rapport au Fils d'aprés S. Maxime le Confesseur', ibid., pp. 173-192.

[135]F. Heinzer, 'L'explication trinitaire de l'Economie chez Maxime le Confesseur', ibid., pp. 159-172.

[136]C. Laga, 'Maximus as a Stylist in *Quaestiones ad Thalassium*', ibid., pp. 139-146.

by Maximus' christological vision;[137] Léthel reiterated the importance of the Lord's praying in the Garden of Gethsemane for the Dyothelite position;[138] J. D. Madden defended the originality, vis-á-vis the preceding patristic tradition of Maximus' concept of *thelêsis*, will;[139] N. Madden approached the *Commentary on the Pater* as a literary work of art, finding its structure to be of a consciously 'geometric' kind;[140] Pelikan spoke on the after-life of Maximus' thought;[141] Piret offered a preview of the interpretation of Maximus' Christological formula about the natures 'of which, in which and which Christ is' which he would lay out at greater length in his *Le Christ et la Trinité*,[142] A. Radosavljevich wrote of the 'presuppositionlessness', in Maximus, of the Incarnation, for which are all things;[143] R. Riedinger suggested, on the basis of lexical considerations, that the original texts of the Lateran Synod were prepared in advance by Maximus and some of his companions, and, after the death of pope Theodore, read out during the Synod to the new pope, Martin I, and his bishops, in a Latin translation;[144] Christoph von Schönborn, in an essay on pleasure and pain in Maximus' ethic, points out that, for the Confessor, while the Christian must separate himself from the sensuous order, such negation has a positive purpose: the integration of the spiritual with the sensuous, which cannot happen on the level of the sensuous alone;[145]

[137]M. J. Le Guillou, 'Quelques réflexions sur Constantinople III et la sotériologie de Maxime', ibid., pp. 235-237.

[138]F.-M. Léthel, 'La prière de Jésus à Gethsémani dans la controverse mono-thélite, ibid., pp. 207-214.

[139]J. D. Madden, 'The Authenticity of Early Definitions of Will' ibid., pp. 61-79.

[140]N. Madden, 'The Commentary on the *Pater Noster*. An Example of the Structural Methodology of Maximus the Confessor', ibid., pp. 147-155.

[141]J. Pelikan, 'The Place of Maximus Confessor in the History of Christian Thought', ibid., pp. 387-401.

[142]P. Piret, 'Christologie et théologie trinitaire chez Maxime le confesseur, d'après sa formule des natures "desquelles, en lesquelles et lesquelles est le Christ",' ibid., pp. 215-222.

[143]A. Radosavljevich, 'Le problème du "présupposé" ou du "non-présupposé" de l'Incarnation de Dieu le Verbe', ibid., pp. 193-206.

[144]R. Riedinger, 'Die Lateransynode von 649 und Maximos der Bekenner', ibid., pp. 111-121.

[145]C. von Schönborn, 'Plaisir et douleur dans l'analyse de S. Maxime, d'après les *Quaestiones ad Thalassium*', ibid., pp. 273-284.

Sotiropoulos explained the principles behind his edition of the *Mystagogia*;[146] Steel put forward reasons for thinking that the twelfth century Byzantine prince Isaac Sebastokrator, to whose intellectual enthusiasms is owed much of the Greek of the texts of Proclus, was also a profound student of the Confessor;[147] H. Stickelberger instituted a comparison between Maximus and Karl Ranner so as to show that the hypostatic union, far from subverting authentic humanity, frees Christ's human nature in its creaturely autonomy;[148] B. Studer explored Maximus' soteriology as an implicate of the faith of Chalcedon;[149] Thunberg's chose to speak on Maximus' eucharistic doctrine which, as both *mystêrion* and *symbolon* he found wholly in accord with his teaching about the Incarnation;[150] K. H. Uthemann looked at changing ways of approaching, in Maximus' century, the relation of anthropology to the Incarnation.[151]

Outside the Fribourg symposiasts, other Maximian students also produced articles of note. In *The Thomist*, P. Plass explored Maximus' view of time: while in the divine plan the creation pre-exists in a quasi-temporal fashion (here Maximus is indebted to the Platonist tradition), more fundamentally, the Confessor adapts an Aristotelian notion of movement, *kinêsis*, to a biblical account of temporality as the entry of creation on its promised destiny.[152] Heinzer published a subtle account of Maximus' concept of will: on the one hand, *thelêsis* expresses the dynamic of human nature, tending to self-preservation and so the rejection

---

[146]C. G. Sotiropoulos, 'Remarques sur l'édition critique de la *Mystagogie* de S. Maxime le Confesseur', ibid., p. 83.

[147]C. Steel, 'Un admirateur de S. Maxime à la cour des Comnènes: Isaak le Sébastocrator', ibid., pp. 365-373.

[148]H. Stickelberger, 'Freisetzende Einheit. Ueber ein christologisches Grundaxiom bei Maximus Confessor und Karl Rahner', ibid., pp. 375-384.

[149]B. Studer, 'Zur Soteriologie des Maximus Confessor', ibid., pp. 239-246.

[150]L. Thunberg, 'Symbol and Mystery in St Maximus the Confessor. With Particular Reference to the Doctrine of the Eucharist', ibid., pp. 285-308.

[151]K. H. Uthemann, 'Das anthropologische Modell der hypostatischen Union bei Maximus Confessor. Zur innerchalkedonischen Transformation eines Paradigmas', ibid., pp. 223-233.

[152]P. Plass, 'Transcendent Time in Maximus the Confessor', *The Thomist* 44 (1980), pp. 259-277.

of non-being, of death; on the other hand, *thelêsis* also manifests the capacity of self-gift, so that Christ's free acceptance of death for man's salvation, as an overcoming of the life-preserving instinct can truly be a *human* act of the divine Son: here the Hellenic and the biblical patrimonies of Maximus are united — but with the palm going to the latter.[153] Berthold, in an article on Maximus and Augustine, begins from the premise that an Eastern theologian, exiled for between twenty-three and twenty-five years in the West could hardly *not* have known of Augustine, as the Latin tradition's greatest divine. Though Maximus never mentions Augustine, Berthold finds it significant that he deals with two favoured Augustinian themes — the *Filioque* and Christ's freedom from original sin. There may also be Augustinian influence from the *de Civitate Dei* on Maximus' positive view of the temporal process, and from the *Confessions* on his notion of liberty.[154] Lastly, Plass evoked Maximus' eschatological concept of 'moving rest': a *stasis* which is a dialectical 'vibration' between time and atemporality: we shall enjoy the stable possession of the divine infinity, yet not cease to be creatures and so 'in movement'.[155]

Finally: the 1990s would open hopefully, with, first, the appearance of the Turnhout edition of Maximus' commentaries on the Lord's Prayer, and on the fifty-ninth psalm,[156] and, secondly, a major study of Maximus' spiritual exegesis, P.M. Blowers' *Exegesis and Spiritual Pedagogy in Maximus the Confessor.* As its title suggests this work aims to show how Maximus' use of the Bible was integrated into his programme of spiritual development — a study, then, in the relationship of biblical interpretation to the practice of the Christian life.[157]

---

[153]F. Heinzer, 'Anmerkungen zum Willensbegriff Maximus' Confessors', *Freiburger Zeitschrift für Philosophie und Theologie* 28 (1981), pp. 373-392.

[154]G. C. Berthold, 'Did Maximus the Confessor Know Augustine?' *Studia Patristica*, Volume XVII, in Three Parts, Edited by E. A. Livingstone, Part One (Oxford 1982), pp. 14-17.

[155]P. Plass, '"Moving Rest" in Maximus the Confessor', *Classica et Mediaevalia* 35 (1984), pp. 177-190.

[156]*Maximi Confessoris Opuscula exegetica duo (Expositio in Psalmum LIX; Expositio Orationis dominicae)*, edidit Peter van Duen (Turnhout 1991, = *Corpus Christianorum, Series Graeca* 23).

[157]P.M. Blowers, *Exegesis and Spiritual Pedagogy in Maximus the Confessor* (Notre Dame, Indiana 1991).

Bibliography

A. Texts

I   F. Combefis and F. Oehler, *Patrologia Graeca*, vols. 90-91 (Paris 1960), with Latin translation.

II   C. Laga — C. Steel, *Questiones ad Thalassium* I, *Corpus Christianorum, Series Graeca* 7 (Louvain 1980); Ii, ibid. 22 (Louvain 1990).

     J. H. Declerck, *Questiones et dubia*, ibid. 10 (Louvain 1982).

     E. Jeauneau (ed.), *Ambigua ad Joannem*, ibid. 16 (Louvain 1988).

     M. van Esbroeck (ed.), *Maxime le Confesseur, Vie de la Vierge* (Louvain 1986, = *Corpus Scriptorum Christianorum Orientalium* 478, *Scriptores iberici* 21).

     Idem. (tr.), *Maxime le Confesseur, Vie de la Vierge* (Louvain 1986, = *Corpus Scriptorum Christianorum Orientalium* 479, *Scriptores Iberici* 22).

III R. Canart, 'La deuxième lettre à Thomas de saint Maxime le Confesseur', *Byzantion* 34 (1964), pp. 415-445.

     R. Devréesse, 'La fin inédite d'une lettre de saint Maxime', *Revue des Sciences Religieuses* 17 (1937), pp. 23-35.

     C. Soteropoulos, *Hê 'Mystagogia' tou hagiou Maximou tou homologêtou* (Athens 1978).

B. Translations

The *Acta*: for the *Relatio motionis* and *Disputatio byzica:* H. Rahner, *Kirche und Staat im frühen Christentum* (Munich 1961).

Quaestiones ad Thalassium:

A. Arguriou, *Saint Maxime le Confesseur, Le Mystère de Salut* (Namur 1964). [Selections.]

Centuriae de caritate:

H. U. von Balthasar, *Kosmische Liturgie* (Einsiedeln 1961^2), pp. 408-481.

A. Cesera-Gastaldo, *Capitoli sulla carità* (Rome 1963).

J. Pegon, *Centuries sur la Charité* (Paris 1945).

P. Sherwood, *The Ascetic Life. The Four Centuries on Charity* (London 1955).

G. C. Berthold, *Maximus Confessor. Selected Writings* (New York 1985), pp. 33-98.

Disputatio cum Pyrrho:

C.-J. Hefele — H. Leclerq, *Histoire des Conciles* III. 1 (Paris 1909), pp. 405-422.

A. Ceresa-Gastaldo, *Massimo il Confessore. Umanità e divinità di Cristo* (Rome 1979), pp. 99-156.

The Ascetic Discourse

P. Sherwood, *The Ascetic Life. The Four Centuries on Charity*, op. cit.

P. Deseille, *L'Evangile au désert* (Paris 1965), pp. 162-193.

A. Ceresa-Gastaldo, *Massimo il Confessore. Umanità e divinità di Cristo*, op. cit., pp. 23-62.

Commentary on the Lord's prayer

A. Riou, *Le monde et l'Eglise selon Maxime le Confesseur* (Paris 1973), pp. 214-239.

G. C. Berthold, *Maximus Confessor. Selected Writings*, op. cit., pp. 99-126.

A. Ceresa-Gastaldo, *Massimo il Confessore. Umanità e divinità di Cristo*, op. cit., pp. 63-94.

Capitula theologica et economica

A. Ceresa-Gastaldo, *Il Dio-Uomo* (Milan 1980).

G. C. Berthold, *Maximus Confessor. Selected Writings*, op. cit., pp. 127-180.

Opuscula theologica et polemica

A. Ceresa-Gastaldo, *Massimo il Confessore. Meditazioni sull'agonia di Gesù* (Rome 1985). [Selections.]

Mystagogia

H. U. von Balthasar, *Kosmische Liturgie* (Einsiedeln 1961²), pp. 363-407.

R. Cantarella, *Massimo Confessore, La Mistagogia ed altri scritti* (Florence 1931).

M. Lot-Borodine, *Irénikon* 13-15 (1936-1938).

J. Stead, *St Maximus the Confessor, the Church, the Liturgy and the Soul of Man* (Still River, Massachusetts 1982).

G. C. Berthold, *Maximus the Confessor. Selected Writings*, op. cit., pp. 181-226.

Varia

E. von Ivanka, *Maximos der Bekenner. All-Eins in Christus, Auswahl, Uebertragung, Einleitung* (Einsiedeln 1961).

C. Secondary works on the Confessor

H. U. von Balthasar, *Kosmische Liturgie. Maximus der Bekenner: Höhe und*

Krisis des griechischen Weltbildes (Freiburg 1941).

Idem., *Die 'Gnostische Centurien' des Maximus Confessor* (Freiburg 1941).

Idem., *Kosmische Liturgie. Das Weltbild Maximus des Bekenners.* (Zweite, völlig veränderte Auflage, Einsiedeln 1961).

G. C. Berthold, 'Did Maximus the Confessor know Augustine?', *Studia Patristica* XVII (1982), pp. 14017.

Idem., 'The Cappadocian Roots of Maximus the Confessor', in F. Heinzer — C. von Schönborn (eds.), *Maximus Confessor. Actes du Symposium sur Maxime le Confesseur* (Fribourg 1982), pp. 51-59.

Idem., 'Introduction', to idem., *Maximus Confessor, Selected Writings*, op. cit., pp. 1-14.

P. M. Blowers, *Exegesis and Spiritual Pedagogy in Maximus the Confessor. An Investigation of the 'Quaestiones ad Thalassium'* (Notre Dame, Indiana 1991).

R. Bornert, 'Explication de la liturgie et interprétation de l'Ecriture chez Maxime le Confesseur', *Studia Patristica* X (Berlin 1970), pp. 323-327.

R. Bracke, *Ad sancti Maximi vitam: studie van de biografische documenten en de levensbeschrijvingen betreffende Maximus Confessor* (Louvain 1980).

M. Candal, 'La gracia increada del *Liber Ambiguum* de san Maximo', *Orientalia Christiana Periodica* (1961), pp. 131-149.

V. Croce, *Tradizione e ricerca. Il metodo teologico di San Massimo il Confessore* (Milan 1974).

I.-H. Dalmais, 'S. Maxime le Confesseur, Docteur de la Charité, *Vie Spirituelle* (1948-2), pp. 296-303.

Idem., 'La théorie des *logoi* des créatures chez saint Maxime le Confesseur', *Revue des Sciences Philosophiques et Théologiques* 36 (1952), pp. 244-249.

Idem., 'L'oeuvre spirituelle de saint Maxime le Confesseur', *Supplément de la Vie spirituelle* 21 (1952), pp. 216-226.

Idem., 'La doctrine ascétique de saint Maxime le Confesseur d'après le *Liber asceticus*', *Irénikon* 26 (153), pp. 17-39.

Idem., 'Un traité de théologie contemplative: le commentaire du *Pater noster* de saint Maxime le Confesseur', *Revue d'Ascétique et de Mystique* 29 (1953), pp. 123-159.

Idem., L'Anthropologie spirituelle de saint Maxime le Confeseur', *Recherches et débats* 36 (1961), pp. 202-211.

Idem., 'Saint Maxime le Confesseur et la crise de l'origénisme monastique', *Théologie de la Vie monastique* (Paris 1961), pp. 411-421.

Idem., 'La fonction unificatrice du Verbe incarné dans les oeuvres spirituelles de saint Maxime le Confesseur', *Sciences Ecclésiastiques* 14 (1962), pp. 445-459.

Idem., 'Place de la *Mystagogie* de saint Maxime le Confesseur dans la théologie liturgique byzantine', *Studia Patristica* V (Berlin 1962), pp. 277-283.

Idem., 'Introduction', A. Argyriou, *Saint Maxime le Confesseur, Le Mystére du Salut* (Namur 1964).

Idem., 'L'héritage évagrien dans la synthèse de saint Maxime le Confesseur', *Studia Patristica* VIII (Berlin 1966), pp. 356-363.

Idem., 'Le vocabulaire des activités intellectuelles, volontaires et spirituelles dans l'anthropologie de saint Maxime le Confesseur', *Mélanges offerts au Père Marie-Dominique Chenu* (Paris 1967), pp. 189-202.

Idem., 'Mystere liturgique et divinisation dans la *Mystagogie* de saint Maxime le Confesseur, *Epektasis* (Paris 1972), pp. 55-62.

Idem., 'Maxime le Confesseur', *Dictionnaire de Spiritualité* 10 (Paris 1980), cols. 836-847.

R. Devréesse, 'La vie de saint Maxime le Confesseur et ses récensions', *Analecta Bollandiana* 46 (1928), pp. 5-49.

Idem., 'La fin inédite d'une lettre de saint Maxime', *Revue des Sciences Religieuses* 17 (1937), pp. 23-35.

M.-T. Disdier, 'Les fondements dogmatiques de la spiritualité de saint Maxime le Confesseur', *Echos d'Orient* 29 (1930), pp. 296-313.

Idem., 'Elie l'Ecdicos et les *hetera kephalaia* attribués à saint Maxime le Confesseur et à Jean de Carpathos', ibid. 31 (1932), pp. 17-43.

M. Doucet, 'Vues récentes sur les 'métamorphoses' de la pensée de saint Maxime le Confesseur', *Science et Esprit* 31, 3 (1979), pp. 269-302.

J. Draeseke, 'Zu Maximus Confessor', *Zeitschrift für Wissenschaftliche Theologie* 46 (1903), pp. 563-580; 47 (1904), pp. 121-130.

Idem., 'Maximus Confessor und Johannes Scotus Erigena', *Theologische Studien und Kritiken* 84 (1911), pp. 20-60 and 204-229.

S. L. Epifanovich, *Prepodobnyi Maksim Ispovednik i vizantiiskoe bogoslovie* (Kiev 1915).

Idem., *Materialy k izuchenii zhizni i tvorenii prep. Maksima Ispovednika* (Kiev 1917).

G. V. Florovskii, *Bizantiiski Ottsy V-VIII [vv]* (Paris 1933), pp. 195-227.

J.-M. Garrigues, 'La personne composée du Christ d'après saint Maxime le Confesseur', *Revue Thomiste* 74 (1974), pp. 181-204.

Idem., 'L'enérgie divine et la grâce chez Maxime le Confesseur', *Istina* 19 (1974), pp. 272-296.

Idem., *Maxime le Confesseur. La Charité, avenir divin de l'homme* (Paris 1976).

Idem., 'Le sens de la primauté romaine selon Maxime le Confesseur', *Istina* 21 (1976), pp. 6-24.

Idem., 'Le martyre de saint Maxime le Confesseur', *Revue Thomiste* 76 (1976), pp. 410-452.

M. L. Gatti, *Maximus Confessor. Saggio di bibliografia generale ragionata e contributi per una riconstruzione scientifica del suo pensiero metafisica e religioso* (Milan 1987).

R.-A. Gauthier, 'Saint Maxime le Confesseur et la psychologie de l'acte humain', *Recherches de Théologie ancienne et médiévale* 21 (1954), pp. 51-200.

D. J. Geanakoplos, 'Some Aspects of the Influence of the Byzantine Maximos the Confessor on the Theology of East and West', *Church History* 38 (1969), pp. 150-163.

M. Geerard, 'Maximus Confessor', in *Clavis Patrum Graecorum* III (Turnhout 1979), pp. 431-456.

V. Grumel, 'La comparaison de l'âme et du corps et l'union hypostatique chez Léonce de Byzance et saint Maxime le Confesseur', *Echos d'Orient* 25 (1926), pp. 393-406.

Idem., 'Notes d'histoire et de chronologie sur la vie de saint Maxime le Confesseur', ibid. 26 (1927), pp. 24-32.

Idem., 'Maxime le Confesseur', *Dictionnaire de Théologie Catholique* 10 (Paris 1928), cols. 448-459.

I. Hausherr, *Philautie. De la tendresse pour soi à la charité, selon saint Maxime le Confesseur* (Rome 1952).

Idem., 'Korreferat zu P. Sherwood, Maximus and Origenism', *Berichte zum XI. Internationalen Byzantinisten-Kongress* (Munich 1958).

J. Heintjes, 'Een onbekende leeraar van ascese en mystick: sint Maximus Confessor', *Studia Catholica* 11 (1935), pp. 175-200.

F. Heinzer, *Gottes Sohn als Mensch. Die Struktur des Menschseins Christi bei Maximus Confessor* (Fribourg 1980).

Idem., with C. von Schönborn (eds.), *Maximus Confessor. Actes du Symposium sur Maxime le Confesseur* (Fribourg 1982).

E. von Ivánka, 'Der philosophische Ertrag der Auseinandersetzung Maximos des Bekenners mit dem Origenismus', *Jahrbuch der Oesterreichischen Byzantinischen Gesellschaft* 7 (1958), pp. 23-49.

Idem., 'Korreferat zu P. Sherwood, Maximus and Origenism', *Berichte zum XI. Internationalen Byzantinisten-Kongress* (Munich 1958).

C. Kekelidze, 'Remarques sur les sources géorgiennes de la vie de saint Maxime le Confesseur', *Trudy de l'Académie de Kiev* (1913), pp. 1-41; 451-482.

W. Lackner, 'Zu Quelle und Datierung der Maximosvita', *Analecta Bollandiana* 85 (1967), pp. 285-316.

Idem., 'Der Amtstitel Maximos des Bekenners', *Jahrbuch der Oesterreichischen Byzantinistik* 20 (1971), pp. 64-65.

F.-M. Léthel, *Théologie de l'agonie du Christ. La liberté humaine du Fils de Dieu et son importance sotériologique mises en lumière par saint Maxime le Confesseur* (Paris 1979).

J. Loosen, *Logos und Pneuma im begnadeten Menschen bei Maximus Confessor* (Münster 1941).

J.-L. Marion, 'Les deux volontés du Christ selon saint Maxime le Confesseur', *Résurrection* 41 (1973), pp. 42-66.

J. Maritch, *Celebris Cyrilli Alexandrini formula christologica de una activitate Christi in interpretatione Maximi confessoris et recentiorum theologorum* (Zagreb 1920).

E. Michaud, Saint Maxime le Confesseur et l'apocatastase', *Revue Internationale de Théologie* 10 (1902), pp. 257-272.

P. Miquel, '*Peira*. Contribution à l'étude du vocabulaire de l'expérience religieuse dans l'oeuvre de Maxime le Confesseur', *Studia Patristica* VII (Berlin 1966), pp. 355-361.

E. Montmasson, 'La chronologie de la vie de saint Maxime le Confesseur', *Echos d'Orient* 13 (1910), pp. 149-154.

Idem., 'La doctrine de l'apatheia d'après saint Maxime', ibid., 14 (1911), pp. 36-41.

L. Negri, 'Elementi criteriologici ed antropologici nel pensiero di S. Massimo il Confessore', *La Scuola Cattolica* 101 (1973), pp. 331-361.

M. W. Peitz, 'Martin I und Maximus Confessor', *Historisches Jahrbuch der Görresgesellschaft* 38 (1917), pp. 213-236, 429-458.

J. Pelikan, 'Council or Father or Scripture. The Concept of Authority in the Theology of Maximus the Confessor', in D. Neiman and M. Schatkin eds.), *The Heritage of the Early Church* (Rome 1973), pp. 277-288.

Idem., 'The Place of Maximus Confessor in the History of Christian Thought', in F. Heinzer — C. von Schönborn (eds.), *Maximus Confessor. Actes du Symposium sur Maxime le Confesseur* (Fribourg 1982), pp. 387-402.

J. Pierres, *Sanctus Maximus Confessor: princeps apologetarum Synodi Lateranensi, anni 649* (Rome 1940).

P. Piret, *Le Christ et la Trinité selon Maxime le Confesseur* (Paris 1983).

J. J. Prado, *Voluntad y naturaleza. La antropología filófica de Máximo el Confesor* (Rio Cuarto 1974).

K. Preuss, *Ad Maximi Confessoris de Deo hominisque deificatione doctrinam adnotationum* (Schneeburg 1894).

A. Riou, *Le monde et L'église selon Maxime le Confesseur* (Paris 1976).

P. Sherwood, 'Notes on Maximus the Confessor', *American Benedictine Review* 1 (1950), pp. 347-356.

Idem., *An Annotated Date-List of the Works of Maximus the Confessor* (Rome 1952).

Idem., *The Earlier 'Ambigua' of St Maximus the Confessor* (Rome 1955).

Idem., 'Maximus and Origenism. *Archê kai telos*', *Berichte zum XI. Internationalen Byzantinisten-Kongress* (Munich 1958).

Idem., 'Exposition and Use of Scripture in St Maximus as Manifest in the *Quaestiones ad Thalassium*', *Orientalia Christiana Periodica* 34 (1958), pp. 202-207.

Idem., 'Survey of Recent Works on St Maximus the Confessor', *Traditio* 20 (1964), pp. 428-437.

A. Siclari, *Volontà e scelta in Massimo il Confessore e Gregorio di Nissa* (Parma 1984).

A. K. Squire, 'The Idea of the Soul as Virgin and Mother in Maximus the Confessor', *Studia Patristica* VIII (Berlin 1966), pp. 456-461.

C. G. Steitz, 'Die Abendmahlslehre des Maximus Confessor', *Jahrbuch für deutsche Theologie* 11 (1886), pp. 229-328.

E. Stephanou, 'La coexistence initiale du corps et de l'ame d'aprés saint Grégoire de Nysse et saint Maxime l'Homologète', *Echos d'Orient* 31 (1932), pp. 304-315.

J. Stiglmayr, 'Maximus Confessor und die beiden Anastasius', *Katholik* 88 (1908), pp. 39-45.

H. Straubinger, *Die Christologie des hl. Maximus Confessor* (Bonn 1906).

L. Thunberg, *Microcosm and Mediator. The Theological Anthropology of Maximus the Confessor* (Lund 1965).

Idem., *Man and the Cosmos. The Vision of St Maximus the Confessor* (Crestwood, New York 1985).

C. N. Tsirpanlis, 'Acta Sancti Maximi', *Theologia* 43 (1972), p. 106-115.

D. J. Unger, 'Christ Jesus, Centre and Final Scope of all Creation according to St Maximus Confessor', *Franciscan Studies* 9 (1949), pp. 50-62.

M. Viller, 'Aux sources de la spiritualité de saint Maxime, Les oeuvres d'Evagre le Pontique', *Revue d'Ascétique et de Mystique* 11 (1930), pp. 156-184; 239-268.

W. Völker, 'Der Einfluss Pseudo-Dionysius Areopagita auf Maximus Confessor', in A. Stohr, *Universitas* I (Mainz 1960), pp. 243-254.

Idem., 'Der Einfluss des Pseudo-Dionysius Areopagita auf Maximus Confessor', in E. Klostermann, *Studien zum Neuen Testament und zur Patristik* (= *Texte und Untersuchungen* 77, Berlin 1961), pp. 331-350.

Idem., *Maximus Confessor als Meister des gesitlichen Lebens* (Wiesbaden 1965).

H. S. Weser, *Maximi Confessoris praecepta de incarnatione Dei et deificatione hominis exponuntur et examinantur* (Berlin 1869).

D. Other secondary works

H. U. von Balthasar, 'Das Scholienwerk des Johannes von Skythopolis', *Scholastik* 15 (1940), pp. 16-38. Reprinted in idem., *Kosmische Liturgie* (Einsideln 1961²), pp. 644-672.

G. Bardy, 'La littérature patristique des *Quaestiones et responsiones* sur l'Ecriture sainte', *Revue biblique* 41 (1933), pp. 322-339.

H.-G. Beck, *Kirche und theologische Literatur im byzantinischen Reich* (Munich 1959).

R. Bornert, *Les commentaires byzantins de la divine liturgie, du VIIe au XIVe siècle* (Paris 1966).

Idem., 'L'anaphore dans la spiritualité liturgique de Byzance, le témoignage des commentaires mystagogiques du VIIe au XVe siècle', in *Eucharisties d'Orient et d'Occident* (Paris 1970), II. pp. 241-263.

E. Bréhier — R. Aigrain, *Grégoire le Grand, Les Etats barbares et la conquête arabe, 590-757* (= A. Fliche — V. Martin (eds.) *Histoire de l'Eglise. Depuis les origines jusqu'à nos jours* 5, Paris 1938).

E. Caspar, 'Die Lateransynode von 649', *Zeitschrift für Kirchengeschichte* 51 (1932), pp. 75-137.

W. Elert, *Der Ausgang der altkirchlichen Christologie* (Berlin 1957).

M. Erbetta, *Gli apocrifi del nuovo testamento. Vangeli I/2. Infanzia e passione del Cristo. Assunzione di Maria* (Turin 1981).

V. Grumel, 'Recherches sur l'histoire du monothélitisme', *Echos d'Orient* 27 (1928), pp. 6-16; 157-177; 28 (1929), pp. 19-34; 272-282; 29 (1930), pp. 16-28.

J. F. Haldon, *Byzantium in the Seventh Century. The Transformation of a Culture* (Cambridge 1990).

J. Hussey, *The Orthodox Church in the Byzantine Empire* (Oxford 1989).

J. N. D. Kelly, *Early Christian Doctrine* (London 1977[5]).

J. Meyendorff, *Le Christ dans la théologie byzantine* (Paris 1969); reviewed in J.-M. Garrigues, '*Le Christ dans la théologie byzantine*. Réflections sur un ouvrage du P. Meyendorff', *Istina* 3 (1970), p. 435-465.

F. X. Murphy, C. Ss. R., — P. Sherwood, O.S.B., *Constantinople II et Constantinople III* (Paris 1973).

J. Plaignieux, *S. Grégoire de Nazianze théologien* (Paris 1951).

J. M. Sansterre, *Les moines grecs et orientaux à Rome aux époques byzantine et carolingienne: milieu du VIe siecle — fin du IXe. siècle* (Brussels 1983).

M. Schiavone, *Neoplatonismo e Cristianesimo nello Pseudo-Dionigi* (Milan 1963).

C. von Schönborn, *Sophrone de Jérusalem: vie monastique et confession dogmatique* (Paris 1972).

M. Tarchinsvili, *Geschichte der kirchlichen georgischen Literatur* (Vatican City 1955).

M. van Esbroeck, 'Les textes littéraire sur l'Assomption avant le Xe siècle', in F. Bovon, *Les Actes apocryphes des apôtres* (Geneva 1981).

A. Wenger, *L'Assomption de la très saint Vierge dans la Tradition byzantine du VIe au Xe sicle* (Paris 1955).

Index of Names

Adam, 142, 166, 196, 208, 235
Albert, 218, 239
Allchin, A. M., ix
Allen, P., 245
Amphilochius, 130
Anastasius Apozygares, 6
Anastasius the Apocrisarius, 225
Anastasius the Librarian, 216, 217
Anastasius the Monk, 14, 225
Anna, 115
Apollinaris, 85
Aquinas, *see* Thomas Aquinas
Arcadius, 6
Argyriou, A., 240
Aristotle, 15, 128, 181, 203, 238
Arius, 64, 80, 86
Athanasius, 65, 84, 85, 115, 126, 163, 194
Athanasius Gammala, 6
Athanasius, priest, 53
Augustine, 174, 176, 177, 234, 252

Balbus, P., 218, 240
Balthasar, H. U. von, 58, 91, 129, 146, 220, 230, 234, 237
Baronius, 221, 222
Basil, 65, 216
Beck, H. G., 216
Bellini, E., 248
Belloc, H., 101, 102
Benjamin, patriarch of Alexandria, 8
Bernard, 218, 229, 239
Berthold, G., 247, 248, 252
Blondel, M., 103
Blowers, P. M., 34, 252
Bonaventure, 231
Bornert, R., 151, 239, 241

Bracke, R. B., 246, 248
Brock, S., 243
Bulgakov, S. B., 144
Burgundius of Pisa, 233

Canart, P., 240
Candal, M., 239
Carnadet, J., 223
Casel, O., 50
Caspar, E., 13
Cerbanus, 218
Ceresa-Gastaldo, A., 240, 241, 246, 248
Chapman, J., 226
Charles the Bald, 216
Chenu, M.-D., 236
Chosroes II, 4
Christou, P., 248
Clement, pope, 31, 176
Clement of Alexandria, 238
Clément, O., 144
Combefis, F., 221, 245
Constans II, 12, 14, 18
Constantine III, 12
Constantine of Apamea, 7
Croce, V., 24–63, 127, 242, 248
Cross, F. L., 236
Cyparissiotes, J., 218, 240
Cyril of Alexandria, 10, 76, 77, 78, 85, 86, 92, 93, 100, 122, 123, 163
Cyrus of Phasis, 6, 8, 9, 195

Daley, B. E., 248–249
Dalmais, I.-H., 190, 230, 231, 232, 235, 236, 240–241, 246, 249
Dante, 111, 181
David, 171

DATE DUE